EVERY BREATH YOU TAKE

"Affecting, tense, and smart true crime."
—Washington Post Book World

"Absolutely riveting . . . psychologically perceptive."
—Booklist

. . . AND NEVER LET HER GO

"Truly creepy. . . . This portrait of an evil prince needs no embellishment." *—People*

"[Rule] might have created her masterpiece."
—The Plain Dealer (Cleveland)

"Even crime buffs who followed the case closely [will] gain new insights."
—The Orlando Sentinel (FL)

"[Rule] tell[s] the sad story with authority, flair, and pace."
—The Washington Post

BITTER HARVEST

"A must-read story of the '90s American dream turned, tragically, to self-absorbed ashes." *—People*

"Impossible to put down. . . . A tour de force."
—Kirkus Reviews

BOOKS BY ANN RULE

Too Late to Say Goodbye
Green River, Running Red
Heart Full of Lies
Every Breath You Take
. . . And Never Let Her Go
Bitter Harvest
Dead by Sunset
Everything She Ever Wanted
If You Really Loved Me
The Stranger Beside Me
Possession
Small Sacrifices

Ann Rule's Crime Files
Vol. 12: Smoke, Mirrors, and Murder and Other
        True Cases
Vol. 11: No Regrets and Other True Cases
Vol. 10: Worth More Dead and Other True Cases
Vol. 9: Kiss Me, Kill Me and Other True Cases
Vol. 8: Last Dance, Last Chance and Other True Cases
Vol. 7: Empty Promises and Other True Cases
Vol. 6: A Rage to Kill and Other True Cases
Vol. 5: The End of the Dream and Other True Cases
Vol. 4: In the Name of Love and Other True Cases
Vol. 3: A Fever in the Heart and Other True Cases
Vol. 2: You Belong to Me and Other True Cases
Vol. 1: A Rose for Her Grave and Other True Cases

Without Pity: Ann Rule's Most Dangerous Killers
The I-5 Killer
The Want-Ad Killer
Lust Killer

ANN RULE

MORTAL DANGER

AND OTHER TRUE CASES
ANN RULE'S CRIME FILES: Vol.13

POCKET BOOKS

New York   London   Toronto   Sydney

Pocket Books
A Division of Simon & Schuster, Inc.
1230 Avenue of the Americas
New York, NY 10020

First Pocket Books paperback edition December 2008

POCKET and colophon are registered trademarks of Simon & Schuster, Inc.

For information about special discounts for bulk purchases, please contact Simon & Schuster Special Sales at 1-800-456-6798 or business@simonandschuster.com

Cover illustration by Tom Hallman; cover design by James Wang.

Manufactured in the United States of America

10 9 8 7 6 5 4 3 2 1

ISBN-13: 978-1-4165-4220-9
ISBN-10:   1-4165-4220-5

For the families and friends of violent crime victims and missing persons.

I salute you for three decades of helping others because you've been through it and you understand.

You have *made a difference.*

Acknowledgments

Most readers have no idea how many people it takes to make a book! There are numerous levels before I finally receive my first copy, which thrills me as much as it did twenty-nine books ago. As always, I feel lucky to have the wisdom, talent, skills, memories, and support from the many who have contributed to *Mortal Danger*. From detectives who worked hard to solve these cases to the families of victims who shared what I realize is very painful to survivors, my gratitude knows no bounds.

And from my editors to my production team to my literary and theatrical agents, I could not possibly have completed this book without you!

My appreciation goes to: Kate Jewell, Susan Hoskinson, David Gardiner, Gold Beach Police Department; Karen Slater, Dr. Randall Nozawa, Lieutenant Brent Bomkamp, Sergeant Ben Benson, Ed Troyer, Pierce County Sheriff's Office.

To the late Dave Hart, Port of Seattle Police Department; Mike Ciesynski, Mike Tando, Hank Gruber, and Bob Holter, Seattle Police Department; and Bruce Whit-

ACKNOWLEDGMENTS

man and Dick Taylor, Snohomish County Sheriff's Office; and Jarl Gunderson, Marysville Police Department.

I thank my publisher, Louise Burke, for trusting my judgment in selecting cases, and my editor, Mitchell Ivers, who—with his sharp eye, literary skill, and deft pen—makes criticism almost fun. His assistant, Jessica Webb, makes things happen on time, and she helped tremendously in organizing the photo sections. The production staff—Carly Sommerstein, Sally Franklin, and Lisa Litwack—whipped all the parts of this book into one cohesive package and sent it off to the printer.

Joan and Joe Foley in New York City have been my literary agents and cheering section for more than three decades. I was lucky when they took a chance on me! Ron Bernstein, my theatrical agent at International Creative Management (ICM) in Los Angeles, is responsible for transforming many of my books into movies and mini-series, and we have more to come soon.

Gerry Hay is still my first reader, and my daughter, Leslie Rule, is a proofreader who catches almost all the mistakes I've missed! My special thanks to Marie Heaney, Donna Anders, Blanche Beanblossom, Marnie Campbell, Brian Heil, Dawn Dunn, Grace Kingman, and Diane Benson, to the "Jolly Matrons of Willamette University and the University of Washington," the "Ladies Who Lunch/Union Meeting Extraordinaire," and to the "Loyal Order of ARFs [Ann Rule Fans]," who never fail to brighten my days.

Contents

Foreword

The format of my True Crime Files series changes constantly. Sometimes, there may be eight or ten short cases. Occasionally, as in this book, there are several long cases and only a few short cases. When I was in college, my professors in writing classes taught me to tell a story until it was told. The trick was to know when that was! It shouldn't be a sentence shorter or a paragraph longer.

In 2007, as it happened, I came across three cases that demanded well over a hundred pages apiece to unveil the many tunnels, dead ends, corners, intersections, and amazing revelations that startled even experienced detectives. And I took all the pages I needed.

There are also two shorter cases in *Mortal Danger.* Readers often tell me that they read my crime files on the bus or a plane. This collection should fit, then, for short or long trips.

Next year, I may choose an entirely different format as I write both new cases and mysteries going back decades. With the evolution of cold case squads in almost all large police agencies, I am learning the answers to many unsolved homicides that I covered at the beginning of my career, and it feels good to be able to write these endings long after we all believed the cases would lie dormant forever.

As I explore each case, I try my best to research the motivation of the killer, going back as far as I can in his (or her) life. I also try to allow readers to come to know the victims as if they were still with us. I look for the moment their two paths cross and tragedy blooms. Sometimes they are strangers who meet only once; sometimes it takes years before the *true* personality of the killer emerges.

As often as I can, I go to the cities and states where the crimes I write about occurred so that I—and then my readers—can know what it is like to live there. What is the weather like? What grows there? How does the air feel? How do people make a living? And even what local culinary treats abound there? In my head, I'm picturing us walking through a heretofore unknown place and, together, observing what happened there.

Many people have the mistaken idea that I write only about the Northwest, but I have spent weeks and months in New York, Georgia, Florida, Texas, Kansas, Missouri, Delaware, California, Idaho, and many other locales where crimes occurred. I have probably attended more than a hundred trials. This book happens to have cases that occurred in the Northwest, where I have lived for many years—yet there are links to the East Coast, too.

Frightening my readers is never my goal, but I do want to warn you of possible danger. I want you to be conscious of what's happening around you and be ready to question odd comments, requests, pleas, life stories, and the people who tell them to you.

You are your first line of defense. Always remember that.

Sometimes I shudder to think of how many stories I have told about cases involving possessive, controlling men and hapless, hopeless women. Although they are all true, and involve scores of couples who don't know one another—and never will—the three-act "play" of each relationship might well have been written by the same author. The first act is all about romance and trust; it moves along so gently that the woman who will soon be captive never senses danger. The second act is a slow progression—he cuts her off from her friends, her family, her job, and her self-respect, until she finds herself dancing to whatever tune her formerly perfect lover chooses to play.

The third act can end one of three ways: (1) the emotionally imprisoned woman gives up and remains with the man who forbids her to leave him; (2) she escapes from him but is left with a constant sense of someone silently stalking her; or (3) their "love story" turns tragic, and she dies at his hand. In the possessive lover's mind, she always *belongs* to him. He finds this perfectly reasonable, and since the trapped woman had the audacity and cruelty to run from him, she deserves to die.

With every case of domestic violence I write, I am hoping and praying that I will warn other women who are on the verge of turning their lives over to a man who has shown them only a mask—a façade. I want to shake them enough to make them back away in time. I also hope that I may give women already captive the strength to leave. But when a woman is entrenched in a sick relationship, it's difficult to escape. She may have no income of her own. She may be very afraid. She has to find someplace to live, some way to support herself, some way to find secure child care. She may also have to locate shelter for beloved pets.

This first case—Mortal Danger—is perhaps one of the strangest and most mysterious tales of obsessive love I have ever encountered. When I began to follow this twisted and interlaced story, I found that each door I opened led to another door.

Did I ever get to the final door? I'm not entirely sure. It may be that there are readers who hold the answers to puzzles that came about because of a man called "Mr. Williams." Maybe someone out there knew him by one of his many names. Maybe the end of the story will come from you.

Time and again, John Williams stated that his true goal in life was to help people—to help bring them health, wealth, and happiness. His full legal name was John William Branden, but he often found it more convenient to use one of any number of pseudonyms. The women he attracted had the same goals: a desire to serve others. He appeared to be a companion who would join with them so that, together, they would be more effective in doing good.

It was only natural that love and respect also came along with Mr. Williams. Or Dr. Branden. Or Jack Hennings. He used all those names—and more. In the beginning, no woman could have asked for a kinder lover.

I make no bones about it—this is a terrifying, cautionary tale. If it saves some lives with its warning, the women who moved through it, caught between life and death, will be forever grateful and know that *some* good came out of telling it. If you recognize yourself in it, *run*! It doesn't matter if a woman who is targeted by an obsessive, possessive lover is a high-school dropout or highly educated, or if she is naïve or brilliant, homely or beautiful, poor or wealthy. The brainwashing that certain men employ can trap any woman until the invisible, silken strands of their webs render her virtually helpless, cut off from those who might help her, her self-esteem squashed, her mind confused.

Ironically, it is quite often the weakest of men who stalk and capture. An insightful friend of mine calls this "the tyranny of the weak."

Strong, confident, men have no need to control. Only those who are empty inside have to—or they cannot survive themselves.

MORTAL DANGER

Chapter One

May 2008

Pacific Northwest residents were enjoying the sixth warm day of the year after a very long, very rainy winter. There was no better place to be on a day like this than in the town of Gig Harbor, Washington. Once a seaside hamlet where almost everyone knew everyone else, Gig Harbor's ideal location made the town's population grow by leaps and bounds. The original town had clustered around the harbor itself, but now there were new developments and shopping malls on both sides of the I-16 freeway that raced from the western end of the soaring Narrows Bridge in Tacoma, Washington, to the Bremerton navy shipyards.

The Washington Corrections Center for Women was located a few miles away in Purdy, but Gig Harbor hadn't known much crime—until recently. From 2006 to 2007, a series of appalling murders reminded people who lived in Gig Harbor that there really is no completely safe place anywhere.

On a balmy spring Saturday in 2006, David Brame, the police chief of the City of Tacoma, stalked his pretty young wife, Crystal, with deadly intensity. She had finally gotten the nerve to separate from him, and he would not allow that. In a crowded shopping mall in Gig Harbor, with their two small children in the backseat of their mother's car, Brame fatally wounded his wife with his service revolver before committing suicide.

Passersby rushed to remove the children from the car and shield them from seeing any more horror than they already had. Brame was dead, but Crystal lingered in critical condition for several days while family, friends, and strangers prayed that she might survive to raise her children. She could not come back from her massive brain injuries, although she fought a good fight.

Ten months later, in March 2007, an older couple died in Gig Harbor in a murder-suicide in their own home. It was difficult to say which tragedy shocked locals the most. The two deadly encounters made headlines in Seattle, Tacoma, and Spokane, and the news flashed throughout the Internet, touching lives far away, too.

Even so, there are still numerous pockets of serenity in Gig Harbor. None seem quite as safe as a small development a half mile from the original downtown. The residents there are all over fifty, and bylaws of the community are strict. None of the homes are sprawling or flashy, all are painted a discreet gray and white. The streets are named with sailing terms, such as Dockside Drive, Tideland Terrace, Windy Way, and Jib Sail, and they wind around in a series of curves and cul-de-sacs. The homes at the front of the neighborhood have wonderful views of the harbor, the

Dalco and Colvos passages that curve west of Vashon Island, leading to Puget Sound beyond. Most of the others have at least a peek at the view, and the tall fir trees in Grandview Forest Park creep up to their backyards, swaying and sighing in the wind off the water.

There are islands in the streets to discourage speeding; they're about fifteen feet across, all covered with bushes and flowers. Each velvet-green yard shows the loving care of its residents: Japanese maples, rhododendrons, azaleas, dogwoods, tulips, daffodils, and heather abound in the spring, and hydrangeas, lavender, petunias, gladiolas, and dahlias blossom in full summer.

But there is one small house that stands empty. Its lot, like all the others, is very small—perhaps eight feet away from the neighbors' windows. It's a sweet house, once the beloved home of an elderly woman. Now it almost seems to vibrate, sending out a chill feeling of terror, oppression, and perhaps insanity.

It was very difficult for me to park in its driveway for even ten minutes. Everything in me seemed to scream: "Leave! Get away from here . . . *now*!"

I didn't listen. I had a story to tell.

Sometimes the month of May felt to her like a replay of one long bad dream, bringing back memories too frightening to explore, too intrusive to ignore. Every spring, the dark-haired woman felt a flash of another recollection, playing across her mind like a video clip. Try as she might, she could never erase it before it finished playing.

May 1999

The sun had become a narrow sliver on the western horizon, and then it was gone, swallowed up by the Pacific Ocean, and leaving the woods dark as pitch as she ran for her life. She couldn't see where she was going, but that meant *he* couldn't see her either. For that she was grateful. He had promised her that this was the night she was going to die, and she didn't doubt his intention. Her only chance to survive was to reach her neighbors' house before he caught up with her.

She was barefoot and naked, but that didn't matter. She barely felt the thorns and little stones on the forest floor, the sharp gravel of the long driveway, the scratches etched in her skin by the fir and pine boughs and the blackberries that sprang suddenly out of the dark all around her. She marveled that she had never run so fast in her life, almost levitating as she plunged through the trees and boulders. Adrenaline surged through her body despite the aching in her lungs; she was a constant hiker on the beach far below, but she hadn't run for years.

Now she ran. She thought she heard him behind her.

It seemed impossible that this was the man she had admired, longed for, and been ecstatically happy with, back when the time they could be together had finally arrived. They had been through so much, and for a while it had looked like all their hopes and plans for the future were actually going to come true. She'd followed his lead without a single doubt, because he was strong, capable, and charismatic. And kind.

Once, she could not even imagine leaving him, but now

she wanted only to be free, and to keep from dying at his hands.

It was May 29, 1999, the Saturday of Memorial Day weekend, when it all fell apart.

Most people who lived on the Oregon coast or who had traveled there for the holiday weekend were having picnics and camping out. It was the first three-day weekend of the year when they could reasonably expect the weather to be warm and sunny, and the whole coastline from Astoria to Brookings was wondrous as summer rapidly headed in. In the winter, Oregon beach towns were subdued, cloaked in misty rain and fog, and year-round residents enjoyed the peace that descended when the tourists left. Gold Beach was no different.

The couple whose lives collided in a scene of horror had believed that Gold Beach would be their Shangri-la. On one of their many driving trips around the country, both of them had been taken with the little town. It seemed almost a Brigadoon of tranquility and natural beauty. Located about twenty miles from the California border on twisting Highway 101, Gold Beach had once been strictly a logging town with rugged roots, but its incredible views of the Pacific Ocean and the sea stacks—rock towers rising high above the surf—drew tourists, too.

Californians flocked to Gold Beach, beachcombing from Cape Sebastian to Cape Ferrelo, enjoying the virtual wilderness just beyond town and the endless surging waves of the Pacific Ocean. Their increasing presence providentially offered a new industry to Gold Beach as the logging faded. Small businesses sprang up, catering to visitors with art, theater, and wine festivals.

Steelhead and trout fishing had long been popular with true aficionados on the roaring Rogue River that coursed to the sea near Gold Beach, but jet boats soon offered sightseeing trips up the Rogue. Hollywood came to the Rogue River to make movies, and a number of famous stars built sylvan retreats there.

Publicity penned glowingly by entrepreneurs pointed out that tiny Gold Beach had more hours of sun on any given day than any other town located on the Oregon and Washington coastlines. Old-timers hated to see the metamorphosis of Gold Beach from a place where everyone cared about one another to a tourist magnet, but they acknowledged that people had to have a way to make a living.

On their first trip, one couple from California drove around Gold Beach, dined at a restaurant owned by locals, and fell in love with the small town. One of their goals was to come back someday, not as tourists but to live there.

And they did.

But by the time they returned to Gold Beach, their relationship was riddled with arguments, disappointments, and quite probably even lies. Moving there was supposed to be another chance for them. Perhaps neither could foresee what might happen if they failed.

Perhaps one of them did.

She sometimes thought back to where they'd begun, when their meeting had seemed so serendipitous. The circuitous route that most people take to meet that one person romantically dubbed the love of their lives makes one marvel that anyone ever finds that person. Sometimes those fated to meet—for one reason or another—cross each other's paths a few times before the timing is right.

Or wrong, in some cases.

Lifelong love or friendship—or endless unhappiness—may result. All perceptions of love and romance seem great at the start.

Kathy Ann Jewell was born in Mount Vernon, Ohio—in Knox County—as the second half of the twentieth century began. Mount Vernon is about halfway between Mansfield and Columbus. As a teenager, I spent one summer in Mansfield visiting my aunt and uncle. All I recall of note was the surprise elopement of Humphrey Bogart and Lauren Bacall, a huge social event for Mansfield. Bogart had extricated himself from his third marriage so he could marry the much younger Bacall. She was twenty and he was forty-five, and their affair was the talk of Hollywood when they were married at author Louis Bromfield's farm estate.

Kathy Ann—who soon was called just Kate—wouldn't remember that, of course; she was only a baby at the time. Her father, Harold Jewell, worked in her uncle's appliance store, as both a salesman and a repair specialist. The first television sets were hitting the market, and the American public was enthralled with the new medium for communication. In the fifties, the sets were black-and-white only, and there weren't many programming choices. Ed Sullivan's *Toast of the Town* variety show and Milton Berle's

Tuesday-night *Texaco Star Theater* drew huge audiences. Some television viewers were so entranced that they found even the test patterns intriguing.

Later, Kate's father worked in the accounting department of the Cooper-Bessemer Company, Mount Vernon's main industry, a company that had manufactured gold-standard compression engines for 175 years.

Kate's mother, Hannelore Erlanger Jewell, was—like most mothers then—a housewife. The Second World War was over and the Korean War seemed so far away. The mood all over America was optimistic, and Mount Vernon's twelve thousand citizens were no different. It was an idyllic town, a good town to grow up in.

Harold Jewell was born and raised in Mount Vernon. He joined the Marines after high school and became a paratrooper, one of the first wave of Marines to hit Iwo Jima. He was also one of a handful of men in his company to survive that assault. Although he rarely spoke about the war, he once revealed that his assignment was to be the last man off the LST (Landing Ship, Tank), an amphibious vessel designed in World War II to land battle-ready tanks. His job was to gather guns and ammo that might have been left behind. Once, he found the lieutenant in command there huddled in a corner, terrified.

"I had to slap him to get him up and moving," Jewell commented. "By the time I finished gathering up all the gear, I was separated from everyone in my company."

A few nights later, Jewell dug himself a foxhole in the black sand and pulled a piece of tin roofing over him, only to be wakened and ordered to the shoreline to fight off an expected Japanese attack. That never happened, but when he got back to his foxhole, he found it obliterated by an air strike. He thanked his lucky stars he'd survived Iwo Jima.

Hannelore, Kate's mother, was born in Germany to a Jewish father, Lothar, and a Christian mother, Minna, although they were not allowed to marry at the time. Lothar's father forbade his son to marry a non-Jew, so Hannelore and her sister, Margo, were sent to live with a nurse from the local hospital. It was only when her parents had a male child that her grandfather permitted Lothar and Minna to marry and Hannelore and Margo went to live with their birth parents.

Her foster mother, the nurse, had a daughter, Katja, fifteen, who adored Hannelore. It was mutual. Hannelore had a happy girlhood until 1939, when she was eleven and suddenly became a pariah—an ostracized Jew—living in fear with her family. Somehow, Lothar Erlanger managed to get his family out of Germany on the last ship before the war began, and they escaped the death camps.

Ten years later, Hannelore found Katja after the war, and she named Kate in honor of her old friend.

Kate clearly came from strong stock. She was a pretty child, who grew to be a lovely woman—tall and slim, with blue-green eyes and almost-black hair. She had a little sister, Connie, eighteen months younger than she was.

Kate became a flight attendant for American Airlines back in a time when they were still called stewardesses and their physical attractiveness seemed to be the primary job requisite. It was a career many young women aspired to, with far more applicants than jobs in what was considered a glamorous profession.

Flying satisfied Kate's quest for new experiences and

adventures not to be found in small-town Ohio. She traveled a lot, both for her job and for pleasure and public service.

Sometimes, when she was on layovers for American, she stayed in luxury hotels like the Fairmont in Dallas, with coffee on a silver tray, a fresh rose, and even a phone in the bathroom. But she also went on volunteer mercy missions, during which she would throw a sleeping bag on the dirt floor of a simple hut or tent in some far-off underprivileged country. She went to Nepal several times, volunteering for the Dr. Tom Dooley Foundation. Many of her fellow flight attendants did the same thing. By Nepalese law, they were only allowed to stay in the country for three months at a time. They could leave and come back, but they weren't allowed to "take jobs" that belonged to citizens.

Kate learned to adapt to almost any situation and was invariably cheerful and content with her life. One of her goals since childhood had been to help people, and the Dooley Foundation gave her an opportunity to do that.

By 1973, Kate had moved to San Diego, California, to fly out of the American Airlines base there. It was a good time to live in San Diego, although the population boom and the inevitable traffic snarls were beginning to emerge. It wasn't surprising that so many people were moving to San Diego County. The weather was perfect, and there were flowers everywhere Kate looked: bougainvillea, jasmine, poinsettias that grew roof-high, and hibiscuses in many colors. Even the freeway shoulders were carpeted with purple ice plants and manzanita bushes. There was the magnificent

San Diego Zoo, as well as San Diego Bay, with the ocean just beyond.

Kate lived in various apartments, moving often, from Mission Valley to La Mesa, back to Mission Valley and, for a short time, in University City. In the late eighties, she found a condo for rent on Solana Beach. It was located on a cliff and had a magnificent, 180-degree ocean view. The rent was reasonable because she shared it with a platonic male roommate. Their schedules were so different that it was almost like living alone. Solana Beach was perfect for her, as she was a dedicated swimmer who would enjoy the sport for the rest of her life. She was in the ocean swimming or boogie boarding most of the days she wasn't flying.

When Kate was in her twenties, she always had plenty of dates, but she wasn't anxious to get married. As she moved into her thirties, she had a few long relationships, but there always came a time when they ended. Sometimes she was the one who wanted to move on; sometimes she realized that the men she dated were averse to any lasting commitment. But she wasn't lonely—she loved her job, and she was still extremely attractive. She felt no pressure to get married or to plunge into a long-term affair.

Kate Jewell had many interests, and one of them was nutrition and its effect on health, perhaps because she had contracted the cytomegalovirus while she was in Nepal, and the virus had never quite gone away. But she'd always believed that what people ate changed who they were. She was a strict vegetarian who studied and worked in nutrition in the early eighties as she maintained her flight status with American Airlines.

In the fall of 1989, Kate was in her midthirties, a time

when most people pause to evaluate their lives. Kate was no different. She had just ended another relationship and realized that if she ever did marry, it might be too late to have children. She wasn't unhappy, but she wasn't really happy, either. She found herself at a crossroads.

Kate started changing her life by literally and figuratively cleaning out her closets, throwing out both clothes and memories that were out-of-date. Then she decided to take better care of her health and feel as good as she possibly could. Always a swimmer, hiker, and exerciser, she had to admit that she was feeling run-down and somewhat weary. Where she had once been slender without effort, recently she had put on some excess pounds. She was subject to hives and had a dime-sized sore on her nose that would not heal; she was quite sure it was caused by the CMV virus and had something to do with her diet.

Kate made an appointment at the Bayview Medical Group on Clairmont Drive in Mission Bay. Dr. John Branden's background appeared to be outstanding. He had come with enthusiastic recommendations from her friends. The Bayview Clinic was modern and well appointed. She studied the diplomas on his office wall: Dr. Branden had a PhD in biochemistry from the University of Santa Fe College of Natural Medicine. He wasn't an MD, but he certainly seemed to have had extensive education in nutrition and alternative medical treatments.

"Hi," he said, holding out his hand to cradle hers. "I'm Dr. John."

On first meeting, Dr. Branden was impressive, although he seemed as young as she was—if not younger. "I thought he was about thirty-five, but he was forty-four," she recalled. "One thing I remember about that first meeting was that he had the most gorgeous—almost glowing—skin."

That in itself was a good advertisement for his expertise. She noted that he dressed impeccably: His jacket and slacks were obviously custom-made, as were his shirts and what had to be a $250 tie. She learned later that his expensive Ferragamo shoes and sweaters were from Nordstrom. He wasn't a handsome man by ordinary standards, only about five foot ten, blond, and slightly balding, with eyebrows that sloped down and a nose that could be described as somewhere between patrician and knobby. Still, he had a definite presence—that of a man in charge of his practice and his life. It suited him. Kate was impressed.

"He wasn't my physical 'type,' though," Kate said. Her preference had always been for the traditional "tall, dark, and handsome man," she admitted, and then added wryly, "who [wasn't] able to make a commitment."

Of course that didn't matter with John Branden. She wasn't in his office looking for someone to date; she just wanted to feel better. And he certainly couldn't make a commitment: He was married. His wife worked at Bayview, too, handling the insurance and the billing with the help of an accountant who was on the payroll. His daughter Tamara scheduled appointments, greeted patients, and was the front-office manager. She was nineteen and obviously thought her father was perfect. Kate learned that his younger teenage daughter, Heather, worked at SeaWorld. "Both his girls were lovely," Kate recalled. "They had that fabulous skin, too."

Tamara was attending the Pacific College of Oriental

Medicine part-time to get degrees in acupuncture and Oriental medicine. When her classes interfered with her job, Dr. Branden's wife, Sue, or his younger daughter manned the front desk. Somewhat jarringly for the wife of a nutrition expert, Sue Branden was quite overweight, and she had a rather glum personality. Or perhaps she was just having a bad day, Kate thought. She seemed very different from her husband and her daughters. They brimmed with enthusiasm and cheerfulness. Kate learned that Tamara would soon be the youngest licensed acupuncturist in California.

The Bayview Medical Group offered an eight-week program, Branden explained to Kate. There would be weekly visits with him, three blood screens, menu plans, and supplements. They would begin with blood tests—titers—and whatever normal and abnormal readings resulted would indicate what her system lacked. He told her that he would personally work out a diet that would be tailored just for her, and he promised to prescribe the proper vitamins. He assured her she would be feeling well in no time, and when he spoke, he looked directly into her eyes.

She believed him. She didn't like the idea of needles in her arm, but she followed him across the hall to the blood-drawing room. At his direction, Kate rolled up her sleeves and lay back on the paper-covered exam table.

Watching him prepare the syringe and vials, Kate said, "I'm warning you that I have deep, rolling veins that don't like being poked or prodded."

He nodded calmly.

"A few years ago," she continued, "a doctor *stabbed* me a dozen times, and he never drew anything but pain."

"No problem."

He palpated her left arm and realized that she'd been telling him the truth about rolling veins. He switched to her right arm, tightening a tourniquet above her elbow.

"I want you to connect with me," he said, looking into her eyes. "Visualize your blood flowing effortlessly from your vein into my needle. I'll insert the needle."

There was an almost sensual feeling as he slid the needle in. With her eyes closed, she visualized what he'd suggested, and her blood draw was complete within moments with virtually no pain.

"That was excellent," he said, once again looking directly into her eyes as he applied a bandage and put pressure on the vein. She couldn't tear her eyes away from his.

She learned that that phrase—"Connect with me"—carried with it a hypnotic power. He was so honest and compassionate that people literally trusted him with their life's fluid.

Kate followed Dr. Branden's recommendations carefully, and her health steadily improved.

"It worked," she said. "I lost a little weight, my skin cleared up, and my virus symptoms were under control. I felt so much better."

During her weeks of treatment, Kate felt she was coming to know John Branden well, and found him to be a "vibrant, interesting, warm, and caring man." They first went over her diet diary, and he chided her gently for what she hadn't done, but more often he praised her. She looked forward to her weekly office visits with him, finding in him almost a kindred spirit. He matched her intellectually and could discuss so many subjects that she, too, found interesting. Kate was a college graduate, a very intelligent woman with a thirst for knowledge. John was fascinating to talk with, and unlike any man she had ever known. There wasn't the pressure that she—or anyone—felt in a dating situation; they were equals, platonic friends, with their own private lives.

Kate finally admitted to herself that she had a crush on Dr. John. She knew he was married and she totally respected his family bonds, so she didn't think there was any harm in her having fantasies about him. She never planned on acting on them.

Once, Kate commented to Sue Branden that she was lucky to be married to such a caring and sensitive doctor. She was startled when John's wife grimaced, rolled her eyes, and shrugged her shoulders, as if Kate had no idea what she was talking about. It was obvious Sue Branden didn't hold John in high esteem. Maybe he was so familiar to her, Kate thought, that she no longer saw his genius.

On the other hand, Sue confided to Kate that she had once wanted to be a stewardess but had married when she was so young, and then had had two daughters to raise, and so many things to do for John.

Kate and Dr. John usually ended her office visits with casual conversations, and he sometimes inquired about the romantic side of her life. She told him she'd had several long-term relationships when she was in her twenties and early thirties, but at thirty-eight, she had finally realized she was okay by herself. "I don't need a man to make me feel fulfilled and happy," she said easily.

In truth, she still hoped to find her soul mate, the one man who would love and admire her, listen to her and take care of her. But she didn't tell her doctor that.

Often, Dr. John gave her little extras, like a very professional shoulder massage. Once, he read her aura. He also told her that she gave him energy. Just being around her made him feel happier. It was a little flirtatious, but she believed it was also innocent.

When Kate's eight-week program was completed just before Christmas on December 20, she headed in for her last office visit and found herself regretting that her friendship with Dr. John was probably over. By its very nature, it was meant to be self-limiting. He was the doctor, and she was the patient, and she was well now. But she would miss him.

She was happily surprised when he gave her a lovely quartz crystal that carried with it curative powers, telling her it was a Christmas present.

"Well," she asked as she sat across the desk from him, "what do we do now? Am I supposed to come back for re-checks every so often?" Now that she had her health back, she wanted to stay on top of it, and John's program was excellent.

"That would be a wise idea," he said slowly. "Probably you should make an appointment for sometime in February."

The room had suddenly become very quiet. She looked up at him, and he wouldn't meet her eyes at first. And that was so unlike him.

John Branden said softly, "I need to say something more." And suddenly this man who was usually so verbal, sometimes spewing out words almost faster than she could understand them, was tongue-tied. When he finally spoke, he stuttered and stammered. It was strange for Kate to see him almost unable to get a sentence out.

"Say it," Kate said, half-dreading, half-hoping she knew what he was talking about.

"I can't."

Maybe he didn't want to keep her as a patient. Maybe she had assumed too much, and he was going to dismiss her and send her to someone else. They had formed some kind of a bond in those eight weeks, but she wasn't sure just what it was. Friendship, certainly. She sensed that he felt closer to her than he did to other patients, but that could just have been wishful thinking on her part.

"Just say it," she said again.

He stood up and walked around his desk. "I think I'm falling in love with you," he blurted.

Now she was speechless and felt stupid when she finally said, "But you're married." It was the kind of response a schoolgirl would blurt out.

He moved toward her and gave her an extremely chaste kiss. He massaged her shoulders and kissed her hair as he shared some of *his* fantasies about her. He asked if he could call her, and she couldn't bring herself to say no. Despite her common sense, her heart and her ego soared.

Kate Jewell was stunned. She hadn't expected this. She had been steeling herself for just the opposite. She actually knew very little about him, and he still wasn't her physical type—but she was drawn to him. It was a ridiculous situation. His wife, who rarely smiled, and who seemed disenchanted with her husband's charm, sat just beyond the examining room door. His two pretty daughters were in and out of the office.

They all seemed to be a solid—if not particularly happy—family, in business together, comfortable with each other, acting out whatever scenarios they had established years before. Now John told her that he had been unhappy in his marriage for years. He said that he and Sue were very close to separating and would probably do so after the holidays. Sue spent so much money on frivolous things, she had put on so much weight, and she insisted on drinking Pepsi—which was anathema to a staunch nutritionist. They had been on divergent paths for a very long time, he said with some sadness in his voice.

Kate hadn't thought about loving John in her real life— or his loving her. She knew a lot of women had crushes on their doctors. She liked him and felt safe in his presence. She had hoped that their friendship and conversations might continue. She knew there would be an empty place in her life if she couldn't see him anymore. He had never touched her inappropriately, not until now. She trusted him, and she would miss him if she should choose to walk away because of those bright red warning lights now exploding in her brain. She doubted she would ever find such an easy relationship with any man again.

She didn't realize how dangerous her combination of emotions could be.

Kate had to admit—if only to herself—that she had fallen in love with John, all unaware.

Right after John's declaration of love, Kate flew an allnighter to Boston and back. As passengers slept, she had a lot of time to think. She'd always trusted her own extrasensory perception, and, for over a month, she had felt strongly that she finally was about to meet her soul mate. Was it John? *No, he's married. But he's unhappy. No, he has a wife. But she doesn't complement, fulfill, or complete him.*

But I, of course, could, she told herself.

Every woman in love with a married man believes that her relationship is "special," that no one else feels as she does, and that her being with him isn't really illicit because the two of them are in love and there are extenuating circumstances. And, with rare exceptions, they all get hurt when they learn that their romance isn't special at all. There is a predictable progression, but it doesn't seem predictable to someone caught up in it. Kate had seen it happen to fellow stewardesses and other friends, and she was cautious. An affair with a married man wasn't something she had ever planned to have. But she was on a slippery slope.

When she left his office that day in December, she didn't know what to expect. Maybe she would never see him again, and probably that would be best. Her mind was reeling with all the reasons *not* to get involved, while her heart sang with joy that this wonderful man loved her.

It was inevitable that John *would* call Kate, and that she would agree to see him. She found him more sincere than any other man she had ever known, and soon it didn't matter that he wasn't her type—because he had become her type, or perhaps her type had become John Branden. They talked for hours when they could find time to be together, and John could almost read her mind. They were that close.

They planned their first date for Christmas Eve afternoon at a health-food restaurant. He seemed shy, and they were both nervous. He told her he had never done this before but he was serious about her and would tell his wife about his feelings after the holidays. He had already told his older daughter, Tamara.

They never went into the restaurant; instead, they spent their time talking in the car. They went to Kate's condo in Solana Beach but drank only cranberry juice.

They did not make love.

They walked on the beach, and John drove Kate back to her car by 5:00 p.m. "I literally floated over to my friends' house to spend Christmas Eve," she wrote in her journal.

Kate continued to fly for American Airlines, usually working as the flight attendant who served as the purser, in charge of the other attendants. She had enough seniority that she could bid on—and get—optimal flights, and she flew San Diego to New York City with twenty-four-hour layovers.

John kept his practice. Their lives, in the beginning at least, were not inextricably entwined. It was a delicate balance, but Kate thought she could keep her equilibrium.

But one day John confided once more that his marriage was virtually over and that he planned to get a divorce. He assured Kate that he'd never been with any woman except his wife and herself, that his feelings for her were an entirely new experience for him. He could not bear to go on in a loveless marriage—not when he felt the way he did about Kate.

When Kate asked him why he'd never strayed before,

since he and Sue seemed so unhappy together, he explained that he needed complete loyalty and commitment from the woman in his life. He had had that with Sue—at first—and he would, of course, need it from Kate. He was a one-woman man, faithful as long as that woman was completely devoted to him. That seemed endearing to her, and Kate promised him she could give him that. It seemed little enough to ask. He assured her that he had remained loyal to his wife for two decades. Now, their goals had diverged, and they had grown irretrievably in different directions.

Sue Branden had treated Kate like any other patient, barely acknowledging her presence when she'd occasionally come to the office for follow-up appointments. Beyond her briefly confiding that she'd wanted to be a stewardess, too, Sue was an unknown quantity to Kate. If she suspected that there was anything between her about-to-be-ex-husband and Kate, she didn't betray her feelings. Kate had the feeling she didn't care what he did.

Tamara and Heather obviously only wanted their father to be happy. His daughters clearly adored him—especially Tamara, who was planning to follow in his footsteps. Tamara actually seemed pleased that her father was happy.

John kept his word. Unlike many married men, he really did intend to get a divorce, and he obtained a legal separation in 1990. His divorce became final two years later. He felt he was being generous with Sue by offering her $50,000. But before their divorce was legal, she asked for their town house, their new car, and generous alimony, and he agreed. Kate didn't begrudge her any of that; Sue had been with him for twenty years, and she'd given him two daughters. It seemed that Sue was almost relieved to have a divorce; she and John clearly hadn't been happy when Kate first met them, and now Sue could have a life of her own.

John still had his practice, and he was full of inspirations about improving it, adding another clinic, branching out to other enterprises, and making even more money than he currently did. Kate didn't care that much about being wealthy, but she supported him completely in his dreams of glory that lay ahead for them. She was anxious to keep her promise to John, and she gave him loyalty and dedication. "He was the brains, and I was the workhorse," she recalled. "I wrote and typed up all of his grand plans, but I was all right with that."

There were occasional bumps in the road, sides of John that Kate hadn't known about before, but she realized that people always reveal new aspects of their personalities as familiarity and trust take over.

In December 1989—even as John was confessing that he loved Kate—he was being sued by a woman who lived in the condominium complex next door to the Brandens in La Mesa, California. She asked for an injunction prohibiting him from "peeping" at her. John never mentioned it to Kate, explaining later that it was merely an annoyance, and not worth worrying her about.

"Early in November 1989," his female neighbor's complaint read, "I was forced to call the police regarding my neighbor, John Branden, and report him as a Peeping Tom. He was watching me over the fence through my windows. This was not the first time he has been caught doing this. Early in the summer of 1989, John Branden was also caught watching over my fence. When confronted, he just runs off. I am afraid he may do me some harm."

31

John was forty-four, and the neighbor was fifty-seven, but she was an attractive woman. He responded to a temporary restraining order granted to her in an affidavit. He explained that he was "a doctor with my own medical group," and he scoffed at his neighbor's claims against him, characterizing her as "emotionally unbalanced" and angry at him for reporting her to the condominium association for having too many cats. Subsequently, seven of her eight cats had been removed. He stated it was "ludicrous" to think he would watch her covertly. He had no interest in her. His daughter Tamara backed up John's testimony, explaining that the woman seemed to be disturbed and angry—to the point of sweeping dirt at them when she and her dad were washing their car, all the while muttering obscenities.

Tamara would always validate anything her father did. He was heroic in her eyes.

A superior court judge ordered both parties to stay away from each other for a period of not less than three years.

He never told Kate about this problem with his neighbor.

More distressing was a suit brought against John, his silent partner (a naturopathic doctor), his daughter Tamara, his estranged wife, Sue, and the Bayview Clinic practice in 1992. Although John downplayed the charges against him—to the point that Kate wasn't aware of any of the details—she saw that he was very worried about this lawsuit.

A former woman patient and her husband were suing John for medical malpractice, sexual battery, failure to obtain informed consent, assault and battery, fraud, and misrepresentation.

John didn't tell Kate what the charges were, and he

waved off her worries, saying the woman was lying. He explained that Mary Ann Lakhvir* was married to a wealthy man from a Middle Eastern culture who didn't understand that in America women could be alone with their doctors without being shamed or ostracized. John said her husband misunderstood the close ties he formed with his patients and was so jealous that the poor woman was forced to tell lies about John to her husband.

The Lakhvirs alleged in their affidavits that they'd sought treatment for serious systemic infections but Dr. Branden hadn't known how to treat them, leading them to endure great physical and emotional pain and suffering when he'd administered mostly ineffective massage treatments and vitamins at the Bayview Medical Group in 1990. They asserted that John Branden was not a medical doctor and was not licensed to draw blood from them or give Mary Ann Lakhvir a pelvic examination.

(The suit was the first step in ending the silent partnership John had with the naturopath, and he later brought in an osteopathic physician to sign insurance claims.) Kate believed that John did have a phlebotomy license and that it was legal for him to draw blood. He'd been very skilled as he'd deftly and almost painlessly slipped a needle into her arm.

But even more troubling were the Lakhvirs' sexual accusations: They maintained that John Branden had made sexual contact with Mary Ann when he'd given her a full-body massage while she was disrobed, and that he'd kissed

---

* Some names have been changed. The first time they appear, they are marked with an asterisk.

her while she'd been naked. They asserted that he had then removed his clothes so she could "practice massage" on his nude body and become skilled enough to give her husband home massage treatments.

Sexual battery, as defined in California statutes, means that a person must intentionally cause harmful or offensive contact with an intimate part of another person. Those parts were listed as ". . . sexual organ, anus, groin, or buttocks of any person, or the breast of a female."

The Lakhvirs stated that Tamara Branden was at fault, too, as she knew—or should have known—that her father was not licensed to massage, draw blood, perform vaginal exams, or prescribe medicine.

He had also given them nutritional counseling—which he *was* adequately trained to do.

The case dragged on until 1993, but Kate knew none of the specifics. She felt sorry for John, because even though he tried to reassure her, she knew he was worried—perhaps even frightened. He went to great lengths to avoid being served papers on the lawsuit. He seemed to be extremely concerned over the suit, which, as he explained to Kate, was over things too minor to even consider. In the end, he gave up his practice, turning it over to his daughter Tamara for a few cents on the dollar. He no longer went into his office at all.

"He changed his appearance," Kate recalled. "He grew a beard, and he let his hair grow so long that he was able to wear it in a ponytail."

Although he didn't live in Florida, John asked Kate's sister and brother-in-law in Sarasota, Florida, to resend all the mail he sent to them, so that it appeared that he was a

Florida resident. With that ruse and his disguise, he felt safe. John was gleeful when people who knew him well walked right by him without recognizing him. He looked nothing like the clean-shaven, well-coiffed doctor he had been.

Of course eventually he had to face up to the accusations of an enraged husband who thought he'd been cuckolded. The case ended in April 1993, almost two years after the Lakhvirs' complaint was filed. It was dismissed with prejudice, meaning that it could not be refiled in the future.

It never was.

"John told me that he made that all go away by spending twenty-five thousand dollars," Kate said. "I'm still not sure whether he paid that to lawyers or to the woman—but we never heard any more about it. He said it was all a misunderstanding anyway, and I believed him."

John was ultimately believable, especially to a woman who loved him and trusted his vows to help people—his vows that both of them would help a lot of people. And the very idea that he might force himself on another woman in any sexual way was unthinkable to her. Not John. He was an honorable and concerned doctor, and simply wasn't like that.

Shortly after they began their relationship, at John's suggestion, Kate invited his best friend—Dr. Stanley Szabo,* a doctor of dental surgery who was also an expert in nutrition—to rent the empty room and bath in her condominium. He was going through a difficult divorce, and it seemed an ideal answer for all three of them. It helped pay her rent until John was able to move in with her and share expenses, and it helped John's good friend, who was working for John at the time.

Kate had never before detected a whisper of jealousy in John, but she caught her first glimpse of his capacity for rage because of this living situation—or, more accurately, as an adjunct to it.

John and Kate had a date one night, and when he walked in the door, he was very angry. He was furious that his best friend, now living in the condo, had parked in the driveway in John's usual spot. John couldn't understand Kate's thoughtlessness in allowing that to happen. How could she expect him to park on the street?

Kate was dumbfounded that such a trivial thing would set him off. John called off their evening and drove away, still angry. But Kate made sure he had his parking space after that, and she put his reaction that night in the back of her mind. John apologized, explaining that his blood sugar had been low and that had made him lose his temper. They resumed their relationship the next day and never spoke of his "parking tantrum" again. It was only an aberration.

She knew John was a perfectionist, even about things that shouldn't matter that much. Kate learned that he dressed so well because he had a personal shopper who bought all his clothes for him. It was one of the more benign things she hadn't known about him.

Early on, she was a little surprised to find that John drank more than she had realized. However, it didn't seem to be a problem, since they were both extremely health oriented and she didn't think John would do anything in enough excess to damage his body. He liked wine, but most Californians did.

Sometimes she saw bursts of inexplicable fury in John, not unlike his anger over his friend taking his parking space in her driveway. Kate blamed it on the times he'd had too much to drink; he attributed it to low blood sugar, fatigue, or some other problem that was out of his control. Once, when they still lived in San Diego, John took a hammer and smashed a ring he'd given her to bits. He put holes in the walls with his feet and his fists. And he was full of road rage, too, furious if another driver cut him off.

But his tantrums faded away as quickly as they came.

When the Brandens' legal separation was a fait accompli, John moved in with Kate. Neither of them was anxious to get married, but they did foresee a bright future as friends, lovers, and partners. When his divorce was final, it seemed that they had smooth sailing ahead, and they really were going to make it together.

With the divorce, John's ex-wife and his younger daughter no longer worked at the Bayview Medical Center. His older daughter, Tamara, had taken over the clinic. Even though the Lakhvirs' lawsuit was settled, John didn't go back.

Somehow, they had accomplished an almost tranquil transition, although John was insistent that he didn't want to stay in his present situation; he had too many plans, and he wanted to travel with Kate, to enjoy life a little now that they were both in their forties.

She was very happy living with him, working beside

him. There was a kind of magic in John that inspired other people, allowing them to see possibilities they hadn't considered. As much as they had talked through long evenings, there was so much about him that she didn't know. Although there were things in his past that he didn't want to elaborate on, he occasionally gave her short scenarios about his years as a boy and younger man. He seemed to have worked and studied very hard to become the man she knew now.

Kate knew that John's father, for whom John was named, had died in 1986, but he didn't care to speak about him much. A pall seemed to descend over John whenever she asked about his father, so she didn't press him. His mother was elderly and ill, and lived close by in the San Diego area. She had lived with John and Sue, but of course they couldn't expect John's ex-wife to be responsible for taking care of his mother any longer.

Kate liked John's mother, and often brought her small gifts she picked up in the cities she flew to. Sometimes Kate brought to work the cozy slippers that the older woman had crocheted, which she would sell to the other flight attendants. That tickled John's mother, and she accepted Kate as a member of her family.

John was a devoted son and very considerate of his mother, who had a series of heart attacks. He visited her in her assisted-living apartment often, and he and Kate frequently took her out to dinner.

When John's mother died of her final heart attack in 1992, she left him a half million dollars in her will. John's sister, Marilyn*, his only sibling, lived in the Point Loma area of San Diego. Kate had never met her—John and she had been estranged for years. Kate wasn't sure why, but John sometimes said she had betrayed him, turning him in to "some" authorities (Kate was never sure if it was the police or someone else) when he and his family had lived with Marilyn and her husband after they'd left Florida. He also said she and her girlfriends had humiliated him when he was only a boy, making him take his clothes off, tying him up, and laughing at him.

But that was such a long time ago, and Kate suspected he might be confused about things that had happened when he was a child.

With his inheritance from his mother, John finally had the freedom to travel and plan what he would do for the rest of his life. He'd closed down his practice at Bayview in 1993, Tamara had set up her own business, and John decided not to start another California clinic.

He and Kate embarked on a long trip. They drove to Arizona to see her father. Then they went wherever the wind took them, heading up the Oregon coast and north along the Washington shoreline on the Pacific Ocean. In some places, now, the beaches became less welcoming and somehow darker and craggier. Nevertheless, the two lovers explored some of the tiny islands off the northwest Washington coast. Both of them loved the sea, and they were sure that wherever they settled down, it would be somewhere near the coast.

It was a carefree journey; they didn't have to be any special place at any given time, and they were together, finally without problems or hopes that seemed impossible to achieve.

Listening to John expound on his concepts and his solutions to any challenge was enthralling for Kate. The temper tantrums she had sometimes seen in him were easy to bury in her memory. She knew he was a good man and he had been through a lot in the past few years. With the pressure off him, she believed the angry scenes would diminish. And they did—for a while.

Kate was thankful that she had waited until she was almost forty to find the companion and lover who was well-nigh perfect for her, and she hoped she was the same for him. She wasn't naïve enough to think they wouldn't have some detours and disappointments along the way, but she didn't worry about them.

Together, they could take on the world.

Chapter Two

Occasionally, Kate came across photographs of John in which he didn't look at all like the confident and charismatic doctor she had first been so attracted to. He was nothing like the man in the photographs, who, with hunched shoulders, appeared to shrink into himself, that almost timid man who ducked his head in a way that diminished his image. John preferred not to have his picture taken, but he occasionally obliged when his photograph was needed for a business brochure, or when she begged him to pose.

Now that they were together all the time, she realized even more that there were basic things she didn't know about John. She knew he'd grown up on Long Island, and that he'd lived in Florida in the years before he'd moved to San Diego, but the details were murky, and there were many almost secret aspects of his life before California. She knew his birthday was February 24, 1945, which made him a Pisces, a Pisces on the cusp of Aquarius. Either zodiac sign fit him in many ways.

John continued his education in 1994 and earned another diploma from Clayton College in Birmingham, Alabama. The document read "The Clayton School of Natural Healing, in Recognition of the Successful Completion of the Requisite Course of Study, Has Confirmed Upon John W. Branden the Degree of Doctor of Naturopathy With All the Rights and Privileges Thereto Pertaining."

Clayton wasn't a typical college; it had no sprawling campus where students attended classes. Indeed, it had been in existence for little more than a decade. There were no classes as such—it was a "distance-learning" institution that allowed students to take classes at their own pace online or through the mail. The actual physical "college" was a small building in Birmingham. Somewhat ironically, Alabama statutes banned distance-learning institutions for its residents, so all of Clayton's students came from out of state.

John spoke of how he'd learned a great deal about his chosen field at Clayton, and he would suggest later that it might be good for Kate to take some courses from the Alabama college, too. She agreed that she would do so if he thought it would make her more valuable in furthering their future plans.

Kate, too, became a naturopathic doctor with a degree from Clayton and a diploma that was identical to John's. Added to her bachelor's degree and with years of personal study on nutrition, she had far more formal education than he did, yet he never acknowledged that. She saw, however, that John did indeed have an encyclopedic knowledge of nutrition, and quite probably knew more than she did.

Slowly, as John began to trust her more, Kate learned

more about John's boyhood in Long Island and his family. His father had been a wealthy real estate investor in Long Island, taking advantage of the housing boom that followed the Second World War. Their family name had originally been Brandenburg, after the city in Germany, but John's grandfather changed it when he came to America. John's father was mostly absent from their Long Island home.

"I only saw him on weekends," John confided. "He was always gone, making deals."

She could see that this lack of interest on his father's part hurt John; he often commented that he'd never really had a father. He grew up in a mostly female family with his mother and sister, and during those sporadic times when his father was home, he was a demanding parent who apparently expected more of his son than John could deliver. The bar was always held too high for him to reach; it probably would have been for any male child. John also came to resent his father because he interrupted his time with his mother.

The family was wealthy; it wasn't that the elder Branden didn't provide well for them, at least financially. As their fortunes grew, they spent half of each year in Florida, where real estate continued to sell briskly. John's father was a tall, well-built man who dwarfed his son in size. He apparently dwarfed John with his personality, too. The skinny boy would never reach his father's height, or compete favorably with his business acumen. He often felt like a failure, but he also privately thought that his father was a failure as a parent. Although he knew he had a biological father, he would never feel he had a "real" father. He had only a man who came home when he had nothing better to do.

John told Kate proudly that he started his own business when he was a teenager, albeit on a much smaller scale than his father's sweeping real estate deals—he mowed lawns. It wasn't a job with much prestige, but he did it remarkably well. Even then, he was a perfectionist, and he bragged to Kate years later that many of his customers assumed he was a landscape architect. For the first time in his life, he was a success at something. By the time he was in his late teens, he was earning far more than most young men did cutting grass or doing other jobs. But he got only grudging respect from his father, who saw no future in his son's mowing lawns, even if John had made an art of it.

John graduated from high school on Long Island and said he started college in Florida at the University of South Florida in Tampa–St. Petersburg, or it could have been at a newer campus near Miami. He was vague about that. Kate wasn't sure how long he attended USF or if he graduated, but she assumed that he had. He told her he hadn't joined the Peace Corps, as many graduates were doing in that era, but he said he'd been active in Head Start programs both in New Hampshire and in Florida.

After college, John entered a fifteen-year period in his life when it was difficult to trace exactly where he was or what jobs he might have held. Kate knew that John married Sue when they were both very young—she was in her teens and he was in his early twenties—but he glossed over many other aspects of his life in Florida when Kate questioned him about them. He and Sue had their two daughters, and for a time John was working at a job that he found stultifying. He was a tax assessor for the county, and he sometimes dabbled in politics on a very low level.

Years later, when Kate did her best to learn everything about John that she could—especially in the Florida years—that job as an assessor was one of the few facts she could verify; she located fingerprints in the county assessor's office employee records that matched John's.

But he had another life, too. Because he always felt he had no father, he was probably vulnerable to some of the charismatic movers and shakers he met in Florida. John was searching for someone to emulate and follow, and there were many candidates for that in the sixties and seventies. It was the Age of Aquarius in the sixties, and America abounded with gurus, messiahs, and even cult leaders of so many new movements that it was hard to keep track of them.

Timothy Leary was espousing LSD "trips" in California, young people flocked to communes, cults were springing up all over, and even the Beatles were making soul-searching visits in 1968 to practice transcendental meditation with their guru, Maharishi Mahesh Yogi.

Two of the outstanding purveyors of far-out self-help were Werner Erhard (born Jack Rosenberg in 1935) and Bill Thaw, both the same age. Erhard and Thaw grew up together in Philadelphia and were mightily impressed with A. J. Silva of Silva Mind Control. According to him, Erhard had a sudden moment of revelation while he was driving along a California beach road. It became the basis for his movement, which swept America: Erhard Seminars Training, known as est. Bill Thaw jumped on board enthusiastically.

Erhard's program basically held that everyone is responsible for what happens to them, and it urged followers to become aware of what should be obvious. They simply had to "get it." The simplicity of it all, Erhard promised, would "blow their minds." In no time, est became immensely popular, as its followers proclaimed they "got it," even though many of them didn't.

The program's training sessions cost $250 a person, and there were waiting lists for trainee classes that usually numbered 250 people. The take for Erhard and his organization was $60,000 a class. This was no small sum in the seventies. The classes were not fun: they were marathon sessions with no amenities and virtually no creature comforts. Attendees were not allowed to eat, smoke, read, take notes, chew gum, or even go to the restroom during their sessions. Those first seven-hour classes were torture for those with weak bladders, so Erhard eventually modified the bathroom breaks and permitted them every four hours.

For a time, the est movement was a huge success, drawing both celebrities and average people who expected to change their lives overnight—or, rather, over two weekends.

It wasn't Werner Erhard, however, that John Branden chose to follow; instead, it was a man who was originally close to Erhard: Bill Thaw. John would often refer to Thaw as "the father I never had," or, more grandly, he would say, "Bill Thaw was my god."

When Werner Erhard moved headquarters to San Francisco, he and Thaw split up. Thaw spearheaded the "psi experience," a very general term for paranormal communication occuring during dreams, or through psychic connections between people when no words are spoken. Thaw found that most humans are fascinated with messages from "beyond," psychic foreshadowing of things yet to come, and communication that cannot be easily explained.

One of Thaw's early disciples still recalls him with the kind of wonder only associated with slavishly devoted groupies.

How much of it is true is anyone's guess, but Bill Thaw was allegedly a quarterback alongside Jim Brown for the Cleveland Browns in the late fifties or early sixties, then worked for the fledgling Dairy Queen chain and made a million dollars. It's said he went to Rome and gambled much of it away. He was reportedly a very handsome, well-muscled man who was a "great dresser" and wore expensive suits. Women were fascinated with Bill Thaw, and he responded. His wife divorced him because she could no longer put up with his affairs.

According to his former follower, Bill Thaw worked at Cedars of Lebanon Hospital in Miami from 1976 until the early eighties as a psychotherapist.

John Branden, the teenager who mowed lawns, the young father who worked for the tax assessor's office, and the man who sought status in local politics, learned much from Bill Thaw and tried to emulate him.

Kate Jewell would always feel that Thaw was the person who inspired John to become the charismatic doctor with scores of grateful patients, and the would-be entrepreneur whose goal was to make a fortune and be widely admired. Perhaps he was. And, quite likely, Thaw taught John Branden shortcuts and even con games that would pave the way for who he was to become.

Who Bill Thaw really was is perhaps more puzzling than who John Branden was, and the details of Branden's connection to Thaw are clouded. Thaw was about ten years older than the young man who saw him as a mentor, and at that point he was far more charismatic than John Branden. Bill Thaw was an enigma, the kind of person whose secrets probably followed him to the grave.

William Michael Thaw, aka Michael William Thaw, was born in 1933, and he was probably the consummate con man. He was an accomplished smooth talker and snake-oil salesman extraordinaire. He could convince almost anyone of almost anything.

In May 1962, when John Branden was still a teenager and years away from meeting Bill Thaw, Thaw was hired by a company called Micronics Corporation of America, with headquarters in Philadelphia. The company made miniature tools for the burgeoning electronics industry, and Thaw was hired to find distributors for these products. He impressed the officers at Micronics, and they agreed when he suggested that he set up his center of operations in Hampton, Virginia.

In his late twenties, Bill Thaw set out with enthusiasm. He began by taking out an ad in the *Newport News Daily Press,* where he offered franchises for Micronics.

A Hampton man named Leon Felcher* contacted Thaw. After he checked out the Philadelphia corporation, Felcher gave Bill Thaw a check for $5,000, made out to the Micronics Corporation of America. Thaw shook his hand and gave Felcher a contract as a "master distributor" for that firm. Smiling, he explained that the check would, of course, be held in escrow to guarantee payment for the tools to be delivered.

Later, Bill Thaw offered Felcher an option besides simply delivering tools and catalogs—he suggested that Felcher join with him and form a Virginia corporation that would be completely independent of the Philadelphia firm. Felcher agreed, and Thaw obtained a charter from the Virginia Corporation Commission for the new company, to be known as American Minitronics Corporation, naming Leon Felcher president and Thaw secretary-treasurer and responsible agent. When that switch was accomplished so easily, Bill Thaw told Felcher that their Virginia corporation could also be awarded the Micronics sales franchise for the entire southeastern territory, from Maryland to Florida. That would mean commissions from all the sales made by distributors in that area.

Leon Felcher wasn't eager to come up with another $5,000, but both Thaw and a man he introduced as his business associate—Donald Hassel—reassured him that this would be a no-fail investment. Somewhat reluctantly, Felcher wrote another $5,000 check to the Philadelphia corporation—for which Thaw had originally worked.

Felcher was right to hesitate. The company that had hired Thaw would never see either check. Bill Thaw had established a bank account with the real company's name, but he'd added "of Hampton, Virginia," opening it with $400 of his own money. Three days after he got Felcher's first check, he put $3,500 in this account and kept $1,500 in cash. None of it, of course, went to the legitimate Philadelphia firm. Within ten days, Thaw and Hassel had drained the account to its last dollar to pay for their motel bills, apartment rent, and other bills unrelated to either the Minitronics corporation or the Philadelphia Micronics company.

Bill Thaw and Donald Hassel expanded their nets. They took out more advertisements in newspapers in the Southeast, extolling the tremendous business potential in miniature tools. "Qualified applicants" who made a $5,000 deposit were guaranteed a place in their corporation and were directed to communicate with Leon Felcher, president of Virginia Minitronics in Hampton.

But the applicants never reached Felcher; instead, Thaw hired a secretary and told her to prepare letters with Felcher's name typed in. And then he instructed her to sign Felcher's name. Wisely, she refused, and the letters were sent out with only the typed name.

Nevertheless, Thaw and Hassel had some takers who expressed interest in joining their nonexistent business. They set up a meeting place for applicants at an upscale hotel in Washington, D.C., and greeted applicants wearing tailored business suits and carrying attaché cases. Their line of patter was as charming as before, but their conferences weren't as convincing to new applicants as they had been with Leon Felcher. None of the new candidates were willing to write a $5,000 check.

Finally, one man agreed to buy the distributorship for metropolitan Washington, D.C., for a bargain price—$2,500. Thaw sold the very same territory to another "exclusive distributor" on the same day. However, he failed to find any further applicants as gullible or generous as Leon Felcher. There were no more $10,000 investors, but there were several who managed to come up with $1,000 to $1,500. Thaw kept all the money for himself and used early applicants to persuade others—until they all realized they had been duped.

William Michael Thaw and Donald Hassel were convicted of mail fraud. They appealed the conviction, but a higher court denied their arguments.

A decade later, Bill Thaw had relocated to Florida, and John Branden was a young married man. John was four years older than teenaged Sue when they married. He always said he had his bachelor's degree from the University of Southern Florida in Naples, and that he had to scramble to pay his tuition as he worked as a landscape architect to pay his way through. He was a dreamer and was constantly looking for ways to rise above the crowd. For a time, politics seemed like a way to mingle with the movers and shakers, but it wasn't.

John told Kate that he had learned to fly small planes when he was a young man living in Florida, and he would sometimes brag that he flew around in Governor Lawton Childs's private plane when he was active in the Young Democrats organization.

Somewhere during that period, he met Bill Thaw. By then, Thaw and Werner Erhard had long since parted ways. John explained their breakup to Kate by saying that Bill Thaw felt that Erhard had become "too Hollywood," having grown far more interested in the commercial side of est than in changing people's lives.

Given the rise and fall of Minitronics, it seems unlikely that Thaw was actually turned off by any enterprise that made big money, but he might have learned to be cautious about franchises and moneymaking schemes that ballooned too quickly.

If John Branden would later dislike having his picture taken, Bill Thaw was adamant about not letting anyone take a photograph of him. Today, it is impossible to find a picture of William Michael Thaw. Something happened to John Branden as he followed his "god," and he undoubtedly learned from Thaw. As John became more savvy, he became more secretive. His jobs and organizational attachments seemed to be conveniently vague—quite possibly as he intended.

The Brandens had their two young daughters and seemed to be an average family of the seventies and eighties, at least to the casual observer. John told Kate that he had a thriving nutritional practice in a woman chiropractor's office in Naples. The way he spoke of his years in Florida, they seemed to be happy and productive.

And yet, they packed hurriedly and left Florida in 1986. John described their exit to Kate in a mysterious way, saying, "We left under cover of night—there was a contract out on me. . . ."

Was there? Kate had already seen that John had a need for drama, but she didn't know if he was testing her or just enjoying telling flamboyant stories.

"Once," Kate recalled, "when I first knew John in San Diego, he told me he had to go up to the northern part of the county to meet two guys who worked for the CIA, and he wanted me to go with him. It was all very hush-hush. And then it turned out it was only two guys who were getting him a hardtop for his Suzuki."

But Kate would always wonder about his tale of fleeing Florida in the dead of night. When she learned that Bill Thaw committed suicide by gunshot in Palm Beach a year after that, Kate began to believe that John *had* escaped from some ominous threat in Florida.

Thaw's body disappeared, according to John, but Kate sometimes worried that he wasn't really dead at all, only hiding from something that might involve John. "Maybe he's in South America," she commented, half seriously. John didn't reply.

John revealed that he had used different surnames from time to time—including his ex-wife's maiden name. He was most voluble when he'd been drinking, but even then Kate noticed that he was censoring what he told her. Still, in their early years together, Kate and John were happy, and she was totally committed to him. She never dreamed that he would hurt her—or leave her. John just loved mystery and keeping part of himself hidden.

It really didn't bother her, and only rarely did she press him for fine points and specifics of his past. Kate would sometimes ask him about his midnight flight from Florida, but he would never tell her why he'd had to leave so surreptitiously. Sometimes she wondered if it was for some illegal activity like gunrunning, and then she castigated herself for being so suspicious. John was a respected professional. He had his PhD from the University of New Mexico in nutritional studies. She assumed that he had attended the New Mexico college on a part-time basis during the time he lived in Florida.

The Brandens left Florida in 1986 and moved in with his older sister, Marilyn, and her husband, Alan*, until they could establish themselves in California. Two years later, John had a booming practice as a PhD in clinical nutrition in San Diego.

(He did not yet have his naturopathic doctor degree from Clayton. There is a legal difference between a naturopathic *doctor* and a naturopathic *physician.* John was never a naturopathic physician. The latter has more medical training and is allowed to write prescriptions. Clayton trained "doctors" who were nutrition and lifestyle counselors. Kate was taught to honor the difference.)

After his mother died, John really had no family except his daughters and Kate. Kate never met his sister Marilyn, and John wouldn't say why the authorities had sought him. Later, he denied that it had been anything very important— just Marilyn's meanness, as she enjoyed getting him into trouble.

As always, Kate believed him.

All in all, their travels were carefree. John's mother's bequest saw him through a jobless period easily, and he assured Kate that the next career he picked would be far more rewarding—both monetarily and in terms of helping people—than any he'd had before. They were in no hurry, and their almost-endless trip erased the stress that they'd both been living with for so long.

John and Kate liked the Oregon coast a lot and were even more taken with Orcas Island, a tiny dollop of land north of Deception Pass between British Columbia and northwestern Washington State. Orcas was reachable only by ferries, and it had kept its windswept, small-town ambiance, which attracted artists, tourists, and salt-of-the-earth longtime residents.

Kate was charmed by Orcas Island, but she pointed out

that the only way to get on or off the island was by ferry, and that could be a hassle. John agreed with her. He preferred Gold Beach, even though naturopaths could not be licensed to practice in Oregon. It was a moot question at this point; they were weighing all kinds of possibilities for bringing nutritional remedies to those who needed them badly. That would mean weeks of travel around America, and perhaps even in Canada. They weren't ready to settle down yet, but they both hoped to live in the Northwest some day. Neither of them liked the rootless feeling of being on the road without a home base.

Kate had no intention of giving up flying for American Airlines, but she had enough seniority to take long leaves of absence.

As the miles rolled away beneath their tires, they discussed John's ideas, and Kate followed his lead. She loved him, admired him, and believed in his innovative plans. If there were any fissures in his perfectly groomed, self-confident façade, Kate saw them revealed only briefly. John always had what seemed like a sound physiological reason—fatigue, low blood sugar, or something else—for his sudden rages.

They had gone through so much to be together, and she finally accepted that she had found the perfect relationship she had longed for all of her life.

Or so she thought.

Chapter Three

By 1994, although happily unmarried, Kate Jewell and John Branden grew tired of the road and were ready to settle down—at least enough to have a home to come back to. John constantly wanted to move on to another of his schemes for success—one more suited to his area of expertise—but they both wanted to live on the Oregon coast.

Kate and John scouted for condos to buy, but those they looked at felt cramped and too close to other units. They were about to give up when they found a perfect spot in Gold Beach. It was a house surrounded by trees, a small shake cottage with a shake roof, Dutch doors, and a yard full of sword ferns and rhododendrons. It was a rental, but they had an option to buy this secluded, woodsy property. They hoped to do that as soon as possible. There was room for a big garden, and neighbors close enough that they weren't completely isolated but not so close that they had no privacy. It was rustic, but not rugged, with thick-piled carpet, new appliances, a modern bathroom, and a big deck.

John's bequest from his mother's estate was long gone, and they couldn't afford to buy the house outright, but

Doris and Bill Turner, the couple who owned it, became their good friends—especially Kate's—and they wanted the younger couple to have the place.

"It was like living in a park," Kate said. "A forested park, and we had a glimpse of the ocean through the trees. We were as likely to see deer in our yard as we were squirrels. We both loved it."

John Branden, however, insisted that they clean every corner of their new home before they moved in. He was fanatic about germs. He washed his hands compulsively—almost like Shakespeare's Lady Macbeth.

"John wouldn't wear clothes inside if he'd worn them outdoors," Kate said. "He insisted on changing so we wouldn't bring in germs. If I sat in 'his' chair with 'street clothes' on, he freaked. I had to be really careful when I washed dishes, and make sure I wiped out the sink 'to get rid of bacteria and water spots.' He usually had to go back and do it over, which was also a way to erode my self-esteem."

John was horrified once when a neighbor brought Kate a cat that had been run over by a car. She cradled it in her arms, trying to find a pulse—but there was none. When John saw the dead cat in her arms, he yelled at her to get away from it. Didn't she know that bacteria and germs jump off animals when they die?

Their futon had to be made a certain way, the bedding folded just so and put away, and their towels had to be folded to John's precise specifications. He drove her crazy when she cooked because he hovered over her, cleaning up and putting away measuring cups before she was finished with them.

But these were irritating and annoying peccadilloes, and not nearly as troubling as his jealousy.

To keep them afloat financially, Kate occasionally returned to American Airlines, flying out of San Francisco. She had so much seniority that she could stay on the American roster, even if she didn't fly as many trips as she once did. It left her free to help John with his plans for a new enterprise. He forbade her to fly very often.

At first, that didn't bother Kate. John wanted her with him, and not in some city at the other end of the country. And they did have plans to make.

John had been seeking an "overnight success" business, although that didn't matter much to Kate. She would have liked to buy their home instead of renting it, and to have a stronger financial base, but she wasn't looking for great wealth and fame. Not at all. She loved to walk the beach, and she enjoyed the muted woods that surrounded their house, making the rest of the world and its problems seem far away.

John wanted more. He began to research companies that sold nutritional supplements, and he read about a Texas corporation that was a rising star in the stock market: Emprise, which soon became Mannatech, Incorporated. Although he read the financial reports on the company, which showed constant growth and millions of dollars in sales, he wasn't particularly interested in Mannatech's checkered background.

Mannatech was founded in the midnineties by an entrepreneur named Sam Caster, a man who had run afoul of the Texas attorney general with some of his earlier ventures. First came an insulation product, which, he said, used

"NASA technology" to dramatically reduce heating and air-conditioning bills. The AG questioned just how much and failed to validate Caster's claims. Next, it was a pest-control device that emitted vibrations that scared varmints and bugs, snakes and scorpions, out of infested households. The AG checked Caster's claims and found no vibrations whatsoever. He went so far as to say, "The device is a hoax and stands on the same scientific footing as a perpetual motion machine."

Undeterred, Sam Caster started Mannatech in 1994, concurrent with the Dietary Supplement Health and Education Act's passage by the U.S. Congress. The new statute made wide marketing of nutritional products much more profitable than it had been.

Mannatech was a multilevel marketing corporation, with a structure much like that of any number of businesses, with constant recruiting of sales representatives by supervisors and officers on a higher level. Makeup, cooking products, spices, erotic underwear, and sex toys are all sold this way. Of course, only those supervisors and officers in the upper echelons of multilevel companies make the munificent salaries.

Mannatech was one of the fastest-growing small companies in America, as its enthusiastic sales force spread to extol the success of its nutritional supplements, skin-care products, and weight-management system. The one aspect of their program that demanded intense delicacy was the fact that salespeople were told to avoid claiming that Mannatech's elixirs, pills, and creams could cure illness. It was all right to say that customers could benefit from "good nutrition," but they were not to promise cures for cancer,

Down syndrome, Alzheimer's, infertility, hemochromatosis, or any other specific disease.

Detractors called Mannatech's supplements "sugar pills" and viewed Sam Caster as a filmflam man. Supporters raved about the benefits of Mannatech and were outraged by doubters. Health care is perhaps more important to the consumer than any other "business," and return customers were anxious to relate their success stories to their friends.

John sold the idea to Kate, leaving out any of the criticism of Mannatech. It was, he said, a natural for them: They were both sincerely interested in nutritional supplements and the way diet could affect life and health. Kate, however, wasn't that impressed with Mannatech. A few years earlier, she had attended one of their functions. She'd been impressed with their products, but she felt that they were overpriced.

John was so forceful in his arguments, pointing out the positive side of their joining a rising star corporation, that she finally capitulated.

They agreed to sign up after attending Mannatech functions, although they hadn't been pressured to join the sales force. The company believed in first defining to future sales staff how their products worked, so the first contact most future salespeople and instructors had with Mannatech was to learn about its products, purchase, and evaluate them. Only later were likely candidates wooed to join Mannatech. John and Kate were hired as "consultants"—not salespeople. It was important that the many products Mannatech sold were adequately explained, and John and Kate had the background to do that.

The upper-echelon Mannatech staff in Texas was very

taken with John and Kate. John seemed so enthusiastic and was clearly well versed in all aspects of nutrition. As always, he made a terrific first impression. He explained that he could not see himself as a salesman or even just a consultant for Mannatech; he was, after all, a doctor and felt he should be accorded a different—and higher—position in the company.

They agreed.

Kate had come to realize that John looked down upon flight attendants in general. He often remarked that they had a "flight-attendant mentality" that didn't demand much brainpower. He could be tactless, explaining that while she was quite capable of doing the "grunt work" in their enterprises, he owned the "intellectual content" of all the work they did together. John always had multiple endeavors in the air, juggling them like plates on sticks. He pressed Kate to finish a project, yet by the time she had, he was already pursuing the next goal. The finished project was then filed with others that had never sold because John was continually moving on to the next idea and the one after that.

Mannatech was only one arm of his ambitious plans. Even though he was sometimes unkind in his zeal, Kate tried to believe that they were a team, working together. "During one of our 'brainstorming' sessions," Kate said, "where we were discussing how to present a particular Mannatech product, I figured out the scientific connection that would work before John did. I couldn't understand why he seemed angry at me, rather than happy that we had the answer we were looking for."

A long time later, she smiled sadly at how naïve she was then.

John hated Kate's airline job, and he coined crude terms for what she did. He told her that men were looking at her crotch when she sat on the jump seat for takeoff and landing. "You're just a flying cunt-hole," he said.

When he was in his mindlessly jealous mode, he accused Kate of sleeping with every pilot she flew with—even with every gay male flight attendant! In August 1998, when he was once again intoxicated, he grabbed a gun from his collection and ordered her to put on her flight-attendant's uniform, and then he forced her to have sex with him. It was a humiliating experience, and she promised him that if he ever threatened her with a gun or his fist again, she would call the police and have him charged with assault.

He didn't seem to believe her, but she was resolute.

Their perfect, symbiotic relationship was shredding rapidly. Emotionally, John kept Kate continually off balance. It was becoming difficult for her to differentiate between the "good John" and the "cruel John."

"He could be so adoring—almost worshipful, so kind," she said, "but the other John sometimes seemed so angry that I was afraid he might be capable of killing me."

And then she shook her head at the very thought. Of course he wouldn't kill her; he loved her more than any man ever had. No man would kill someone he truly loved.

"John kept coming up with the ideas, and then I did 90 percent of the work, writing up the educational material," Kate said. "That became a pattern for us. We made an audiotape for Mannatech called 'Let's Give Them Something to Talk About,' drawing on the Bonnie Raitt song that Mannatech had permission to use. That got us launched with the company."

John and Kate attended Mannatech conventions and sold the tape and other educational brochures and booklets they'd created to help associates sell the products with correct information. At the same time, they produced a CD-ROM with Ed DeMarco, Kate's brother-in-law. They called it "Your Own Diet." The company liked it so much that they remarketed it as "The Mannatech Optimal Health Plan."

Although they left Mannatech for a year or so, they returned to the company in 1996.

Signing on with serious commitment meant that they would be gone from home more. At this point, the company saw John and Kate as perfect candidates to represent Mannatech on a speaking tour around America. They were attractive, extremely personable, and intelligent.

John was an excellent salesman. He told Kate that he could be whatever or whoever someone needed him to be just to "close a sale."

Dwight and Susan Havener held top positions in Mannatech in the southeastern states, and they invited Kate and John to visit them in Jupiter, Florida, just north of Palm Beach. John seemed to have no qualms about returning to Florida, but he flatly refused to go without Kate.

In many ways, it turned out to be a great trip. The Haveners had a wonderful estate on the water with its own guest cabin that was nicer than most people's homes. Jupiter drew many millionaires. Burt Reynolds had his home and theater there, and it was heady to be guests in such a posh environment.

At first, the visit went well, and Susan Havener particularly liked John. She was amazed by his knowledge and his charisma.

"John convinced the Haveners that we were the greatest thing since sliced bread," Kate remembered. "Their business was already booming, and he assured them it would 'explode' with us joining their organization."

But John bruised this first impression by going too far, too fast. He was full of ideas on how to improve Mannatech, most of them criticism about the current corporate structure. It didn't seem to occur to him that the company was already a huge success the way it was currently functioning. Why should they want to change it? Kate felt embarrassed as she saw their hosts exchange glances, obviously irritated with John's grandiose plans for changes in Mannatech.

It was clear he had walked in with an ego almost beyond comprehension and wanted to start at the top. Even so, aside from his unsought critique, the Haveners could see that John might well be an asset as a consultant/ lecturer. His charm might have a tendency to tarnish on very long acquaintance, but on one-night stands around the United States and Canada, he would be very imposing.

The Haveners had some vitally important meetings set in New Jersey, and they asked John to accompany them on a driving trip there. They were taken aback when he flatly refused to go.

"He wouldn't go," Kate said. "It was almost impossible

to make him realize that, for the moment at least, he wasn't the boss."

Beyond dismissing Mannatech's business structure as not nearly as profitable as it could be if they followed his suggestions, John insisted that the Haveners owed him $1,500. Kate was mortified.

Despite that, Dwight and Susan Havener continued to believe that Kate and John would be an asset to Mannatech. They were sent on a lecture tour extolling the benefits of the company's four main products, particularly Ambrotose, the lead product, "a glyconutritional dietary supplement ingredient consisting of monosaccharides, or sugar molecules," according to Mannatech.

Critics doubted that Ambrotose had any health benefits, because they believed the human body lacked the kind of enzymes needed to break down the plant fibers in the highly touted supplement.

The differing opinions ended in a stalemate year after year, and a decade later, ABC's *20/20* aired a show on the controversy.

But John and Kate both felt it had benefits. And if it wasn't as much of a cure-all as some believed, it didn't harm anyone outside the pocketbook or if substituted for more accepted medical care in the treatment of life-threatening diseases. Mannatech continued to insist that its representatives refrain from promises that their products targeted and cured particular illnesses.

The couple from Oregon was a hit. Each of them was the very picture of health, vivacious and encouraging, and they didn't employ any hard-sell tactics. They didn't have to. Despite their private disagreements, they believed in what they were doing. One of the things that had originally attracted Kate to John was his desire to make people's lives better. That drove her, too.

John and Kate lectured together. As they left the West Coast to begin their first speaking tour, they had had six weeks to prepare. John was the experienced speaker, and Kate asked him to tell her how he wanted to handle their presentation. He put her off continually. Only when they were on their flight to Georgia, where they would begin their series, did he hand her an outline of what he wanted her to say.

When Kate, using her airline passes, flew as a passenger with John, he seemed very comfortable with flying and showed no fear. "The only thing that upset him," she would remember sardonically, "was when we couldn't get seats together. If I sat next to a good-looking stranger, John was convinced he was making moves on me or that I was flirting."

With so little preparation on their first venture, Kate was very nervous. Fortunately, the audience was kind and receptive, and complimented her after she spoke. She felt confident, but later, in their hotel room, John belittled her and berated her for "screwing up." She could see he resented even her small success. First she was mortified, then furious.

As long as she was with him, he remained calm and confident. He had told her in the beginning that his wife had always been there for him, and that he would expect that of her, too. And she'd promised to stand beside him. However, she hadn't realized how dependent he would be on her. Sometimes, he was almost like a child who needed to hold his mother's hand. But in front of an audience, he could be a magnanimous and totally competent performer who held a roomful of people in thrall.

"There came a trip," Kate recalled, "when everything went wrong. We'd recently returned from the Canadian tour, and I had my 'speaking outfit' dry-cleaned. I picked it up, threw it in my suitcase, and we left to fly to Lansing, Michigan. The morning of the presentation, I put on the outfit only to discover it had shrunk considerably!"

There wasn't time to buy anything else, so Kate slid the pants down to her hip bones so they reached her ankles. This didn't leave even a full inch for her tunic top to cover the waistband of her slacks.

She got on stage feeling ridiculous, knowing she had to maintain perfect posture, as she had no room for error lest her bare stomach show.

"I was so nervous. I decided just to 'zen' the situation," Kate said, "so I simply spoke from my heart. Apparently I connected with the audience, who were most complimentary to me, but a couple of people added almost as an afterthought, 'You were good, too, Dr. John. . . .'

"That was the last time I was allowed to take the stage."

She still loved him, but try as she might, Kate could not avoid seeing emerging aspects of John's personality that continued to disturb her. She'd known from the beginning that he had a strong ego; back then, it had been part of his charm, but it wasn't so much any longer.

Why did he have to build his ego by sacrificing hers?

They stayed with Mannatech for five years after returning to the company, and they didn't mind the sporadic traveling. They went home to Gold Beach when they could. It was much like the kind of book tour I do as an author—a different city every night. They began their first Mannatech tour in Florida and Georgia, crossed Canada in five days, and headed east to Michigan, where their tour ended. Kate and John flew from city to city most of the time and stayed in nice hotels when they landed. Many of the Mannatech presentations had a festive—almost partylike—air.

Still, Kate often longed for their quiet cabin in the woods in Oregon. It was a place where she felt serenity and safety, where even the wild deer and their fawns felt little fear. She flew her two-day trip for American once a year and remained on the active roster.

John loved Oregon, too, and they were able to stay in Gold Beach most of the time. They were getting by financially, but Kate could have made more if she'd flown full-time. John wouldn't hear of that. He was restless. Kate had long since accepted that it didn't matter what he was doing; he grew bored easily and began to formulate plans for new enterprises. He was like a butterfly—lighting on a firm base, then launching himself too soon into the air and flitting on to the next perch.

Kate only knew him from his San Diego days. It was almost as if he'd had no life before then. What had happened to him earlier remained a mystery. Every so often she wondered about the real reasons he and his family had fled from Florida. He didn't want to talk about it, so she let it go. The only time he referred to that last night, even obliquely, was when he'd been drinking. Even then, he never gave specific details.

"There were times," she mused, "when I thought he might even have been involved in some kind of crime. But that seemed ridiculous, and I blamed my own imagination."

There *were* things about John that were odd, beginning with the story he had told her about meeting with CIA agents when he'd only been buying a convertible top, and on to the midnineties, when he occasionally behaved as if he'd been in a spy movie. There was the time he had donned a disguise to avoid being served with the suit for improper sexual advances. He also had a kind of code he used when he wrote letters, apparently for no particular reason. He used Kate's last name—Jewell—intermittently. He sometimes alluded to being involved with important political figures in Florida, but, again, gave her no names or details.

"Every night," Kate recalled, "John had to lock the door and then rattle the doorknob exactly seven times to make sure it was really locked. That drove me nuts."

Maybe he was a frustrated secret agent, she thought. No, it was just one of John's idiosyncrasies. Kate was far more disturbed when John hit her for the first time, after they'd had an almost innocuous argument in a campground on one of their trips. Later, he berated himself. He swore he'd never meant to hurt her, to leave marks and bruises on her.

And she forgave him.

John seemed more horrified than she herself was that he'd hit her.

But it happened several times, usually when he'd had too much to drink.

Their lives were far from the idyllic match that John had once painted for her. Kate accepted the fact that John would probably never be happy unless he was recognized and financially rewarded for his "intellectual capacity," and all the "wonderful ideas" he came up with. John believed that his intelligence was far superior to most people's, and he assumed others should be grateful to bask in his presence. It wasn't a stance that endeared him to others. John had told her as much about his idol, Bill Thaw, and she recognized that John was identifying with his dead hero more all the time.

"It seemed that every time we reached a solid jumping-off place for one of John's grand ideas, he changed his mind—and he was off on something else," Kate said. "We lasted the longest with Mannatech."

Always investigating many possibilities, John chose one new career after another. One of his ideas was to teach other doctors and dentists how to build their practices. He and Kate could continue to work side by side, utilizing the strong points each possessed. He'd made a success of his San Diego clinic in less than a year, and he was positive he had the know-how to point out mistakes doctors were making without realizing it.

Resurrecting flagging clinics was challenging enough for John for a while. When he took on a new client, he spent hours talking and questioning what it was the doctor hoped to achieve. Again, it was Kate's job to write and type—to whip the client's expectations and John's advice into a cohesive portfolio. She was an excellent writer, far more talented than John was.

Occasionally John told her he couldn't succeed without her, but he would obliterate that compliment the next day by saying he could hire a two-dollar-an-hour typist to do what she did. (She often wondered where he could find *anyone* who would actually accept such meager pay.)

Sometimes, she grew weary, and a little resentful. "It would be two a.m. and I'd be typing away, and John and the clinic owner would be shooting the bull. Sometimes, I thought I was doing all the work."

And, in truth, she was. John enjoyed pontificating and playing the expert, and sometimes he tended to view Kate as only his secretary. She, too, was good with people; any good flight attendant has to be. They were to have been almost-equal partners, and she would have enjoyed joining the conversations with their clients.

Still, John could not stand to share the spotlight. He pointed out that *he* was the only one who could read each new client and respond in a way that convinced them he could multiply their income with his wisdom and experience. He believed that the "good old boy" routine was the best way to do that.

John's new advisory business didn't last long, and it wasn't making much money. He was soon chasing two or three other ideas that he was sure would be wildly successful. Kate signed up to fly more trips as a flight attendant/purser with American Airlines. She drove to San Francisco and flew into New York City. He didn't like it, of course, and he grew more and more jealous of any time she spent away from him—particularly when she flew away as a flight attendant.

On her layovers in New York City, John called Kate as soon as she walked in her room. Then he would call her every ten minutes for several hours to make sure she was still there. If she went to the deli across the street to get something to eat, she had to accomplish that in a twenty-minute time frame. When she occasionally joined the crew for dinner, she knew she would face an inquisition, and when he was angry about something, he called her all night long.

"Once," Kate said, "the hotel operator connected him to the wrong room at two a.m. He woke up a man who'd been sound asleep and spoke with what John thought was a black dialect. John went ballistic."

She hated to even think it, but being away from John was often a relief. She could breathe again.

Chapter Four

Dr. John Branden was insanely jealous of Kate, and more so when she was traveling without him. His possessiveness wasn't just over other men—it extended to *anyone* who took her focus away from him. John was even resentful when he felt she chatted too long on the phone with her best friend, Michelle, who lived in San Francisco.

"He accused us of having a lesbian affair, which was absurd," Kate said. "But he resented my having anything of interest to talk with her about. He read my mail, and now he started to tape all my phone calls. There wasn't anything I'd hidden from him, but Michelle was going through a difficult divorce, and the fact that John was taping our calls frightened her. Neither of us knew what he might do with the tapes."

There were times when the only peace Kate could find was when she took long walks on the ocean beach. There, with the sound of endless breakers crashing over the rocky outcroppings, and with the clean, almost medicinal smell of salt water clearing her head, she could think. She admitted to herself that their relationship was dissolving. Initially, John's fanaticism and ravenous ego had been virtually hidden, but just as constant drops of seawater wear away sandy cliffs, John's jealous clinging to her carved rivulets of doubt into their love affair. The drops were often becoming deluges that sluiced and dissolved the very structure that had once seemed so sound.

If John was jealous of her best friend, he was tyrannical when it came to other men. Kate was faithful to him—completely faithful—but she had many male friends; over the years she had met a lot of men working for the airline. She was no longer romantically interested in any of them, but John always thought she was.

Often, he embarrassed her. If a man smiled at her or touched her hand lightly, she saw the flicker of rage darken his eyes and prayed he wouldn't explode. Usually, he maintained control until they got home, and then the eruption she knew was coming burst through. She had bruises, but he struck her carefully so that they would be hidden by her clothing.

Kate had such high hopes when John agreed to go to a formal party for American Airlines employees. Their evening started out well enough, and she was proud of him, hoping he would show off his charming side to her friends and coworkers. They made a handsome couple as they posed and smiled for the camera, then headed into the party. Kate wore a red satin strapless gown and a black cape with a high collar, and John wore a black tuxedo and a red bow tie. This time, she thought, everything would be all right.

And they *were* having a good time—until a pilot who

had been her friend for a long time stopped at their table to talk. He was a tall, very attractive man, and Kate saw John tense up as he approached them. When the pilot touched her bare shoulder and rested his hand there for a moment, Kate knew that it was going to be a long, unpleasant night.

John insisted the pilot had let his hand slip to Kate's breast, and he was quietly angry. He sulked for the rest of the evening, but he waited until they got to their hotel room before he detonated the dynamite inside him, accusing Kate of flirting and enjoying the touch of another man. It did no good at all for her to speak rationally to him, and she had bruises blossoming by morning.

She realized that she couldn't let John into her American Airlines family; he saw threats to himself in every man in the room. That was the end of the parties she had once enjoyed a great deal.

It seemed to her that they often worked at cross-purposes. John still attempted to be romantic and gallant, but his timing was all wrong.

Kate had to fly, however infrequently, to maintain her status with American and to keep her airline benefits for both of them. A cross-country trip with three changes of time zones was exhausting. John didn't understand that. After he'd been alone for a few days, he thought her homecomings were the perfect time for romance.

"He'd go out and buy all kinds of deli food and wine, and insist that I eat that salty, fatty stuff and drink the wine," Kate recalled. "But when I came home from a flight, I was bloated and worn out, and my brain was in another time zone. I wasn't hungry and I didn't feel like drinking.

He wanted to have sex, and I just longed to get some sleep. John was incapable of recognizing signals about what other people wanted. He did what *he* wanted. Always."

Like all couples who spend years together, traits that once seemed endearing to John and Kate no longer did. In the beginning, John had seemed to Kate to be a man completely in control, stable, and understanding—someone who would care for her. But that side of him dwindled more and more as the years passed. For instance, he would never accept blame for anything that was wrong in their lives or in their relationship.

"He always had an excuse. In the beginning, it was the pressure of his divorce. Sometimes it was that his blood sugar was low, and he said he had no control over his rages because of that. He had many, many 'biochemical reasons' for his moods—and I bought them for a long time. But as I got more educated in the effects of nutrition, I doubted his excuses.

"Whatever went wrong, it was somebody else's fault," Kate remembered with a sigh. "More often than not, it was my fault."

Kate just tried harder to please him. She had never been married, and he'd been married to Sue for twenty years. She assumed initially that he knew more about marriage than she did, and she followed his lead.

"John always expected extra attention," Kate said. "He'd told me that he expected the woman in his life to be completely loyal and committed to him, and I promised him that I would of course be that kind of partner. I just didn't realize all that included. When we were out in a restaurant, he expected me to break open his rolls and butter them for him—because Sue always had. Finally, I told him to butter his own rolls."

But when it came to more important requests, Kate appeased John. "It was much easier not to make waves."

If she did, John would blame Kate for not being supportive enough of him, and that meant another skirmish that would *always* be her fault.

One day, she would have to wonder if giving in to him might save her life—or at least prolong it—but at this point she had no idea what terror lay ahead.

But that came later. For years, Kate hoped to marry John. Sometimes, she still did—if only to reconnect with the man she once knew. They had been together for almost a decade. Maybe it wasn't too late. It was 1998, and Christmas was coming. John bought Kate an engagement ring and asked her to set a date to get married. She was hesitant. "I told him, 'I will marry you if I can find the John that I fell in love with.'"

"Okay," John said quickly. "Then that's who I'm going to be."

She hoped that he meant it. "When John was good, he was really good," Kate remembered. "When he was bad, he was a little bit worse each time."

Over their ten years together, Kate left John several times—but never for long. If he couldn't find her, or get through to her with his blandishments and apologies, he hounded her family, her friends, the people she worked with, calling them at all hours of the day and night, dropping in unexpectedly, demanding to know where she was. She worried about the way he disrupted the lives of people she loved.

John wouldn't let her go. He stalked her, phoning her constantly. If he couldn't find Kate, he called or confronted everyone in her life, making her relatives feel as trapped as she herself did. "He bothered the people I lived with, bothered my family, my friends," Kate sighed, remembering. "Bother, bother, bother. Call, call, call. He insinuated himself into the lives of everyone I cared about. It got to the point that everyone hated John—except John. He didn't care about anyone else's feelings, and he felt he was so much smarter than anyone else. It wasn't the way to make friends. . . ."

Whenever he found Kate, he begged her to come home, telling her that he couldn't live without her. Once, he even showed up at the airport in San Francisco to meet her flight, his smile beaming through the crowds of disembarking passengers. He couldn't understand why she wasn't thrilled to see him. Once again, she was mortified at John's behavior and found herself apologizing to all the people he called when he was desperate to find her.

"I'd finally decide I had to go back," Kate said. "I was committed to him—when I think of it, I realize I was probably more married than most women who were legally bound to their husbands. We'd been together almost all the time—we were practically joined at the hip, and he was totally lost by himself. People in Gold Beach assumed we were married, and it was easier to say nothing than to explain what was really unexplainable."

John's jealous moods were exacerbated by his drinking, and Kate attended some AA meetings to see if that would help her deal with him. It didn't. But her eyes were opening about the futility of trying.

For years, she'd been living with domestic abuse, but

she hadn't recognized it fully. She was classically in denial. Kate remembered only her promises to stay with John, and her conscience overrode the emotional battering, the bruises, the stalking, and his rages, which had grown steadily in frequency with every year they'd been together.

"I always concluded that we should try one more time, and that we should have therapy to try to make our relationship work." In the end, it still seemed easier for her to return to their little house in Gold Beach to try to work it out between them. She'd been captured in the cycle of violence that thousands of women come to know all too well. Kate lived with guilt over John. "I felt like I had brought this man into the lives of my family and friends, and it was my duty to go back to see if there was a way I could either make the relationship work—which I sincerely doubted— or *amicably* end it. We had done so much work together, and it was hard to let go of the dream of helping people."

As the year turned over to 1999, Kate felt more hope than she'd felt for the past few years. She even wrote to John's daughters, Tamara and Heather, to tell them that she felt she and John were going to make it after all. It was a new year and, she thought, a new relationship.

Kate had never thought of herself as a victim of domestic violence. "Those were cases, I believed, involving poor women who were barefoot and pregnant—uneducated. My parents never fought, and for a long time, I was sure that *I* was doing something wrong, that it was my fault we had so much trouble. And John certainly reinforced that by blaming things on me."

She knew now that he was bipolar, and that he swung

79

wildly between euphoria and depression. But he had promised to change. He even moved to an apartment temporarily, and he began seeing a psychologist. John saw the therapist in person, and the doctor consulted with Kate by phone.

"Charlie, John's psychologist, warned me not to get John upset," Kate said. "He told me to 'just let it go' if John began to act in a volatile way. I wasn't to argue with him, because it would just make it worse. That was pretty much the way I'd always reacted to John's angry moods, so I took his advice."

Kate was afraid to ask Charlie what John was capable of if she should speak up for herself. He hadn't said that appeasing John was for her own safety, but he'd implied it. For the first three weeks of 1999, everything went well. She hoped the pattern would continue; she didn't want to throw away a relationship that had inspired ten years of trying.

Their financial situation was bleak at best. Kate insisted that she had to keep flying. Although John detested the thought, he knew it was necessary.

"And I was helping John as I always had by typing up his newest plan for success, and discussing just how we could sell it. But we'd be almost finished with his 'Idea Number 22' and ready to launch it when John lost interest and he was off to 'Idea Number 26.' "

John saw occasional nutrition "patients," and he had blood studies done by Bonnie Crichton,* a young woman nutritionist who lived in Napa, in northern California, with her husband, Joe,* and their children. John had few friends, but he became close to the Crichtons. As part of his "Doctors' Practice Builder Plan," he taught Bonnie how to read blood chemistry, assuring her it would enhance her practice and her income.

By now, Kate had created a standard written report for blood test results. It provided a comprehensive review for each patient. John suggested to Bonnie that she send him and Kate her patients' blood test results. Kate would insert the information and send it back to Bonnie so she could share it with her patients.

John promised Kate he would present her with $250,000, and she would see that she'd done the right thing by staying with him. She didn't want the money, and she recognized his ebullient offer as a symptom of the manic side of his personality. Still, she hoped against hope that it wasn't too late for them.

It was.

The aberrations in John's thinking began to seep through his façade like poison. He couldn't maintain the "new John." The "heroic figures he admired were disturbing," Kate said, shaking her head. "He thought Ted Kaczynski was a hero—and he thought the two kids [who] shot up Columbine were brave. He might only have been baiting me, but he seemed serious."

January wasn't over when John had another tantrum, this one the worst Kate had experienced. Kate had met Paula Krogdahl at a swimming pool, and they shared rides. Paula was an assistant district attorney in Curry County. (This, by coincidence, was the same Paula Krogdahl I wrote about in *Small Sacrifices*. Fifteen years before she met Kate, she'd helped Diane Downs's daughter, Christie, recover from being shot by her mother, and counseled the girl on how to feel safe when she testified.)

In the intervening years, Paula had become an expert in domestic violence. She had an uncanny knack for spotting abusive men, and John Branden frightened her. She was discreet, and asked Kate very tentatively if she was in trouble. Kate shook her head. She wasn't ready to discuss her relationship yet.

Paula recommended a beauty shop in Gold Beach run by a husband and wife. Kate had such thick hair that she'd had trouble finding a place to style it. On January 20, she had an appointment to have a shampoo, cut, and set. John insisted on going along, but he agreed to wait in the car for her. As it happened, the male owner had the first opening, and he started to wash Kate's hair. For once, it didn't hurt to have the snarls combed out, and she relaxed.

It didn't occur to her that John was watching every move through the window, and when she came out, he was very quiet.

"I made the mistake of saying that the guy had given me the best shampoo I'd ever had, and I should never have mentioned that I'd enjoyed it.

"The shampoo and cut took a long time, and John was fuming. He told me the salon owner was 'coming on' to me," Kate recalled. "He said washing hair was a 'sensual act.'"

"I'll never let you go back there again," John snarled.

At first, Kate resisted, saying he was imagining things, but John was adamant.

They went next to a Fred Meyer store to get some shopping done, but John wouldn't let it go, and he hounded

Kate to tears in the aisles, berating her for being seductive in the beauty shop. The afternoon was ruined, but it was more than that; their relationship was ruined. She had been waiting, albeit subconsciously, for the other shoe to drop, and now she realized that John had just been hiding the same old suspicions. That effort seemed to have made his rage more vicious.

Kate had reached the point where she could never go back to a time when she had loved John.

When they were back at the cottage, she blurted out that she was leaving him. Once again, he pulled out a gun. He threatened to shoot her cat, Mittens, and then her. She looked into his eyes and believed that he didn't mean it. Just to be sure, she did the only thing she could—become submissive. That usually settled him down, and he didn't object when she grabbed her kitten and went to sleep on the floor of the room they used as an office, locking the door and barricading it with a dresser. He shot at the door lock but soon gave up trying to get in. He went to sleep on the futon in the living room.

Kate remained resolute. By the next morning, she knew she had to leave John. He hadn't changed. Each angry outburst escalated to a more threatening level. She was truly frightened for both of them if they stayed together. Even so, she expected to find that his rage had passed as it usually did overnight. She put on sweats and slippers, and was surprised to find him still "crazy-mad."

Kate wasn't going to back down about their breaking up, and she said quietly, "Don't worry, I'll be fair about the money—"

Before she could say anything more, he had the gun in

his hand again and was pinning her with his arm as he held the gun muzzle against her head. Bizarrely, John remembered it was her father's birthday.

"This will be my birthday present to your father," he breathed. "His dead daughter . . ."

"He threatened again to kill Mittens and me," Kate said, "and I believed he meant it. I grabbed Mittens and jumped in my car. As I was backing out of the garage, he was ranting at me and trying to jump in my car."

A heavy rain sluiced over her windows, too much for the wipers, and Kate squinted to see the road. Mittens was in the backseat. Somehow, just as they turned onto the highway, the cat managed to put his paw on the window button, and the side window lowered all the way down. Kate reached out to grab Mittens before he could jump out. She caught him by the scruff of the neck and hauled him back in the car, fortunately without having an accident.

When she got to a public phone, she called the Domestic Violence hotline and spoke to a counselor at Oasis, the shelter for women fleeing abuse in Curry County. Paula Krogdahl had told Kate about Oasis, but Kate had never thought she would be calling there for help.

The counselor told Kate to park at the hospital, and she would meet her there. Like most domestic violence shelters, Oasis had no facilities for pets. Kate knew a woman named Ursula Elliott, who fed homeless cats down at the jetty, and she agreed to watch Mittens while Kate was hiding at Oasis.

(Women in sudden need of a safe haven can take their children, but many stay in dangerous situations because they can't bear to leave the animals they love. Today, there are good Samaritans who provide temporary homes for dogs and cats of families in trouble, but there is a need for more.)

Kate stayed at Oasis for four days. She learned later that John had called a cab to look for her, and the first place the cabbie had taken him to was Oasis. She wondered how he'd known where it was, and she learned that the local paper had unthinkingly printed the address and a photograph of the shelter when it opened. Fortunately, her car was parked behind the hospital and not at the shelter, so John thought she wasn't there.

On January 21, 1999, Kate filed a formal complaint against John alleging domestic violence, and she asked the judge for a restraining order. She asked the Court questions about the efficacy of such an order and realized it would not protect her in California or New York or anywhere her American Airlines layovers took her. In fact, the judge couldn't give her any answers that would make her feel safer with a restraining order. She withdrew her request.

After four days, she agreed to go back to the cottage, but *only* if John removed all his guns from the premises. He went along with that, and stored them with a friend who had an auto-repair business in town. She confirmed that they were safely locked away there.

A long time later, she learned that John retrieved his weapons only two weeks later.

Kate had gained stunning knowledge about domestic violence at Oasis, and she was grateful the center existed. But she had also learned how little women can do to protect themselves. She felt somewhat safer, because John wouldn't be in Gold Beach much—he was working on yet

ANN RULE

another "major venture" down in San Diego. He had joined with a dentist there in selling vitamin supplements. He'd told Kate that he was putting together a training program for potential sales reps and that the first session would net him at least five thousand dollars.

He rented a small apartment in Coronado, assuring her that this would be a new start for them. But Kate no longer believed it.

Chapter Five

The watershed point of a relationship comes at different times for different people. In the spring of 1999, Kate Jewell reached the point of no return. "I realized that I had to leave him if I hoped to keep some little shred of me alive." She wondered if anyone would even believe that she was serious about leaving. She had promised to leave John so many times before.

They were halfway separated now. The millennium was approaching, and the last few years of the twentieth century were creeping by. Kate would mark her fiftieth birthday in April. If she was ever going to retake possession of her own personality, the part that was truly *her,* it was time. She could support herself if she returned to flying full-time, and she could live with friends in San Francisco.

Kate tried to follow John's counselor's directives. Charlie, John's therapist, had advised her to keep John calm, to see that they had enough income to pay their basic expenses, and to quell the feeling of foreboding that sometimes caught her unawares. That sense of danger got worse after she saw a television movie about the Ira Einhorn case in Philadelphia. She saw too many close parallels between

Einhorn and John. Einhorn had been so like the younger John—a charismatic and convincing counterculture activist at the University of Pennsylvania in Philadelphia. When Einhorn's girlfriend, Holly Maddux, disappeared suddenly in 1977, her family and friends lived in dread; Holly hadn't been able to get away from Ira, either. She had stayed, believing things would change for the better.

Some months after Holly vanished, her mummified body was discovered in a steamer trunk in a roof closet connected to Einhorn's apartment. He glibly denied knowing anything about her death, but he jumped bail and left the United States in 1981 just before he was to go on trial for first-degree murder. Einhorn was convicted of Holly Maddux's death *in absentia* in 1993.

(In 1993, no one knew where Einhorn was; only later, in 1997, would he be found living the good life with his Swedish wife in France. After much negotiation, he was extradited to America in 2001. Despite the pitiful finale of Holly's life, he had become almost a fascinating antihero. Kate could visualize John skating just as free as Einhorn, using his charm to draw supporters to him.)

One of Einhorn's judges summed him up in a way that Kate Jewell recognized: ". . . He is an intellectual dilettante who preyed on the uninitiated, uninformed, unsuspecting, and inexperienced. . . ."

And that was Dr. John Branden, a man Kate now saw revealed as a hater of women, who thought he was so much smarter than the masses who believed his lies and his embroidery of the truth. She believed that she could be as easily sacrificed as Holly Maddux had been.

On April 24, Kate wrote her will, and she wrote a letter

to her landlords and friends Bill and Doris. "If you are reading this, I am gone," it began. "I do not want to die, yet must write how I am feeling. I have had a sense of death for the past few days. . . . In six days, I will be 50. In 3 days, John will come. I hope I make it to my 50th birthday.

"After all the violence I have experienced with John—physical, mental and emotional—I still hope and try to believe that somehow if I stay with him, we can bring something valuable to the world. . . . I believe [the work] can help the world accept responsibility and know how to respond to health concerns. Unfortunately, I also think it tends to drive someone to the point of insanity."

She was, of course, writing about John. She wrote of a nightmare John had had the night before, and of how upset he'd been when he'd called her to tell her about it. ". . . 'This man attacked me at my car and strangled me with piano wire.' I believe this man is John, in his sub or unconscious. The loving side of him is warning me about the vicious, angry side of him. If that angry side comes out while he is here, I fear my death."

John was telling a number of their mutual friends how angry he was at Kate and how he blamed her for all of his troubles. "I guess slowly but surely the violence has destroyed my feelings for him," she wrote. "I have desperately wanted to believe (and still do) that somehow we can make this work."

But she knew they couldn't, and she wrote about her lost dreams. "I have always wanted to share my life with one special man. I have long sensed that my true soul mate died in Vietnam before I even had a chance to meet him. I have a tiny sense that if somehow I survive this with John, there may be someone to live the rest of my life with in PEACE and SAFETY . . . God willing."

Kate wrote out messages to the most important people in her life—family and friends. Good-bye messages. These were clearly *not* suicide notes but the desperate words of a woman who was quite sure she would soon be killed by the lover she had tried to trust.

It was too late for her to realize her hopes to have children, but she begged Bill and Doris to take care of her beloved Mittens if she died.

Her birthday passed without an overt fight with John, but something odd happened. They'd hiked to a secret place their landlord, Bill Turner, had shown them—some rocks that rested over a waterfall between the high spots of Cape Sebastian. It was very complicated to get to. They'd had to hike through the forest, hack through brush, and then wade through a creek.

On this day, Kate had no energy at all, and her stomach felt queasy. She actually fell asleep on the trail while John was using the machete to cut brush. At the waterfall, Kate fell asleep again on the rocks.

They were scheduled to meet Bill and Doris for a picnic at a place where Bill had carved an ocean view through the trees and placed a picnic table. Kate felt too ill to move, and John said he had to pick something up at their cottage and that she should wait for him. He never came back for her, but she finally felt well enough to drag herself to the picnic spot, where she found Bill and Doris, who were very worried about her.

"I was afraid John did something to you when we saw

him coming up the trail without you, swinging that machete," Doris said, with real relief in her voice. "He said
he'd chopped you up with the machete and thrown you
over the cliff."

John grinned, signifying it was only a joke. They all
laughed, but weakly. After they ate, Bill offered to give Kate
a ride to the cottage, and he put his arm around her to help
her into the truck because she was too weak to step up.

"I caught hell for that later," Kate recalled. "John said
Bill was coming on to me. But that was so absurd. Later,
Doris told me that she thought John probably had poisoned
me, but just didn't use enough."

Kate had the same suspicions. They were all jumpy.
Kate wondered if her own apprehension was catching, or if
Bill and Doris could see John's dangerousness.

Kate had received a package for her landmark birthday
from her best friend, Michelle. It arrived early, and she
forced herself not to open it when John brought it home
along with the other mail from their post office box. She
found out later that Michelle had shopped very carefully,
trying to find something that matched Kate's taste.

"But I never saw her gift," Kate recalled. "The package
was empty. Michelle sent me a sketch of it; it was a lovely
amethyst and silver necklace, with matching earrings that
she'd ordered from Bangkok. I was pretty sure I knew
what had happened to it. John was always jealous of the
time I spent talking to Michelle on the phone, and I think
he just threw my present away, although he denied it, saying he had no idea what I was talking about."

*　　*　　*

Kate Jewell laughed when she said it, but even the most obtuse listener could have caught the tinge of anxiety in her voice as she described some of the "gaslighting" techniques John used to throw her off balance emotionally. "I got to the point where I either had to take a trip or sign up for a stay in the loony bin."

The tension between John and Kate grew. Her days were laced with trepidation about what he might do next. Even though he was in San Diego, eight hundred miles away, she felt his presence in the cottage and half-expected him to pull one of his surprise visits. Five months earlier, he'd been extremely upset that she'd filed domestic violence charges against him when he'd threatened to shoot her on her father's birthday, and he was still angry over that. She'd thought she knew him completely, but she was no longer sure what he might do if his emotions tilted too far.

Kate needed to get away, if only for a short time. Ironically, their lovely cottage, which had seemed like a safe haven from the world, was now menacing. Kate unfolded a map of Oregon on her kitchen counter and looked for some kind of sign that would show her a spot she should seek for a time-out. She scanned the southern Oregon coastline and found nothing promising. Then she looked north. Just east of Astoria, she saw a small town: Jewell, Oregon. Her own name.

She had her sign.

"I thought that I would go to Jewell to see if I could find *me*. 'Cause I wasn't happy. I had looked inside myself and I wasn't there anymore. I felt like John had sucked my soul out. I was empty, frightened, miserable, and lost."

That was a massive understatement.

Kate told Bill and Doris where she was going, and she promised to check in with them every day by phone. She didn't plan to tell John where she was headed, knowing full well that he was likely to track her down wherever it might be. She would tell him only that he could call their landlords, and they would let him know she was fine.

"I just meandered up the coast on 101," she said. "I took the 'cape route' north, and I walked every beach, and followed every trail I wanted to. I was gone a week, but I checked in every night with Bill and Doris."

Heading north, she stayed in a "funky little cottage" in Oceanside and used the only pay phone in the two-block town for checking in. But the connection was bad, and the message was garbled. Misunderstanding, Bill played it for John—and John picked up "Oceanside."

Kate had already moved on when the manager of the cabins received a call from a man identifying himself as the "Oregon state police." The officer asked the manager if Kate Jewell had been there, who she was traveling with, and if she'd left any drugs or alcohol behind in the room. He also asked which direction she'd been traveling in.

It wasn't the Oregon state police; it was John Branden, tracking her, trying to control her.

"I found that little spot in the road called Jewell," Kate said. "There was the Jewell School and the Jewell Elk Preserve—with not an elk in sight—and that was about all."

During her walks on the beaches along the way, Kate had finally allowed herself to recognize that a decade of her life was gone, and a sea change was washing over her. Whatever she and John had had together was finished and couldn't be resurrected. If only she could convince John of that. It was taking such a long time to peel him from her life.

She got back to Gold Beach on Monday, May 24. John was due to return the next day. She called him from the road and was vastly relieved when he appeared to have come to the same conclusion that she had. Staying together was too painful for both of them. They were through. He didn't accuse her as he usually did. He sounded only a little sad.

She would be free of him, after all.

"I thought I had finally achieved what I had been working for years to accomplish—a friendly separation. And he said it first, just the way I'd hoped it would happen. John actually said, 'I can't take this anymore, you can't take it anymore—so let's just end it.' He wasn't angry, and I thought we both felt relief that it was over. I think he even said, 'Let's be friends.' I promised to be at home in the cabin if he came up from San Diego."

She felt happy and calm for the first time in years. They could work together without recriminations. They could still help people with health problems but let go of the anguish of a doomed love affair.

The next few days were fine. John respected Kate's space, and he was "wonderful" to her. She didn't totally trust him, because she knew how quickly his mood could change. They lived platonically, talking calmly about their plans. Kate still hoped to have a work relationship with John, and a friendship. Seeing the "good John" for those days at the end of May, it all seemed possible. They blazed a shortcut trail to the fire road that led to the beach—John with a weed whacker and Kate with a machete.

They had planted a large garden on the lower terrace of their rental property, and on Saturday, May 29, John was busy cleaning up brush and weeds on the upper level of the property. Whether either of them would be there to harvest the garden was anyone's guess, but it seemed important to both of them to do the yard work.

Kate was idly watching soap opera videos in midafternoon without paying much attention to them. She felt guilty because John was working so hard and she was being lazy. When he walked in, she sensed he was annoyed with her, probably because she had taken a break from weeding. She changed the subject and unwittingly picked the wrong topic. She told him that she planned to volunteer at Oasis, and he was instantly angry. Of course he would be, she understood too late. That was where she had gone for help in January after he'd threatened her life. She had been put off her guard because John had been so understanding and reasonable for several days.

She apologized for not helping him more in the yard, and he nodded. They were back to having a pleasant conversation, and she breathed an inward sigh of relief.

Kate started outside to help with the yard work. Grabbing a machete from the garage on the lower level of the cabin, she headed down below the garden path to trim back the salmonberries. She concentrated on the task before her, and they didn't talk for most of the afternoon. John was cutting a path to the beach with a weed whacker, and it made so much noise they would have had to shout. After a long while, Kate heard the machine's engine cut off. Now there was only the sound of the waves far below and the last buzzing of insects and chirping of birds as the sun lowered on the western horizon.

At sunset, Kate headed uphill toward the garden, and she stopped at the faucet there to water the drooping vegetables. John yelled down at her, "Oh—I thought you'd been killed."

Maybe he was making a sick joke, but it was the second time he'd talked about her dying violently in a week.

Kate watered their garden, turned off the hose, and climbed up the sandy trail to where John was sitting in a lawn chair near their huge pink rhododendron. She saw smoke rising from the fire he'd built in the pit there.

It was a lovely evening, and she was tired. At this point, Kate had no sense of foreboding at all. But then John leaned back in his chair, and it tipped completely over backwards. She looked at his face and the clumsy way he was trying to get to his feet and right the blue plastic chair, and she felt a chill. Now Kate saw there was a one-and-a-half-liter bottle of Chardonnay, three-quarters empty, sitting on the picnic table next to their cabin. She'd seen John drink two large cans of beer during the afternoon. He was very drunk.

She walked over to the basement garage to put her machete down, and to pour cat food out for Mittens. She was dusty and soaked with sweat from her yard work, and she wanted a shower. She headed toward the stairs but he called her over, asking if she wanted to sit with him. Kate knew this mood he was in all too well, and she didn't think he meant it; even though their lawn chairs had been stuck together, he had obviously disentangled them and only carried one chair down from the deck.

"No," Kate said. "I think I need to head for the shower. I don't want to sit down right now."

"That figures," he said sarcastically.

Kate knew better than to argue with him when he was like this. She took care of Mittens, then walked over to John and stood beside him.

Suddenly, John's hand reached out and held hers fast. He looked her directly in the eyes, and she saw someone she didn't know, someone so cold that she wondered if he even recognized her.

"You're going to die tonight."

And she knew he meant it this time. "His eyes were always safe until that night—and then they weren't. . . ."

Chapter Six

John explained quite calmly that with his training in karate, he could kill her with his bare hands. He could do it with a "chicken chop" to her neck and break it instantly. "You can scream," he warned, "but it won't do any good. No one will hear you."

He began to muse about the way she would die, and how easy it would be for him to explain her death. He mentioned the barbecue they had planned for the next day with friends, and said he would tell them that he and Kate had gone hiking up Cape Sebastian and that she had slipped and fallen to her death in the ocean. John kept up a hissing, guttural stream of ugly words, telling her that he would, of course, throw her off Cape Sebastian. No, he decided, he would chop up her body and throw it off in pieces.

There it was again. For the third or fourth time. He had dreamed of her death and obviously thought of ways to kill her, most of them grisly. There was no question; John had been intent on totally obliterating her, and she hadn't realized it until this moment.

She tried to reason with him, but he said, "There's nothing you can say—you're going to die tonight," which he repeated over and over, like a mantra.

Kate's thoughts raced. What *could* she do to save herself? She prepared to fight for her life. She would knee him in the groin and put her fingernails in his eyes if she had to. He wasn't a big man, but he was very strong, and now he seemed possessed of inhuman strength. There was madness in John's eyes.

He cocked his fist and hit Kate squarely in the mouth, and then on the side of her head, knocking her to the ground. He spit on her. She tried to kick him in the groin, but that only made him more determined. Kate was no longer in much of a position to fight. He was straddling her, and choking her with both hands. She tried to wrestle away from him, but they tumbled around on the ground, his grip never loosening.

Another scene flashed through her mind. She thought of Nicole Brown Simpson. *This is how she must have felt when a man who professed to love her was killing her*, Kate thought. She tasted blood trickling down from her nose and teeth, and she knew she had to keep her brain intact if she hoped to have any chance of surviving. "I had to get him to stop beating me in the head. I was running out of air, so I lessened my struggle."

Somehow, she managed not to pass out, but her eyes bulged and her ears rang. When John saw the blood, he said, "Now, you've ruined it. There's no going back now."

She'd ruined it by having the temerity to bleed? As always, he was blaming her for anything bad that happened. They hadn't had sexual relations for a long time, and he told her he planned to "finally have sex with you after you're dead." However, he'd decided he would also take her while she was still alive.

He tore her panties and one shoe off in the yard, throwing them somewhere among the pink blossoms that had fallen on the ground next to the fire pit. Then he dragged her into the basement and up the steps to their living room. She either had to crawl on her knees or stumble on the stairs as he held one arm tightly in his grip.

"Get down on the floor and take your clothes off."

"I'm cold. I'm cold," she said. And she was—from shock, from the sudden chill that blew off the ocean now that the sun was gone.

"I don't care," he said flatly.

Kate's mind searched desperately for a way to survive. *Why* hadn't she kept the machete with her? What could she do to snap him out of the weirdly icy mood he was in? He looked at her but didn't make eye contact.

"I have to go to the bathroom," she said. Maybe she could lock herself in and somehow wriggle through the small bathroom window.

"It won't matter."

She had no doubt that he meant it wouldn't matter because she would be dead soon.

John explained to her that he was going to rape and kill her mother when he was through with her, and kill her father, and her best friend, Michelle, and Michelle's daughter, Missy. He promised to find Kate's niece and keep her captive for a week until he had her completely addicted to cocaine. He was going to find Paula Krogdahl and kill her, too, because she had supported Kate's stay at Oasis after his January attack on her.

It was as if the top of John's brain had opened and all the pent-up violence and ugliness inside had spilled out; Kate had never seen such a depth of depravity in him before. She doubted that he used cocaine; she'd certainly never seen it, but he was possessed with something that had taken over his mind.

Maybe it had been there along, and he'd been able to hold it inside until now.

He had a knife against her throat now, sometimes moving it to her breast. It was one of their knives from the butcher block in the kitchen. She had used it a hundred or more times when she'd cooked for him. She kept asking to go to the bathroom, and he finally relented, but he went with her, standing a few feet away from her, blocking the door. She knew she had no chance to escape before he stopped her.

He led her back to the living room, the knife pressed against her flesh. He *was* going to rape her. As he forced himself into her, he held the knife in one hand. She didn't dare fight back. Bizarrely, he used herbal lubricating jelly from their bathroom. She was in the middle of menopause, and even if she had wanted to have sexual relations with him, her vaginal tissues were dry. He was going to kill her at any moment, but he apparently didn't want to hurt her as he raped her. Or—she quickly corrected herself—probably he didn't want to hurt himself.

Kate kept looking into his eyes. "I tried to find 'John' in those eyes—but he was gone."

His hands moved over her insistently as he interrogated her about everything she had done since she'd reported him to the police in January. For the first time in a decade, he hadn't been with her continually, and his jealousy and possessiveness raged. She hadn't been with any other man, but this crazy John didn't believe her.

They were on the rug on their living room floor, next to a futon where they had had consensual sex dozens of times. Ironically, in the late seventies, Oregon was the first state where a husband was charged with the rape of his wife while they were still living together. The Greta and John Rideout case generated huge media interest, and even though he was acquitted of the charges at trial, most people don't remember that. (Kate and John weren't married, but everyone in Gold Beach thought they were.)

The attack went on for a long time—probably hours—or maybe it only seemed that long. He raped her endlessly, thrusting with each question he asked. Nothing he did to her seemed to satiate him. This ending was her fault. "I've lost everything," he said. "There's no way out. I've lost everything, and you are going to die."

She marveled that she was still alive.

Now he told her that he was going to have anal sex with her, but first he needed to go get a condom. To be sure she couldn't get away from him, John ordered Kate to flip over on her stomach. He attempted to tie her hands behind her back with his handkerchief, but it wouldn't stretch that far. His hernia truss was hanging from a chair, and he grabbed it and bound her wrists with that.

Kate's mind raced. She knew that John had had several guns, including an AK-47, in the room over the garage.

She'd found out that he'd brought them back without her knowledge. He liked guns. He'd brought another gun up from California in April, and she'd demanded then that he give her the clip. She didn't know if those weapons were still in the house. Was he really going to get a condom, or was he going to get one of his guns?

Testing, Kate realized she could wriggle her right hand free, and she worked her bound hands inside the hernia belt, frantic to get them out before he came back. She wasn't sure exactly where he was. She knew she would have only one chance, and that it would be gone within a minute or so. She would have to run across a room where she thought he was. If he saw her, she had no doubt he'd kill her with the knife.

But she had to try.

Suddenly, she was on her feet, running through the living room and kitchen. Thank God, the safety bar wasn't in the track of the sliding glass doors yet, but the door was locked. She eased the lock open, holding her breath. She didn't see or hear John.

Their deck was creaky. She was sure he'd hear her, and she wondered if she should make an attempt to cross it.

"I heard God's voice, saying, '*Go!*' " Kate recalled. "And I did."

It was pitch-dark outside, save for one outside light. She didn't know where Mittens was, and she didn't dare stop to find her kitten; she prayed Mittens was hiding somewhere in the garage where John couldn't find him.

Kate ran up a strip of grass between the two graveled ruts in their driveway. The closest neighbor was downhill, but Kate's friend there was a single woman with little children, and Kate felt she couldn't expose them to a man gone mad, a man who had a butcher knife, and probably a gun, too. Instead, she headed uphill, trying to stay in the shadows of trees and bushes and out of the moonlight, where John could see her.

Another driveway met theirs in a V, but she decided against taking it. Her goal was to somehow get to the highway and attempt to get someone to stop. It didn't matter that she was naked. Better to be naked in front of strangers than dead.

She was sure that John was close behind her, but when she paused, there were no sounds except for her own ragged breathing.

She turned left and into another driveway. It led uphill to where friends of hers—a man and wife—lived. They usually rented out their mobile home, which sat at the bottom of their driveway, but she thought the tenants had moved out. There weren't any lights on inside. Not daring to delay, she raced on up the steep driveway.

Kate ran diagonally across the yard of her friends' bright blue bungalow and was relieved when she saw several cars parked there, although there were no lights on. She darted along the side of the house, trying to keep out of sight, and rounded a corner, heading for the front door.

She tried the door. It opened. She closed it behind her and quietly locked it. If anyone was home, they were asleep. She didn't know what time it was—the evening had been endless; it could be two o'clock in the morning. Now she faced another danger. She was the intruder, and Mike, the husband who lived there, probably had a gun. He would be within his rights to shoot her if he didn't recognize who she was.

And John was probably just outside, looking for a way to get in.

As Kate's eyes adjusted to the dark inside her neighbors' house, she saw a child sleeping nearby. A television was on somewhere in the house, and she saw the screen flicker. As gently as she could, she eased a sleeping bag off the bed where the child was sleeping and wrapped it around herself, calling out for her neighbors—Mike and Maria—in a whisper.

No one answered.

But then she saw they were sleeping on a porch next to the room she was in. She raised her tortured whisper a little. "It's Kate," she called. "John's trying to kill me. Call 911!"

Finally Mike woke up. They all huddled in the hall, where they wouldn't be open targets if John had grabbed one of his guns. Apparently, John didn't know which house Kate had gone to for help.

Mike saw him on another neighbor's porch, banging furiously on their door. The resident who lived there had a police scanner, and it was quite possible that John had heard the dispatcher sending units to the cottage. At that point, it seems that John had either returned to his cottage or to Kate's car. The headlights were off, so it was difficult to see if anyone was in the car.

Three law enforcement agencies had responded to the

911 call for help. It was 10:30 p.m. when central dispatch in Brookings directed Curry County Sheriff's Sergeant John Sevey to an address on Bellevue Lane. He was joined by Oregon State Police Trooper Dan Stennit and Officer Wally Hartman of the Gold Beach Police Department. Records show that they arrived at 10:49 p.m.

As Hartman left his patrol car and walked toward Mike's house, the officers saw headlights sweeping the driveway. At the same time, Kate saw other headlights dim, move out of the neighbors' driveway, and head toward the highway. It was John, driving her car. He must have known the sheriff was coming, and he'd been biding his time so he could escape without running into them.

Kate wondered where he was going.

Hartman and Stennit raced to their units and attempted to catch up with John, but his head start was just enough to let him disappear before they got to Highway 101. They couldn't tell which direction he'd turned there.

Inside Mike's house, Sergeant Sevey looked at Kate, and she could see the concern in his eyes. She was naked, except for the sleeping bag she'd wrapped herself in. There was dried blood on her mouth, her lips were badly cut and swollen, particularly on the right side, and her entire face was puffed up and scratched.

And, of course, she was in shock. "Jewell was extremely frightened," Sevey wrote in his report. "To the point of near-hysteria. She was cowering in the corner of a hallway, afraid Branden was going to see her from outside and come inside and get her. She would cringe at every sound she didn't recognize."

Even though she had seen John drive by and head toward the highway, she was terrified that he would come back to kill her.

Sevey called the lieutenant and asked for assistance with the investigation. Deputy John Ward was then directed from Brookings to be present for an interview with Kate at the hospital.

After taking a brief statement about what happened, Sergeant Sevey called for an ambulance at 11:01 p.m. and requested that Kate be transported to Curry General Hospital. Deputy Ward followed in his patrol car behind the ambulance just in case John should double back and try to cause an accident on the way.

Once Kate was safely on her way to the hospital, Sevey and Trooper Stennit entered the cottage she'd fled from. It was midnight, and they entered cautiously, wondering if John Branden had returned on foot and was hiding there. They were also looking for weapons, but they found only one handgun that Kate told them she had hidden a few days before. Lieutenant Boice joined them, and they found some items outside—including Kate's key ring. She had told them she believed John's arsenal of guns was in a locked loft over the bathroom.

None of the keys on her key ring opened that lock. She had given them permission to force the door if necessary. They did, but whatever guns had been in that room were gone.

They took photographs of the crime scenes and gathered items that might serve as physical evidence later, bagging and initializing them.

At the hospital, Kate's horrible night continued. The doctor who was called in to do a vaginal exam for the rape charges did that, but grudgingly.

"He treated me as if *I* was immoral, and he obviously resented being bothered. Although I asked him to look at my facial injuries and the contusions on my head, he wouldn't do it. He actually told me to take two aspirin! He didn't seem to care if I had a concussion or other injuries. There was a nurse there, but she had no experience at all with the rape kit, and I left there feeling even worse than when I went in."

It is an attitude evinced by some physicians—fortunately fewer than in the past—and it makes women hesitant to report sexual attacks, particularly by someone they know.

Kate couldn't go back to the cottage. She had no idea where John was, and she was frightened that he might come back to finish killing her. She believed there was one reason only that he wouldn't return: He didn't want to be arrested. Bill and Doris insisted that she move in with them until her father arrived to stay with her. The sheriff's office ordered her not to go back to the cottage alone. They would provide an escort for fifteen minutes a day so she could go back and feed Mittens, who was in hiding, too.

Mittens was living in the bushes, smart enough to stay invisible, as if he knew that John might come back.

Oregon authorities moved swiftly. On June 1, 1999, two days after the attack on Kate—the first business day after the Memorial Day holiday—the Circuit Court of the State of Oregon, County of Curry, issued a warrant for John William Branden's arrest. He was charged with four felonies and three misdemeanors: rape in the first degree, kidnapping in the first degree, attempted murder, attempted sodomy, menacing, and harassment.

His bail was set at one million dollars.

John's name, aliases, and the warrant information were entered into the National Crime Information Center (NCIC).

Whatever trouble he might have fled from in Florida a dozen years earlier surely paled in comparison to what had just happened in Oregon. Or did it? Kate still didn't know what had happened there.

But once again John Branden had escaped punishment, and Kate Jewell spent her days and nights wondering what he was planning next. She was afraid. More than that, she was angry. He had pushed her to the wall, to a place where she could either give up or fight back. And even though she was frightened, she chose to fight back: Curry County Detective Dave Gardiner was assigned principal responsibility on her case, and she knew he was doing everything he and his department could to find John. Sometimes, however, she felt that she was the only one who could locate him, and stop him from hurting her—or anyone else—ever again.

He had tried very hard to erase her from his life by erasing her from her own life. Scarily, it had always been Kate who'd left an outgoing message on their answering machine, but when she called her own number, she heard John's voice asking callers to leave a message. How odd that he would have taken the time to change the settings after she'd fled from him in a panic. Then a chilling thought surfaced: Maybe he had planned to kill her as he built the bonfire and drank wine, and decided to put his voice on the phone then, sure in his mind that she wouldn't be alive after that night.

As she poured out food for Mittens, she saw the light blinking on the answering machine. She rewound the tape, and John's voice filled the room.

"Kate, it's me. I just wanted to let you know that your car is safe—unharmed—and I'd like to get your car to you, so let me know by leaving a message on my San Diego answering machine. I want to apologize and do whatever we need to do. Take care. Talk to you soon. 'Bye."

He sounded so normal, as if the world hadn't changed two days earlier. She didn't call him; she was afraid he actually might come driving up in her car, although his sense of self-preservation would probably keep him from doing that.

Within a week, Kate's father arrived from Arizona, and she could finally go back to the cottage.

She didn't sense that John was anywhere nearby now. What would he do? Where would he go? She wondered if he might commit suicide, but she doubted it. He had told her she had ruined his life—that his life was over—but blaming her seemed to Kate to be nothing more than his tendency for high drama again. Her biggest fear was no longer for herself; she feared that he would hurt someone else, probably another woman.

She made up her mind to do her best to find him, to see that his out-of-control behavior could be stopped. Hopefully, it would take a combination of confinement and psychological treatment.

But where was he?

*   *   *

Dave Gardiner moved ahead with the investigation into John Branden's attempt to kill Kate. Gardiner didn't doubt that it had been a serious attempt, and that Kate would probably be dead if she hadn't managed to escape.

With Paula Krogdahl present, Gardiner took a video-taped statement from Kate. Safe inside the sheriff's office, with Paula and Gardiner beside her, she managed to recall the events of May 29 in detail. But, later, as they walked around the property where she and John Branden had lived for so many years, where she had come close to dying, the tension in her voice was obvious. Sergeant John Sevey, in uniform, sat in the same lawn chair in the same spot where John had waited for Kate that night. It was difficult to see the tall lawman sitting there and not see the ghost of John superimposed on him, but she blinked her eyes and John vanished. She and Gardiner walked from the lower part of the property, up the sandy path to the cottage, videotaping as they went.

It was clear that Kate's mind was back in that night as she pointed out where John had hit her in the face, explain-ing now that the nerves to her front teeth had been severed by the blow. Her clothes had been torn off and left on the ground near the rhododendron, but they had disappeared, along with John. Her shoe, however, was still caught in its branches.

"Maybe the raccoons took my clothes away," she mur-mured faintly. More likely, John had taken them with him when he'd left, perhaps to hide the blood staining them.

As Kate and Dave Gardiner entered the house, she shuddered. Nothing had changed. The knife used to keep her from resisting was missing from the butcher block; the others were all in place. John's clothes from that night—black sweatpants and a green sweatshirt—were gone. The guns that he had once kept in his hiding place were gone. She couldn't be sure how many he'd secreted there. She wasn't an expert on guns, but she had seen so many: a Colt .45, Smith & Wesson .38, an AK-47, some long guns that she couldn't identify. John liked guns.

There were phantom presences in the rooms now—Kate and John as they had been in their final night together. At least Kate devoutly hoped it had been their final night.

She had a little money, but she had no job. She had no place to live. She feared that he was out there somewhere within a few hundred miles, able to get to Gold Beach in a few hours if he chose to, stalking her or planning how he could follow her every move. It wouldn't be just a matter of her finding a little house or an apartment somewhere; she would have to relocate someplace where John wouldn't be able to find her. She could go back to American Airlines, and she would. But would the airline be able to hide her from John?

She had to find him, because he was terribly dangerous while he was loose. At the same time, she had to be sure he wouldn't find her.

It seemed impossible.

Chapter Seven

Kate wasn't surprised when she saw the envelope in her post office box. She recognized John's handwriting on the envelope at once—large printing with a Sharpie pen. It was postmarked in a small town in Oregon, but she knew he wouldn't be there. He was never in the places where his letters came from, especially when he was in trouble. She recalled how he'd had her sister mail letters for him from Sarasota during the Lakhvir trial. The date on this letter was stamped "June 9, 1999." She wondered who he'd persuaded to send it on for him.

> Kate
>   I am so sorry for what has happened between us. I hope and pray you are okay.
>   I'm doing the best I can. I'm scared but decided it's best to stay in Oregon, attempting to find the courage to deal with this.
>   I need time right now to sort things out and put my affairs in order.
>   This has been hard on everyone. Please continue to be kind to Tamara and Heather—I know you will.

You need to know that whatever happens to me you are safe (and so is everyone else). All this has brought me to reality. I want you to be able to go on with your life in peace, prosperity and happiness. I know you will.

Please accept this letter, as my wish that you be in Joy, not sadness, as you read this. Please think of all the great times we had as John & Kate (And Dr. John and Dr. Kate). I am thankful for all the happy & fulfilling years we had together.

In spite of things, please know that I Love you and Always will—No matter what.

Love your,

John

Kate sighed. It was still all about him, and he didn't have the faintest idea what love was. How could he possibly expect her to feel safe? She wondered what he wanted from her—probably a way out of the trouble he was in. *He* was scared. *He* wanted time to put his affairs in order. And *he*, as always, was trying to make her feel guilty.

But his manipulations didn't work any longer—not with Kate.

She tried to think where he might be. Since John had emphasized in his letter that he was in Oregon, Kate was sure he *wasn't* there. She knew he would be working frenetically to protect himself and to avoid arrest. She guessed that he was probably in California, heading south. He might be trying to get into Mexico. It was unlikely that he'd go north. As far as she knew, he didn't have any contacts in Washington, and it would probably be more difficult for him to get across the Canadian border than to slip into Mexico, even though he had his ever-present assortment of driver's licenses in different names. There was a "stolen" bulletin out on her car, and she was working with Dave Gardiner to bring the FBI into the search for John. There was every possibility that he had crossed state lines by now.

Kate and her father had gone to pick up an extra-strong cell phone from the sheriff's office (ordinary cell phone signals didn't penetrate the Gold Beach area) when they spotted her car. Her 1999 Suzuki Grand Vitara was parked in the Fred Meyer store lot, right behind the sheriff's office. There was no way to tell how long it had been there.

Had John had a pang of conscience, or was he afraid of being stopped in a stolen car? Whichever it was, she was happy to have her new car back.

She doubted that John had much money, and the only vehicle he'd had in Oregon besides hers was a 1971 Ford pickup truck that had once belonged to his father. It was virtually undrivable and it was still parked at the cottage. Somehow, he must have made his way out of town, possibly even by hitchhiking, although that or a bus ride would have been iffy with the dragnet of deputies and state police looking for him.

John's daughters were in the San Diego area, and his best friend—Stanley Szabo, the dentist who had lived in Kate's condo so long ago—was in Florida. Kate tried to figure out who would be most likely—and most able—to help him continue his escape. His older daughter, Tamara, had always backed John up. Even if what he was doing was illegal or morally wrong, Tamara covered for him.

Kate was quite sure Tamara would be first on the list of all the people he would run to.

She had lost touch with Dr. Szabo and didn't know exactly where he was. John had helped Stan out when Stan had been struggling back from an expensive divorce, and she thought he might help John, *if* John could even find him. "Stan used to sigh and say, 'He who has the money can pull the strings,'" Kate said, "and back in the days at Solana Beach, it was John who had the money, and he did help Stan."

But Kate felt that Tamara Branden was the most likely to protect the father she idolized. Kate sent an article to Tamara about John's spate of violence. It had appeared in the *Curry Coastal Pilot* and was entitled "Man Sought in Rape Case." She followed it up in mid-June with a phone call. She couldn't get through to Tamara, but she did speak with Dan,* Tamara's fiancé.

It was an oddly stilted discussion, during which she sensed that Dan was choosing his words very carefully. He complained that they'd had to move all of John's "crap" out of his apartment near San Diego and turn off his phone there. That proved to Kate that John had been in touch with them.

Kate explained that John had begun to send questions and "demands" to her through his psychologist, Charlie, and Dan seemed quite aware of that. He didn't come right out and say it, but he admitted that he had sent a big duffel bag full of John's possessions to Oregon.

She hoped that wasn't true, but she said nothing. She knew in her gut that John wasn't in Oregon, but that gave her faint comfort. She and her father were packing her belongings, but she still didn't know where she was going, and it would be weeks before she could wind up her affairs in Gold Beach. It was so hard to stop in the middle of life and completely change direction. She thanked God for her dad, who promised to stay with her until she moved.

The big questions in Kate's mind were how John was managing to stay hidden and who was giving him money.

"Is Tamara concerned about where her father is?" Kate asked Dan.

"No," he said too forcefully. "She's pissed as hell. Heather's about ready to write him off, too. She's like, 'If I get a call, I'm real seriously thinking I never want to talk to him again.' Tamara's not quite that extreme, but, ahhh, we're all *extremely angry*. Kate, I would say that you're the most sympathetic ear he has."

She didn't respond to that.

In the next breath, John's son-in-law-to-be surmised that the next time John tried to kill Kate, he would succeed. He agreed that John was probably in dire need of psychiatric help, but Kate almost felt that Tamara was standing nearby, telling him what to say. Still, Dan muttered that it might be better for everyone if John killed himself.

Maybe he meant it. He seemed sincerely annoyed with all the upheaval in his and Tamara's life because of John.

Kate suggested her theory that John had found someone within a 450-mile radius and had charmed them or made them feel sorry for him. "I think it's someone you guys know; it's not a business acquaintance," she added.

"Someone's gotta be taking care of him, all right," Dan agreed.

"I think he's always expected a lot of Tamara," Kate said, but Dan wouldn't bite on that.

"Well, he's going to be disappointed," he said. "I don't know what he's doing or who's giving him advice, but, as usual, he's making a bad situation worse."

Dan said he didn't know why John and Sue and their daughters had left Florida more than a decade earlier, but he thought John had stayed in hiding for a year, and that everything they'd owned had been put in Sue's name then.

He danced on the edge of confiding in Kate—if indeed he knew anything. Kate repeated that John had probably charmed someone just to keep a roof over his head. "I would figure he'd head to Stanley Szabo," she said. "The other thing would be Mexico, but if he did that, he must not be planning on coming back. I can't imagine that, as racist as he is, but I guess it's a possibility."

"I don't know how he would get to Mexico—we have his Hyundai, and it's not even running," Dan replied. Then he stressed that he and Tamara were leaving for Alaska in three days, and that he was happy to "get away from this mess."

"If you feel as if Tamara's not saying something—"

"Yep," he said, which didn't answer her question at all. "Yep. Yep."

Kate urged Dan to have Tamara call Dave Gardiner in Curry County, but Kate knew Tamara wouldn't. She was positive that Tamara knew where her father was, that she was probably helping him stay free. His daughter thought John was a saint, and loved him, Kate thought, but he was a loaded gun out there. Who knew how many people would die before he was captured? Didn't Tamara know that in this case blood shouldn't be thicker than water?

Apparently not.

"Well," Dan said, "you have a pleasant evening."

The line went dead as Kate thought, *How weird!* It would be a very long time before she would have a pleasant evening.

Kate suggested to Dave Gardiner that he check the passenger list for the Holland America cruise scheduled to leave Portland, Oregon, for Alaska on June 18. John's name—or any of the fake names he was known to use—wasn't on the manifest.

On June 29, exactly one month after John's attempt to kill Kate, David Terry, an ACLU attorney, called her to say that John had contacted his agency. Terry had approached the Curry County district attorney's office to feel them out. If John turned himself in, could he count on a plea bargain that would net him far less time behind bars than the three or four hundred months the charges against him called for? They weren't enthusiastic.

"He's very, very scared," Terry told Kate, "and given the position of the DA's office, he has reason to be."

"So I've been told," Kate said without expression.

Would Kate intercede with the prosecution to help John get a more humane resolution to his case? Terry asked. She didn't know; all Kate wanted was to have John locked away someplace where he wouldn't do any more harm. She wanted to be able to walk free without constantly glancing over her shoulder, or waking to the smallest rustle in the night.

John's temporary attorney said he realized that John had been deluding himself about the way he'd treated Kate.

"He minimizes—," she began.

"Oh . . . hugely." It didn't take anyone long to see how manipulative John could be, and the depth of his need for absolute control. Kate herself had been so caught up in keeping some vestige of peace that she hadn't realized how tightly John had trapped her in his power over her.

Even though she never wanted him back in *her* life, Kate still hoped that he would get some kind of psychological treatment, albeit in prison. She asked Terry if he had a way to contact John, and there was a long pause on the line.

"If I did, I would not be at liberty to share that with you, because that would be a confidential communication. . . ." Terry then reminded her that at the very minimum John faced twenty years in prison. "My personal observation is that he's continuing his abuse of you by doing what he's doing—"

She sighed. "Some things never end. I'd like my life back, and I'm doing the best I can to take it back."

"You're familiar enough with therapy and with self-empowerment to know that you are the person who is going to do the heavy lifting there."

"Yep," she said wearily. "And I'm in the process."

She promised to call Terry if she had any questions or wanted a message passed on to John. But she had no messages to pass on—unless she could make herself believe that John had the capacity to feel regret for what he had done, and, even harder, make herself believe that he wanted to change, to get better, and think of someone other than himself.

Kate concentrated on who might be inclined to help John stay free of arrest. Tamara, of course, but her fiancé, Dan, not as likely. She talked to John's dentist friend, Stan Szabo, and hung up with the feeling that Stan knew where he was, and that he, too, was protecting John.

Sometimes, it seemed to be a conspiracy of silence.

Tamara and Dan were practicing Buddhists and therefore against violence of any kind. She wondered why they were helping John hide when *she* was the victim of his rage, both emotional and physical.

She thought about whom she and John had been in frequent contact with in the past year. They had been close to Bill and Doris, of course, but John wouldn't contact them because they were helping her. Then Kate recalled the young woman with a practice in Napa, California, whom John had taught to do blood screenings. She hadn't sent any reports since the end of May, nor had she called. With all that had happened, Kate had almost forgotten about her.

Napa was in wine country, about twenty-five miles north of Oakland, and some three hundred and forty miles from Gold Beach. Suddenly, Kate felt the little hairs on the back of her neck stand up: *John was hiding in the Crichtons' house in Napa.* She was so sure he was there that she accepted it even before she called Bonnie Crichton. When she did, Bonnie's voice was wary, flat; and Kate visualized John standing there next to her, telling her what to say.

He must have convinced Bonnie and her husband, Joe, that he'd been falsely accused. Then he'd preyed on their sympathies. He was so skilled at playing that part.

As soon as she hung up, Kate called Dave Gardiner. "Don't ask me how, but I know where he is. John's in Napa, California, with some people named Crichton. . . ."

Kate gave Gardiner the address, and he immediately called deputies in Napa County. It was mid-June, and no one had reported seeing John for more than two weeks. Joe Crichton answered the door. When he saw the uniformed officers, he turned aside and said something quietly to one of his children.

"He told him to warn John," Kate recalled. "And he did, and John took off running out a back door."

The dogs the deputies had with them weren't search dogs; they were trained to follow a moving target at their master's commands. John had a good head start on them. They circled the yard, looking for a scent. When they finally had it, they stopped in confusion at a fire road, surrounded on all sides by acres of grapevines.

John Branden was gone, just as surely as if a spaceship had dropped down to pick him up. The California officers kept searching, continuing their tracking on more than a dozen properties that Bonnie Crichton's family owned.

They never found him. Either he was dead or he'd found a secure hiding place where law enforcement officers couldn't locate him. The Crichtons insisted that they knew nothing about any attack on Kate; they'd only been giving a good friend a place to stay. Maybe the authorities believed them, maybe they couldn't prove otherwise, or maybe the Crichton extended family's clout in the community stood them in good stead. Bonnie and Joe weren't charged with harboring a fugitive.

Kate wondered if he had managed to come back into Oregon and was nearer to her than she knew. If a car followed her for more than a few turns, or the phone rang, only to have no one there, or she heard a noise she didn't recognize at night, her pulse beat rapidly and she felt a familiar fear.

Chapter Eight

As the summer passed, Kate tied up the ends of her life in Gold Beach—her life with John Branden. They had been renting their cottage from Bill and Doris with an option to buy, but Kate never wanted to live there again, and heaven only knew where John was. He wasn't dead; she was sure of that now. Through some third parties—whoever they were—John was communicating with his daughters, his therapist, and his attorney.

It was a hot summer. The garden below the cabin became choked with weeds and went to seed. In the fall, Kate executed a deed in lieu of foreclosure back to Bill and Doris, releasing all her interest in the cottage property. Their attorney drew up a summons in Curry County, addressed to John, asking him to appear and pay the balance of the house contract: $150,000. Legally, it had to appear in the Public Notices section of the local paper four times.

There was only silence from John. The perfect cottage, with its trees, flowers, and a view of the ocean would be returned to Bill and Doris.

In mid-July, the FBI entered the case, and the search expanded. *America's Most Wanted* producers received letters from Dave Gardiner and Kate asking that information on John be broadcast on John Walsh's show. The producers promised to consider their request.

"But I got the feeling," she said with some bitterness, "that *America's Most Wanted* wasn't very interested in my story because I didn't die. It would have made for better true-crime television."

The sense that John was hovering in the background, sending directives to those he still manipulated, often washed over Kate. But she thought that might only be her imagination.

Her father pulled her through. He vowed to stay with her until he was sure she had relocated to the safest possible place, and he carried a gun with him wherever they went. She felt very lucky to have him with her.

Kate realized that John expected her to stay in Gold Beach; he would be shocked when he heard that she wasn't there any longer. He was undoubtedly planning to return, smooth things over as always, and then convince her to help him get the charges against him reduced.

Kate hadn't yet decided where she would go, but she knew it had to be someplace isolated for her own safety, and near water for her serenity. She would be leaving dear friends behind and starting over. That is the fate of women who live in fear. She would probably have to change her name when she got to wherever she was going. The first part of her life seemed to lie on the floor like ropes cut off without being tethered to anything.

She believed John was probably someplace in California, but she had no idea where. It was a big state, but even so, she was afraid to move there. She didn't feel safe in

Oregon. John was so good at tracking her, wherever she was. Kate and her dad headed north in the first week of August 1999. She figured that Orcas Island far up in Washington State might be a place where she could start over. John wouldn't be likely to look for her there; they'd decided not to move there because of the restrictions imposed by ferry commuting. It would be one of the last places he would choose to live himself.

She talked to a deputy sheriff on Orcas Island, and he told her that no one had ever been murdered there. She took that as a "good sign," and somehow that made her feel safer, although she knew that was no guarantee for the future.

If she could fly out of Sea-Tac Airport in Seattle, she could live in insular obscurity and earn a living, too. They found a little house, which was basically a summer cottage. It wasn't fancy, but it would do. Kate loved the ambiance of Orcas Island, the serenity of it, and the woods and acres of fields, bounded on all sides by water. Knowing it was too expensive, she rented it anyway, and planned to be living there before winter storms closed in.

She signed her "new" name on the lease: *Chris White.* That seemed suitably common, and it could be either a man or a woman.

Back in Gold Beach, Kate packed up those possessions that were mementoes of her family—her grandmother's antique secretary and small items that predated John. She held a yard sale for the rest.

The cottage was still full of John's things. She wanted to put them in storage, but her father stopped her. "Put them in a pile down in the garage," he said. "You don't owe him anything. He can arrange to have them picked up if he wants them."

As they cleared out the cottage room by room, they searched for John's gun collection. Finally, Harold Jewell opened a wardrobe box in the camper of John's old truck and found the cache of weapons. It gave them both a chill to see the handguns, shotguns, and rifles there. There were Smith & Wesson .38s, Colt .45s, an Israeli gun, and the AK-47. Why had John found it necessary to own so many guns?

(Eventually, Bill Turner heard from Tamara's fiancé, Dan, who said he and a friend would be coming up to get John's stuff, asking Bill to put it in storage in Brookings, Oregon. The old Ford truck also went to Brookings, a small town five miles from the California border.)

As they hurried to leave Gold Beach, Kate's dad was burning trash, and Kate made a number of trips with papers and other things she didn't intend to take. She was carrying a high stack of papers when she stepped in a hole and broke her leg. Her father heard the snap of the bone breaking and saw her fall. He thought it was a gunshot; he panicked, because he'd left his gun in the house.

"He thought John had come back and he'd shot me, and he didn't have a gun to shoot back. That's how jumpy we both were."

Now Kate had to hobble up and down the many stairs on crutches. This was not the luckiest summer of her life.

She felt like one of the walking wounded. Although her bruises and cuts had healed, her dentist still believed the nerves to her front teeth had been severed when she'd been hit in the mouth.

John had left so precipitously that he'd failed to take many of the documents and papers he'd hidden from Kate. The court records on the suit brought by the Lakhvirs were among them. For the first time, she learned about the charges that the Middle Eastern couple had brought against John. They were far more serious than he'd told her.

On September 3, three months after Kate barely escaped with her life, she found another letter from John in her post office box. It had been postmarked two days earlier in San Francisco. She stared at it, feeling the heft of it. It was quite thick.

She hadn't wanted to hear from him ever again. She didn't want to read it. But she felt compelled to, knowing that he had had time to land on his feet by now, and that his rhetoric would be choreographed to entrap her. What could he possibly have to say to her?

It was nine pages long, printed in the same dark Sharpie ink as his first letter, his capital letters large and flamboyant, the *t*'s and *l*'s crossed with his familiar downward-curved umbrella shape.

Kate,
I can feel you so strongly this morning as I can so many mornings . . . I can feel you sending me messages (so you can go inside your heart and know I am alive and okay).
It's hard for me not to just find a phone and call

you (to know how you are doing). So we will have to trust our way of communicating via the Universe.

He was very confident, his words from the beginning indicating that they were in this together, sharing a deep love, sharing all the blame. His magical thinking had returned to him, and he saw "the Universe" as he chose to see it. He wrote of how much they had both lost, although he ended that thought vaguely: "as a result of *things* . . ."

He blamed his May 29 "nervous breakdown" on his fear of losing Kate and his need to control everything in his life, including her. "I've come to the realization that I created the most extreme situation to realize the extremes of the loving, compassionate side of me that wanted to be there for you, and love and care for you forever. Versus the scared, cruel side of me that survived my past hurtful experiences through control and manipulation. It finally exploded within me. I snapped and lost control. I had no right to do so."

For pages, he repeated his apologies for manipulating her to his will, and she almost wondered if he *had* had some kind of watershed moment where he finally saw the truth. Then she caught herself. It was an old technique for him: *Mea culpa* and then pleas for forgiveness.

"I saw you run out of the house," John wrote. "I was in the bathroom, and when I looked in the bathroom mirror, I realized that what was happening was wrong and I had to stop."

John assured Kate that he didn't blame her and had no anger for her. *Blame her for what? Calling the sheriff? Going to the hospital? Giving a victim's statement?*

"I acknowledge you," he wrote on page four, "for all

you gave to me and our relationship. All your love, loyalty, truth, honesty, compassion, and passion. All your hard work, creativity, and wisdom in All we have created together. Please keep doing the work and carry on what we began."

She had wished for such sentiments for a decade; now they were only ashes.

"Please remember all the neat and beautiful things we did together from Bodega Bay to our last time together at the waterfall with Mittens. From time to time, look at our photo albums and be happy for all we shared. . . . I have written you so many long letters, but never sent any of them. What I write is for your eyes only. I hope you will honor our private communications."

He had apologized, explained why he'd acted the way he had, declared his love and admiration for her, boasted that he'd deliberately spared her life, and then attempted sharp tugs on her heartstrings. He was a master of persuasion.

He had, he wrote, only "One Request." He feared disasters when "Y2K or something similar" happened, and he begged her to give shelter and safety to his daughters in Oregon. He wanted her to remain close to Tamara and Heather, because "they love you."

And there was another matter. Although he admitted that what he had done to her was wrong, and he accepted responsibility and wanted to "give myself up," so he could serve "some reasonable time and be provided counseling," he hadn't been happy to hear from his attorney that the woman DA who was handling his case would not negotiate. He bemoaned the fact that "local law enforcement and

130

court want me to spend the rest of my life in the state prison."

If only he and Kate could have talked, John suggested, and worked with a neutral attorney so they could have negotiated with the state. "That way we could bring this to closure and both go on with our lives. *Without your help,*" he stressed, "any resolve is impossible."

But, alas, his life was over. It was too late. Most of his "deals" were gone. But he still had the biggest one in action—the sale of urine kits. "I've kept in touch with these people in spite of things."

He wanted to see this endeavor succeed so that all the profits could go to Kate, and she could have a good income for many years. "The State is costing you the loss of earning a living," he suggested. "Even with me out of the picture, I still love you and want you to be financially secure."

The implication was clear. If Kate would only plead for him to get a shorter sentence—or no sentence at all—he would see that she would be rewarded financially . . . with urine kits. How romantic.

Once again, he switched gears, and the next two pages returned to the love letter form:

> *I wish it were possible for me to hold you in my arms once again, To look into your beautiful eyes, and kiss your wonderful lips. We always kissed so beautifully, We did it so perfectly. Waking up with you in my arms, holding you at night, Just being with you. Walking with you, giving you a hug. Just sharing life with you. What an incredible loss, knowing*

this (likely) is the only life we will ever have to be together. To have found each other and now we no longer [are] experiencing all we have and feel for each other. . . .

My mind and feelings never stop. My every thought and every breath are painful. I am so alone, what a punishment I have imposed upon myself. What will happen to me now? I have no idea, I just live one day at a time, never knowing when or how it will end for me.

I am glad you have a place to live (our house) and the support of Bill and Doris and your supportive group of family & friends. I have none of that. What I do have are all my thoughts and memories of us. I lost all my personal belongings at Bonnie's. The only personal item I still have is the ring you gave me. I have always considered that my Wedding Ring from you. I still wear it and am loyal to you and have not been with anyone else. I love you always! . . . The next time in another time and place, I will do it right. You will know it's me when I say "Connect With Me."

It was his time-tested clincher: *"Connect With Me."*

Kate felt goose pimples prickling on her arms, even though the day was warm. John believed that she was going to remain in the cottage, that she would come to understand his explanations for his violent behavior, and that she would surely connect with him and plead for a lighter sentence for him at the Curry County district attorney's office.

He clearly felt he still had the ability to control her, and he thought he was pulling all of her strings in this letter.

Kate folded the pages and slipped them back into the envelope. John seemed convinced that she would stay in the cottage. That was good; she would have a better chance of moving to Orcas Island, and she and her dad could probably leave Gold Beach without John's knowledge. John might be clever about pretending to be a police investigator, but if he had no idea where to start calling, or hadn't followed close behind her, it wouldn't do him any good.

Before she left Oregon, Kate used one of John's tricks. She wrote letters on Nepalese stationery to her friends and family, and sent them to a friend in Nepal to remail for her. "That way," she pointed out, "if John showed up looking for me, my friends and relatives could show him the physical evidence that I was far, far, away living in Nepal."

In October, Kate and Mittens started their new life on Orcas Island. Her mother and father stayed for a month but left before Thanksgiving—long enough to realize, along with Kate, that the "cute" summer cottage was drafty and cold in the winter.

She didn't know anyone, and she was living under an alias—"Chris White." But then she learned that on this lightly populated island, there was already a Chris White— a male optometrist. So she changed the spelling of her first name and became "Kris White."

On many days, she felt as though she was in a surreal world. "I didn't know who to say I was," she said. "I would introduce myself as Kris. When I got to know people and was comfortable enough with them to mention my story, I told them my real name was Kate. But it was a really unsettling, confusing situation."

At American Airlines, Kate kept her real name, as well as her actual Social Security number; she was concerned that the government might not credit her with all the years she'd worked when it came time to collect her Social Security.

"I finally decided that my name was basically all I had left, and I'd be damned if John Branden was going to take that away from me, too. He'd already taken my house, my new career, my mind, my soul, and almost my body!"

After she went to great lengths to explain to American how dangerous it would be for her if John ever managed to find her, they agreed to protect her by putting DNGO [Do Not Give Out] next to all her information. They wouldn't tell *anyone* that she even worked there, no matter what. That made her feel somewhat safer.

"But it's hard to get people to understand," Kate said. "No one really does understand domestic violence unless they've experienced it themselves."

It was a long time before she could fly again. Her new rental had lots of stairs and a very steep driveway, and her leg took a while to heal. Her plans to return to American Airlines and fly out of Seattle didn't work out at first, because she couldn't fly with a broken leg. Moreover, her "hardship transfer" request to Seattle hadn't yet been approved. Since the postmark on John's last letter in September read "San Francisco," she didn't feel safe flying regularly out of there.

When her leg finally was strong enough, Kate was granted her transfer to Sea-Tac Airport in Seattle as a home base.

She was Kris White now to most people on Orcas. A woman living alone with her cat, someone who worked off-island much of the time. She kept in touch with her family, but very carefully. She didn't want to place them in any danger. When she flew, it meant a long ferry ride and a one-hundred-mile drive to the airport, but she was gainfully employed again.

Sometimes, at night, Kate woke from a sound sleep, frightened by some noise she couldn't immediately identify. A tree limb cracking in a high wind. Footsteps in the leaves, or just deer looking for food? Something scratching at her door? Her phone ringing, but when she answered, nobody was there. That would be John's style.

Like a fox, he had gone to earth somewhere. He could be far, far away—or he could be creeping around outside her cottage.

In the daylight, she was quite sure he had no idea where she was. If he did, he would have come forward, sure that he could convince her he was a changed man.

Despite all her rationalizations, Kate Jewell/Kris White still lived in fear.

Weeks passed.

Then months, and finally, a year.

She made new friends, and she sometimes worked with people who wanted to know more about healthy eating.

But she always heard silent footsteps walking just behind her.

Kate still didn't think that John Branden was dead. He

was alive—somewhere. And she was just as sure that he would be a threat to the next woman who came into his life. Her one regret about disappearing from Gold Beach—and from his life—was that she wouldn't be able to warn the next woman. Sometimes she had nightmares about that. She felt that John was living in a protected environment, and that his daughter Tamara was helping him, but Kate couldn't risk calling her. She just prayed that Tamara would do the right thing and turn him in once she accepted how hazardous he was to women.

Buddhists were nonviolent. Maybe that would make the difference, and Tamara would understand that her father had gone beyond normal behavior. He needed to be locked up.

For two years, John's movements could not be traced, and there was simply an empty spot in the masquerade that was his life when no one seemed to know where he was hiding.

Chapter Nine

Turid Lee Bentley was born in Stavanger, Norway, on January 28, 1941, as war was brewing in Europe. She came to America with her mother and father—Liv and Magnus Lee—and her sister, Bodil, and lived her whole life in the Tacoma–Gig Harbor area. She attended Mason Junior High School, and the castlelike Stadium High in Tacoma, and then the brand-new Woodrow Wilson High School, also in Tacoma. She stayed close to friends she made when they were all teenagers. She was a true Scandinavian beauty, slender, with green eyes and thick brown hair, which turned white as she passed middle age.

Almost always called "Turi," she resembled Kate Jewell in that they both had fine bone structure with similar facial features, although Kate's coloring was darker. They had other things in common: Both Turi and Kate had a passion for helping others achieve optimum health, and they wanted to change lives for the better as much as they could. Turi and her husband, Lorne Bentley, married when they were quite young. After decades in a marriage and living in a circumscribed region in Washington State, Turi was far more naïve than Kate, who had traveled the world, but she had a good business head, and she worked as the office manager/bookkeeper in her husband's building contractor business. In the early days of her marriage, Turi also worked for the *Tacoma News-Tribune* typing classified ads. She was a lightning-fast typist, who typed her children's school papers.

Turi always worked. Like Kate, she sold Mannatech products. She was also a sales associate for Shaklee products. Money itself meant very little to Turi, but it allowed her to support numerous charities that she believed in—in many diverse areas. When her daughter Susan went through her files, she was amazed to find how much money Turi had given to charities like a crisis pregnancy center, Gospel for Asia, World Vision, and the Reverend David Wilkerson, a country preacher who walked the hazardous streets of New York City, armed only with his Bible and his belief that even the most troubled and threatening dregs of society could be rescued. His book, *The Cross and the Switchblade,* became a classic.

Turi helped people closer to home, too, but she didn't talk about it. She was always there for friends and even strangers who needed a listening ear, a casserole, a pie, or a place to stay. She attended church regularly for many, many years, but she was sometimes impatient with church politics and pettiness in the congregation. She believed in living her Christianity by helping, in practical and caring ways, those who needed it.

"She would drop everything to listen and lend support to the many God sent her way," her daughter Susan recalled. "Often those the rest of the world had given up on.

She had that rare gift of seeing the heart where many people got stuck on the exterior trappings."

Still, Turi had a sense of humor, and she could be feisty, particularly when she stood up for someone else. "She had an incredible faith in God," Susan said, "but it was a relationship and not a religion, and that makes all the difference in the world." Quite possibly it was Turi Bentley's devout faith in God that saw her through life's pitfalls. As a young woman she'd befriended in Gig Harbor remarked, "[Turi] was 'sold out for Jesus'!"

Turi Bentley never aimed to get "more stars in her crown"; she simply stepped in where she saw she was needed.

Turi and Kate Jewell never met at Mannatech meetings or sales promotions; the company was huge, and they lived in different states. Turi had sold its products for years, and she, too, sincerely cared about her clients' health. Even today, those who were close to Turi in 2001—including her family—aren't sure how or where she met John Williams. In all likelihood, it was through the Mannatech roster of associates who were willing to participate in three-way phone conversations with prospective clients and give personal testimony on the efficacy of the curative powers of Mannatech products.

Lorne and Turi Bentley were listed in 2001. If they were called, they could explain—as laymen only—how Mannatech was effective against bronchitis and prostate cancer. The chances were that Lorne was only a silent partner who wasn't nearly as involved in the Mannatech "family" as Turi was.

It was a moot question anyway; the Bentleys' marriage was drawing to a close that year.

At some point, Turi's children noticed that she was corresponding with a John Williams. Her marriage was over, although there would be a long, drawn-out division of their marital property, which her son, David, oversaw. For the most part, Lorne kept his contracting business assets, and he was awarded their yacht. Turi got the family home they had built near Point Defiance. She eventually sold it and moved to an apartment in Tacoma. She kept up a cheerful front, but she was vulnerable to an intense man who managed to be suave and kind at the same time. John Williams could read who people wanted him to be, and he was adept at putting on whatever mask coincided with their expectations.

Turi and John Williams probably met in Washington or California; he had reasons not to be in Oregon. It's unlikely that she met him in church. It's more probable that they met through Mannatech or Shaklee, some business they both believed in. It would have been easy for John to strike up a conversation with Turi there, exchanging business cards, phone numbers.

She was still lovely, with a serene beauty that few women manage to maintain into their sixties. She didn't feel old, but she no longer felt as if she was the center of anyone's life, either.

Kate had never heard of Turi Bentley, of course, but she was the nameless, faceless woman Kate had wanted so much to warn and protect. John couldn't manage alone;

she was sure of that. He needed a woman to hold his hand, to sand the sharp edges off life's problems—a woman who would devote herself to him. He had explained his demands to Kate in the early days of their affair. And Kate knew he would eventually enslave whatever woman fell for his blandishments and believed his lies.

Kate had attempted to convince his daughters—particularly Tamara—that their father was dangerous. The next woman he became involved with might go through what she had—and quite possibly endure an even worse fate. She never managed to get through to Tamara in person, having been reduced to sending messages through Tamara's fiancé. Maybe his daughters really *didn't* know where he was. After that, it became too risky for Kate to even try. She didn't want John to be able to track her down on the windswept island where she was hiding.

After a few years on Orcas Island, Kate tentatively began to feel a bit out of harm's way. There was no way to get off-island without the ferries, and new faces in town drew attention. But she would never feel completely secure until she knew John was behind bars. And she dreaded hearing what he might have done, wherever he was.

That is, if he was still alive.

He was. In the first years of the twenty-first century, John Branden emerged from hiding, as shiny and renewed as a snake who'd just shed its tattered outer skin. He was close to sixty now, five years younger than Turi Bentley (although he looked older), and his hair had thinned to baldness with a few "comb-over" strands. But his eyes were just as bright and hypnotic as ever. As always, he was full of moneymaking ideas and grand plans. He wasn't John Branden any longer, though; he was John W. Williams. He'd always had his clutch of driver's licenses and identification cards, and he still did. He had plenty of "paper" to support his image as John Williams. He didn't call himself a doctor now, except to a very few people close to him, in whom he confided that he was a naturopathic "physician."

He was simply "Mr. Williams."

Turi was sixty-one when she met John, and like most older women who are alone, she doubted that there would be another man in her life. Her three children were grown and on their own, and she was a very loving and proud "Grambar" to ten grandchildren. She had too many friends to count, and she was full of joy in her life despite the disappointments she had known.

After meeting John Williams, she began to hope that she might have a second chance at love.

Shortly after the turn of the century, John was living in a cabin in Northern California near Mount Shasta. He may have led Turi to believe that he owned it, along with the meadows surrounding it. In truth, he was the house-sitter. The true owner lived in Switzerland and trusted John to take care of his property. How John met the property owner is anybody's guess. Without having his permission to do so, John rented out rooms to strangers and kept the rent he collected. He would later brag to a friend in Gig Harbor that he not only had a free place to live but he also had an income of about $800 a month from the rent.

In his phone conversations with Turi, he spoke mysteriously about the six months he'd spent living in a Buddhist monastery, trying to sort out his life. That was apparently before he moved to Mount Shasta.

Tamara Branden was a Buddhist. Perhaps he'd hidden on her property, which was rife with many of the religious icons and tranquil gardens favored by the religion. Perhaps that was what he meant when he said he'd been in a monastery. At any rate, he had outrun the dogs tracking him in Napa, California, had apparently spent time in some sort of religious retreat, and lived quite comfortably on the Mount Shasta estate.

John Branden-Hennings-Jewell-Howell-Williams preferred pretty women with good figures, and Turi Bentley certainly fit that category. He sought out those who would indulge him, and Turi was kindness and consideration personified, always concerned for others. He cared only that she doted on him. He wasn't interested in her religious beliefs and was annoyed that she interacted with her family and with so many friends of all ages. Her brilliant smile drew people to her and made them remember her.

Turi was an intelligent woman who had never been a goody-goody. She could be quite bold and witty. She taught her daughters to always speak the truth and face their fears head-on. Because *she* told the truth, she didn't recognize that John had lied to her from the beginning. She didn't even know his real name, and it's possible that he planned his scenarios so she never would.

John convinced Turi to invest in "his" Mount Shasta property. She paid to have the garage attic remodeled into a nice apartment where John could live—while he rented out the entire cabin. The owner was so far away that he didn't know what was going on. Turi's financing of the garage remodel actually enhanced his property, but she and the absent owner were conned.

The very fact that Turi was trying to help John be more self-sufficient financially indicates that she knew he wasn't wealthy. It didn't matter to her; they were going to bond together to help people, which was far more important to her.

As always, John could be charming, and he was never more charming than during his courtship of Turi. And of her family.

"He was odd—but nice enough," David Bentley, Turi's son, affirmed. David's children were entranced with John, especially when he showed them how to carve their initials in a tree trunk. Their real grandfather, Lorne, had been too busy most of the time to do things like that.

David Bentley, who lived most of the time in the Virgin Islands, where he had his own business, only met John Williams five or six times. He never met John's daughters, who lived in California, although John spoke highly of them. He understood that his mother's fiancé was "some kind of doctor," but he assumed he was retired, as he didn't work. He found John to be a nervous man, who admitted that he was "scared of germs and flying."

John Branden had never before evinced any fear of flying. But he was a wanted man, and after 9/11, airport security had become much tighter than before. He probably didn't want to try passing through airport security with one of his phony IDs, and he could avoid that simply by pretending to be terrified of flying.

Beyond his phobias, John had good reason to be nervous. In December 2001, the FBI put John William Branden's Wanted poster on their website, noting that a federal judge had issued an Unlawful Flight to Avoid Prosecution arrest warrant for him. He was described as being five feet ten inches tall, weighing 180 pounds, with gray hair and blue eyes. One of his early publicity photos from Mannatech appeared on the poster, and his careers as a holistic healer, clinical nutritionist, and naturopathic doctor, along with his many aliases, were noted.

Special agents visited some of the places he had once lived, talked to his friends from the past, and came away empty-handed.

"He should be considered potentially dangerous," the online poster warned.

Turi Bentley would have been shocked beyond words to know that the man she loved was wanted for a number of violent crimes. Or that he might have the potential to cause her harm. She considered John a wonderfully kind man who loved her, and who was prepared to work beside her to help those in ill health and who were troubled.

John proposed to Turi over the Christmas holidays in 2001, but it wasn't an actual marriage proposal. He told her they didn't need to deal with "all the paperwork" that a legal marriage would bring, since Turi had so many assets in her name. It made him seem even more genuine to her; he obviously wasn't after her money. His real reason for wanting a fake wedding was probably that he didn't want to show up on any public records or have to prove his identity to obtain a marriage license. He had been in hiding for

ANN RULE

most of the past fifteen years, and he wasn't about to risk his anonymity and his current complete absence from public records.

"We'll know we're married in our hearts," John assured Turi. "That's what matters. We don't need to bother with all the other stuff."

Turi agreed with him. On January 18, 2002, they had a church "wedding" with all the frills. John rented a tuxedo, Turi wore a lovely dress, and the pastor presided as they said their vows. Turi's daughter Susan sang. As far as anyone else knew, they were married. It was the only time in her life that Turi had evaded the truth, and John had talked her into it.

David Bentley was somewhat concerned about the marriage, as his mother was worth quite a lot and her new husband had no visible assets at all. But he had no need to be concerned. Their marriage wasn't legal; at most, it was a lavish dress rehearsal.

After a few months had passed, Turi's daughters, Susan and Sonja, who both lived in Washington, were even more worried about Turi, especially when the gregarious and friendly side of John Williams vanished. It was like night and day, and the dark side of him wasn't very nice at all. He became a know-it-all, a man who monopolized every conversation—so much so that it was difficult to get a word in edgewise. He paused only to draw a breath, then continued talking before anyone could respond to his pontifications.

They thought he was a boor and a bore. Turi's daughters

146

could see that their mother's hopes were already being severely blunted. John didn't let her offer an opinion any more than he let anyone else speak.

He was an intellectual snob, too. John Williams looked down his nose at most people, whom he found less intelligent than he was.

Susan only heard her mother voice apprehension once—shortly after she'd "married" John. They were visiting Liv Lee, Turi's mother and Susan's grandmother. "I don't know what I've gotten myself into," Turi told Liv, with anxiety shimmering in her voice.

After that, Turi didn't express concern. She might have been embarrassed by her faulty judgment about John. She had never wanted to worry her family, but she had reasons to regret moving in with John. One was the worst of all: When the first blush of romance in their relationship wore off, he wasn't always kind to her. Following the classic pattern of abusers, he began isolating her from her friends and made her family feel uncomfortable if they visited too often—too often by *his* calculations. For a woman whose whole life had revolved around her family and her friends, this was unthinkable. Turi had always reached out to people. She was, in every sense of the word, a Christian woman who lived her religion.

John resented time spent on anyone but him, and he liked his privacy. It was against his nature to make friends with anyone unless he had something to gain from it. Although he boasted of wanting to help others, he didn't mean it, and he could not for the life of him understand why Turi bothered with some people when she didn't get favors or business in return.

ANN RULE

It would have been increasingly difficult for him to keep up his friendly, "Mr. Wonderful" façade. Kate had seen that he could read people very well and was quite willing to dazzle them for as long as it took, but he could only pretend to be magnanimous for a limited time.

Once he felt secure with Turi Bentley and had her pledge of complete devotion, it would have been safer and more convenient to have her all to himself, outside of any sphere of influence from others. Despite his lies about owning the cabin on Mount Shasta, John really had no property at all—but Turi did. And, though he denied it, that certainly appealed to him; he needed a woman to stand between him and difficulties he didn't care to deal with, but he also required a sound financial base so he could be free to be the entrepreneur he'd always aspired to be. His mind worked feverishly now—even more than before, consumed with what he believed were brilliant and innovative ideas.

Turi had some investments gathering interest from her divorce settlement. John soon told her of his dreams for retirement—to have a homestead in a virtual wilderness where they could live in privacy and peace. And, in case of war or a natural disaster, they would always have some place to run to. Turi thought he meant they would have a stress-free vacation property, and she agreed to look for land with him. They drove 650 miles to Montana to view acreage for sale, but there was nothing there that seemed right to John.

He *was* enthusiastic about a compound of homes near Priest River, Idaho. It was planned for four families, with twenty-two to forty acres of land apiece. At the time they made an offer, there was only one family living there full-

MORTAL DANGER

LEFT Dr. John Branden's intelligence, education, and charisma impressed Mannatech executives, and they quickly hired him as a spokesman. But problems with his overweening ego soon surfaced.

Dr. John Branden and his daughters, Heather (*left*) and Tamara (*right*). He adored his girls and worried about what would happen to them if the world became too dangerous—either from natural disaster or invasion. He asked Kate—and then Turi—to provide a safe place for them.

LEFT Kate Jewell was thrilled to graduate from American Airlines' Stewardess Training classes at the age of twenty-one. She longed for travel and adventure, but she found more of both than she had bargained for, and she lived with a bleak terror she could never have foreseen.

Dr. John Branden and Kate Jewell celebrate her birthday by going to Disneyland. She was thrilled when he declared his love for her, believing that she had found the perfect man.

Kate Jewell and John Branden, attending an American Airlines party.
Kate was a longtime flight attendant for AA. She soon learned that
John watched her constantly at parties, jealous and furious if she
talked to any other men.

ABOVE John and Kate, ready for a costume party. John enjoyed being in disguise, but the gun in his holster was real. He could be charming and witty, and they made new friends in Oregon. Kate, however, dreaded the violent scenes that often followed parties.

LEFT When Dr. John Branden was sued by a patient, he closed his office and disguised himself as a "hippie." With his long hair and a beard, his own brother-in-law failed to recognize him. He was pleased.

The charming cottage Kate and John rented in Gold Beach, Oregon. They had a view of the Pacific Ocean, almost-tame wildlife in their yard, and, at first, a sense of serenity. They'd left John's troubles behind in San Diego.

Kate and John in coastal Oregon, caught in fierce winds. They hiked often and climbed Cape Sebastian with the ocean roaring far below. On one ascent, Kate fell ill and found herself all alone. She wondered why John had left her there.

Doris and Bill Turner, and John Branden *(from left)* on the deck of their cottage in Gold Beach. The older couple were both landlords and close friends, but they were shocked when John arrived at a cookout and said he had killed Kate and cut her up with a machete. It was a sick joke. After that, the Turners tried to protect Kate from her erratic mate.

Harold Jewell *(left)*, Kate's dad, and John in yet another disguise. The two men got along well at first, but later Harold moved in with Kate in an effort to keep her alive. The two lived a nightmare existence, wondering where John Branden was.

Gold Beach, Oregon, Detective Dave Gardiner. He investigated a man he knew as John Branden, almost caught him in California, and learned the final denouement of the case eight years later. Kate Jewell lived in terror for years, and Gardiner protected her.

Dr. Randall Nozawa from the cover of his book, *Inside Dentistry: Everything You Need to Know.* Ironically, this photo, taken before the car accident that half blinded him, shows him in high-powered dental glasses. He was forced to give up his practice when the crash destroyed his keen vision.

LEFT Turi Lee, eighteen, at her high school graduation in Tacoma, Washington. She was a beautiful young woman who married soon after and had three children.

BOTTOM Turi Lee, in her sixties, was still lovely. When she met John Williams, she felt that she had a second chance at love. They shared many interests at first, but John became more and more controlling and difficult to live with.

Brian and Bev Mauck, newlyweds. They were the perfect match, with nothing but happiness ahead. (*Slater Family Collection*)

Brian and Bev, who shared a jubilant sense of humor, laughing on their couch. The same couch is visible in crime-scene photos. (*Slater Family Collection*)

Bev and Brian Mauck were married in "paradise" in Mexico on the beach, and then left to go scuba diving on their honeymoon on Turks and Caicos. They were both superior athletes. (*Slater Family Collection*)

Bev and Brian Mauck on their honeymoon on Turks and Caicos. It was probably their favorite "getaway" vacation spot. They planned one more trip before they had children. (*Slater Family Collection*)

Beverly Slater Mauck
March 16, 1979 - November 17, 2007

Brian Mauck
October 25, 1977 - November 17, 2007

TOGETHER FOREVER

United in Marriage May 5, 2006

This photo of Brian and Bev appeared on television news bulletins and in area papers—to the shock of their many, many friends.
(*Slater Family Collection*)

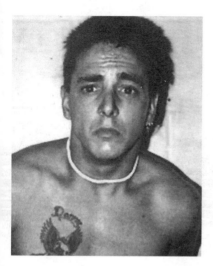

Daniel Tavares, twenty-five, poses for the mug shot camera in Massachusetts, after being arrested for a horrible crime.

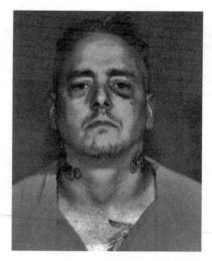

Daniel Tavares, now in his forties, had many more tattoos in this mug shot taken in Pierce County, Washington, in November 2007. He'd sustained a black eye and facial cuts from a feisty victim, fighting for life.

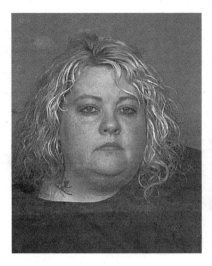

Jennifer Lynne Tavares fell in "long-distance love" with a man she met through a convict website. Fascinated by his tattoos and macho image, she married him a few days after he came to Washington from Massachusetts. She would live to regret it.

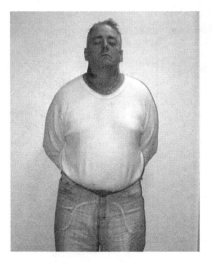

Daniel Tavares in a police photo after his arrest. He left irrefutable physical evidence linking him to a cruel and mindless crime. Jennifer was there to help him cover up and lie for him.

Brian and Bev's new house, which they worked two jobs to pay for. Both their vehicles were in the driveway, the panel was knocked out of their front door, but they didn't answer any of their three phones and neighbors were worried about them.

Daniel and Jennifer Tavares lived in this travel trailer with a lean-to and a "honey bucket" bathroom outside. Although they were a football field's length from the Maucks' home, they told Pierce County detectives that they had seen suspicious men at the victims' home.

Bev Mauck almost made it out her front door, and she fought valiantly, leaving bruises and cuts on her killer. The killer left clear shoe prints in the blood, tying himself forever to the double murder.

Pierce County Officers saw bloodstained blankets covering the bodies of two victims just inside the front door, where a panel had been kicked out. In the upper right, the wall is speckled with back-spatter blood, but there is a tall blank spot, the "phantom image" of the shooter, showing where he (or she) stood.

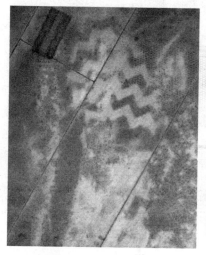

Detectives and forensic investigators photographed a clear photo left by the killer's shoe in the blood that marred the Maucks' floor, even though they thought the guilty person would dump the shoes as soon as possible.

When a suspect in the Maucks' murders walked into Pierce County Sheriff's Headquarters, he stepped in a puddle and left distinct imprints in the concrete and tile walkway. A detective following behind recognized the pattern, and ordered photos before the water prints dried. They matched the prints left in blood at the Mauck homicide scene.

time. It was very isolated, and there were few road signs. Locals learned to find their way by looking for landmarks like general stores, taverns, barns, and particular clumps of trees.

A long driveway led into the area of land parcels for sale, with the brush and trees growing thicker as it wound into the wilderness. The first spread they came to was owned by a female park ranger, who kept a number of horses on her land. Two more unoccupied, ranchlike homes were next, and then—at the very end of the road—they came to exactly what John was looking for.

The price was something Turi could afford, particularly when they were offered forty acres instead of twenty. This land in northern Idaho, long the bastion for survivalists in America, fascinated John Williams, who had always wanted to find someplace where he and his daughters could find safety in the event of some cataclysmic event. One of his requests in his letter to Kate—when he'd been on the run—was that she give shelter to his daughters in Gold Beach, Oregon, in case of a Y2K disaster. In the intervening three years, he had grown even more paranoid.

Married to Turi—even though it wasn't legal yet—and with the Priest River property, he hoped to build an impenetrable fortress.

Turi was less than enthused, but if John wanted to live in Idaho, she was willing to at least give it a try.

Chapter Ten

By 2004 John Branden-Williams had seized on another moneymaking idea. He and Turi became associates of a company called Isagenix. It was a multilevel marketing corporation very similar to Mannatech. He, of course, couldn't go back to Mannatech, and if Turi signed up as an Isagenix associate, she would have to give up her longtime relationship with Mannatech. Some of the more zealous associates there would feel she had betrayed their company.

John explained to those he considered smart enough to understand that Isagenix was a "nutritional cellular cleansing program" that would remove toxins and body fat. It was an herbal cleansing formula, and he believed it would revolutionize naturopathic medicine, and be something he could proselytize in health clubs. He couldn't spearhead Isagenix himself; he was still a wanted man, and he sure didn't want to put his photograph on ads for Isagenix. He needed someone to join with him in this new venture, someone who could be the public "face" of their branch of Isagenix.

Turi and John had eaten at a small restaurant down in

the harbor, where they'd met the proprietor, Debra Nozawa, a woman who was committed to the benefits of nutrition and herbs, just as they were. Debra soon arranged
for them to meet her husband, Dr. Randall Nozawa, a retired dentist, who was forty-six at the time.

Randall Nozawa had suffered more than his share of
bad luck in his life. In 2003, a year earlier, he'd been in an
automobile accident that had ended his dental career. He'd
been run off the road by a car full of teenagers, and a tree
branch had taken out one of his eyes, damaged the other,
and become stuck in his brain. After delicate surgery, he'd
recovered, but he'd no longer been able to see well enough
to practice dentistry: After eleven years in practice, he had
to retire in 2004. He couldn't drive, either, but, ironically,
Randall was in perfect physical shape—he'd always been
a body fitness devotee—and he soon started teaching Pilates and yoga at the Gateway Fitness Center in Gig Harbor, walking to work or anywhere around town he needed
to go. He was very popular there with both the staff and
those who came to work out at Gateway.

Despite his injuries, Nozawa was a walking advertisement for fitness and good health, and he, too, believed that
nutrition was the key. He wanted to find a profession where
he could do some good for people, and he was remarkably
optimistic.

John Williams and Randall Nozawa first met in October
2004, and Randall was one of the few people John seemed
to consider a friend. He often told Randall, "Smart people
like us need to stick together."

Randall was intrigued with the concept of Isagenix. It
was based on what he considered sound premises, and it

seemed almost an answer to a prayer. He had two young daughters and a wife, and he was doing everything he could to provide for them. His marriage was going through a rough patch, and he had nowhere to stay. Turi offered to pay for an apartment for him until he and Debra worked things out.

Believing that John had two PhDs in nutrition, Randall was flattered that John found him worthy as a potential partner. Yet he, too, found John eccentric. "He had a fiery temper that had to be held in check, as if he was a child," Nozawa recalled. "In and out in the snap of a finger."

Wherever he had gained his knowledge, there was little question that John Williams was a genius. He knew everything about nutrition and how to evaluate blood draws. He promised to teach Randall what he had learned in his many years of college. Randall could deal with John's moods. "Lots of people who are very smart have their peculiar ways."

John trusted Randall, and now *he* could play the role of mentor. He clearly wanted to be Bill Thaw to the younger man. John didn't talk about Thaw now. Rather, he extolled the brilliance of another dentist friend, this one in Florida: Now, it was Dr. Stanley Szabo, whom he called his mentor. Szabo may well have been one of the first to teach John body chemistry and nutrition.

John Williams confided in Nozawa—or at least Randall thought he did. John had created a whole new background, and he was convincing at first as he spoke of his earlier years. Randall had gone to the University of Oregon, and John said he had, too. Randall had no reason to doubt John, who named some of the outstanding buildings on the Eugene campus and seemed very familiar with the layout of the university. John said he'd joined the Peace Corps after leaving the university.

"He told me he was from the San Francisco Bay area," Randall Nozawa recalled. "And that he'd worked there for thirty years in his own clinic. Eventually, he sold his nutrition business in San Francisco. I believed him for a long time, and then sometimes I wondered, because the dates and the math didn't quite match up."

Of course it was a lie about any San Francisco clinic, and a lie about being in the Peace Corps, and a lie about attending the University of Oregon. John was adept at making up convincing new backgrounds for himself.

John mentioned his ex-wife, Sue, and his daughters, but he said very little about them. "He said that he'd left his wife because he just didn't want to be married anymore."

Where John had told Kate that he'd never been with any woman except for his wife and herself, he bragged to Randall Nozawa about many, many seductions, saying, "I was always finding naked women in my office at the end of the day, and I had to look around the parking lot to see if jealous husbands and boyfriends were lurking."

This skinny, balding man seemed anything but a love god, but John explained the simple reason women were so drawn to him. "I got to screw a lot of women," he bragged, "because it all came down to the personal thing. I just let 'em talk. I listen, and they think you're a great guy."

John sometimes spoke of a woman he'd been with for a long time. He never called her by name to Randall, but he said she was a stewardess, adding, "All stewardesses are whores."

He seemed ambivalent when he described her. "This was a true 'ten.' But then, after a night of great sex, she's standing over me, with an expression of disdain on her face."

This nameless woman—who was really Kate—had, according to John, betrayed him and caused him all kinds of grief. "She was having an affair with the police chief in this town we lived in and they drummed up phony charges against me."

His hatred for the flight attendant was all-consuming, and he apparently blamed her for everything that was wrong with his life. Randall could understand John's loathing if it was true that she'd been unfaithful and then conspired with the police chief. That was really rubbing his nose in it.

John told Randall about being in a monastery for six months. Had he been hiding out from the charges trumped up by his cheating mistress and her lover? John didn't explain just why he'd been in the monastery, or in what time frame that had occurred. But he did marvel at the wisdom and almost psychic intuition that he said some of the monks had had.

"When I left," John said, "one monk looked at me and said, 'Don't do it.' "

"Don't do what?" Randall asked. "What did he mean?"

"Wow, those guys can get in your head!" John said, still not spelling it out. "He told me, 'It's not worth it.' "

Randall found little mystery about what John had been contemplating—he'd wanted to kill the woman who'd betrayed him in Oregon. And somehow "the monk" had known that. If, indeed, there had been a monk. The whole scenario of the monastery might well have emerged from John Branden/Williams's fertile imagination, no more true than his stories about San Francisco.

John and Turi lived in Tacoma when they were first together. Turi's mother, Liv Lee, had resided in a house in Seascape Hills, a retirement community in Gig Harbor, for fifteen years, but it became apparent in the early nineties that she could no longer live alone safely. Turi found an assisted-living facility in Tacoma. Together with her daughters, she helped her mother move. That left the house on Lost Beach Road in Seascape Hills vacant. It didn't sell, and that worried Liv.

Turi missed Gig Harbor—she had so many friends there—and really wanted to move back. The house was very nice, worth close to half a million dollars as the housing market boomed in Washington State. Any property with a view of the water was desirable, and this gray-and-white house was much larger inside than it appeared to be from the street. It had two bedrooms, two luxurious bathrooms, an expansive modern kitchen, a large living room with a fireplace, and a backyard that opened onto a greenbelt. The only flaw, as far as John was concerned, was that Liv's house was very close to neighbors on either side—probably not more than a dozen feet away from them. But he and Turi could drive into the garage and enter their home from there, so there was no need for him to interact with any neighbor on their street.

They could step through the sliding glass doors in the kitchen, sit on their deck at the rear of their home on warm evenings, and hear the wind in the tall fir trees. It was the reasonable move for them to make. Turi soon made friends with people who lived in Seascape Hills, but John remained aloof and discouraged Turi from getting too friendly with the neighbors.

They did go to the Gateway Fitness Center to study yoga with Randall Nozawa, but John didn't mingle. Randall was a frequent visitor in their home. He lived only a few blocks away and would often walk down to see John and Turi when they invited him.

Turi was relieved when Randall visited, because he seemed to calm John down when he was agitated. It became a habit for her to call Randall when she saw trouble coming with John, whose emotions ran up and down the spectrum from depression to ebullience, from rage to joy.

Randall was happy to help her out, but he soon saw that Turi lived in John's shadow. This lovely, kind woman seemed cowed by her husband! Nozawa was shocked at the way John treated her. He used demeaning swear words in front of her and called Turi derogatory names. He seemed to want to have complete control over her, and her boundaries grew more and more confining.

"John had no friends," Randall said. "He had a very unlikable attitude, an aloofness that turned people off."

Randall worried about Turi. "She wasn't allowed to talk. He kept such a tight lid on her that when John left the room, she would whisper quickly to me, trying to get a few thoughts out before he came back. It was a burst of words, as much as she could say."

John scarcely let *anyone* talk, as he constantly monopolized the conversation. He was worse than ever about that. Of course, Turi's daughters saw that, too. Once he had their mother under his control, he dropped his charming mask. He was arrogant and insufferable, with an opinion on everything, and as far as he was concerned, his opinion was always the right one.

"He was totally nonsupportive of Turi," Nozawa said with a sigh. "She was there to handle the computer, to look up what John wanted, and keep the books. And if John wanted access to the computer, she had to get up and let him use it—no matter what she was working on."

Randall Nozawa probably knew John Williams as well as anyone else did, and he grew used to John's neurotic compulsions. Most of them revolved around his need to be in command of his own life—as well as other people's.

"He was obsessive about cleaning," Randall said. "He did the cooking and he washed the dishes to be sure that the food was to his liking and that the kitchen was up to his standard of cleanliness. When I was there for meals, he would start wiping the table while I was still sitting there. He'd come back to wipe the table three or four times before he was satisfied."

John also made the beds, because he didn't think Turi did it correctly. And he did all the shopping. None of this made Turi feel confident or capable.

"He made long, precise lists of what he wanted to buy," Randall recalled. "He told me that he couldn't go shopping without a list. One time, we drove all the way to Port Orchard—thirty miles—to shop at Wal-Mart. When we got there, he realized he didn't have his list with him, and said we couldn't go shopping."

Randall suggested that they could probably reconstruct the list, but John was adamant—they would just have to go home. He couldn't possibly remember all the items that were on the list, and he didn't want to waste time. To Randall's consternation, they turned around and went back to Gig Harbor without buying anything.

John's was the worst obsessive-compulsive disorder he had ever witnessed.

When John did have his list, he was a speed shopper. He wouldn't look at anything that wasn't on the list, and he forbade whoever was with him to be distracted by anything that wasn't on his list—even if there were tempting sales.

"He would speed-walk through the store, checking off things on his list," Randall remembered. "He told me that looking at other items interfered with his 'chain of thought,' because he had a 'sequential mind.' I guess he meant he had an 'A-B-C' kind of mind."

Randall knew that John drank port wine to help him "tolerate life when he got depressed." He hid the wine bottles from Turi in their house in Seascape Hills, and, later, when they began to clear the property in Idaho. It kept him calmer, although Randall Nozawa never saw him drunk. He wouldn't characterize him as an alcoholic. John apparently knew he could lose whatever control he had if he drank too much.

John and Turi drove to California two or three times a year. Turi did all the driving, one of the few times when John handed her the reins. Why they went to California wasn't clear; perhaps they visited his daughters, or they might have gone on Mannatech or Isagenix business. John distrusted cell phones, preferring to stop at pay phones—especially in Oregon. When Randall asked him why he used only pay phones on the road, he replied inscrutably, "I want to stay safe."

He never said what it was that he feared. It makes sense that he wouldn't have wanted to drive—especially in Oregon—because he must have known there were still felony warrants out for him there. His fear of cell phones verged on paranoia. Did he really expect that police channels might pick up his conversations? Turi didn't know his real name or much about his past—at least until almost the end of their relationship—but she accepted his peculiar aversion to cell phones.

She frequently told Nozawa that she only wanted John to be happy, and she kept trying to find ways to bring that about—even though he could be "difficult" at times.

Randall also learned to live with John's neuroses. He was still enthusiastic about the possibilities inherent in Isagenix. He, John, and Turi had many discussions about the best way to begin their sales campaigns. It was agreed that Randall would be the face of Isagenix, and Turi would do all the bookkeeping and correspondence, and talk to prospective clients and associates. John would continue to fine-tune the way they sold Isagenix products and come up with ideas as only he could.

They would begin at the new Gateway Fitness Center in Gig Harbor, where Randall already taught yoga and Pilates. Gateway was pleased to join with them; they thought highly of Randall already, and they were impressed with John and Turi. Turi was gracious and kind, and John was presenting himself at his most charismatic. To advertise the Isagenix program, the fitness club wanted to put their photos up on the wall at Gateway, but John absolutely refused. He was prepared to be the "brains" behind the venture, but he wanted to be a virtually invisible partner.

"He was *extremely* likeable when he wanted to be," Randall said, but he noted that John wanted little interfacing with potential clients. "He left that up to Turi. He had nothing good to say about the people who called for information, and considered most of them beneath him in intellect and social stature."

Whenever John did answer the phone, he turned people off, at best. At worst, he was rude to them.

Turi tried to point out to John that they were essentially *teachers* and Isagenix was meant to help others. "You have to be more compassionate, John," she said softly. "They're calling for information, and even if you don't think they're suited to work with us, you should be kind."

Turi had come to a place where she had virtually no life that didn't include John. Once, the thought of having John by her side must have been as hopeful for her as it had been for Kate Jewell two decades earlier. And, like Kate, Turi had become entrapped. She was forbidden even to go shopping by herself.

When Turi had visits with her attorney over her divorce settlement from her marriage to Lorne Bentley, John would not go in with her, but he parked outside or sipped coffee at a restaurant across the street, always watching, and he questioned her carefully when they returned to Seascape Hills.

"They would talk about her property settlement when I was there," Randall said. "I was somewhat embarrassed, as it was none of my business, but it didn't seem to bother John."

Saying grace before meals was extremely important to Turi Bentley; it was an essential part of her Christian life. It annoyed John, and he kept telling her to shorten her prayers. It finally came to a point where Turi was allowed only to say rapidly, "Thank you for this food," before John cut her off and started eating. Turi rarely got to have lunch with her daughter Susan as she had in the past. There was a natural food restaurant in tiny Ruston, Washington, a midpoint between Tacoma and Gig Harbor, where Turi and Susan had once loved to eat, then browse through antiques. Now John discouraged these visits so much that Turi felt it wasn't worth risking his anger to go.

Her world steadily grew smaller.

Soon, John had plans to take her hundreds of miles away from her daughters and grandchildren. Convinced that the world was going to come to an end, he wanted to move to their property in northern Idaho as soon as possible.

Chapter Eleven

Ironically, Kate Jewell had once considered moving to Gig Harbor. It had been on the short list of her choices as she'd prepared to leave Gold Beach, Oregon, in the fall of 1999. In the end, of course, she moved to Orcas Island. Heading due north from Gig Harbor—by sea and land— she was less than a hundred miles away from John and Turi.

In 2006, Kate was almost ready to retire from American Airlines. She had carved a good life for herself on Orcas, made friends, bought a little house. American's base in Seattle had closed in 2002, so she commuted to Los Angeles to fly the Tokyo routes. She stayed at her parents' house and drove to LAX. By flying three Tokyo legs, with four of them back-to-back, she only had to fly two weeks at a stretch. Then she could go back to Orcas and have a week to catch up with her life there, before she started all over again.

Her father was having major health problems, so she tried to help her parents during her twenty-four-hour layovers in California. Sadly, her father died on March 30,

2006, while Kate was in Guatemala on an airline ambassador's mission.

She still had Mittens, and she adopted a few more homeless cats. Mittens had been through so much with Kate that he demanded special treatment. When she traveled by car, Kate often let Mittens ride shotgun.

Was she still afraid? Yes—but not to the degree of terror she'd felt seven years before. Sometimes she felt that John knew where she was, those times when the phone rang in the night and no one spoke. She still scanned faces on the ferries to Anacortes and back, and she occasionally did computer searches to see if his name had appeared in news stories. But John Branden seemed to have vanished from the face of the earth.

Maybe he *was* dead, but she thought she would know somehow if that were true. She had long since stopped trying to correspond with his daughters or his friends for fear they would have clues to where she was and possibly tell John. He could be so persuasive and convincing that Kate was positive he could talk almost anyone into giving him information about where she was.

Kate dated some, but she had lost much of her ability to trust that men were who they purported to be. She couldn't reveal her past, and she didn't want to lie. She also had a subconscious fear that if she was having coffee or lunch—or whatever—with someone, and if that was the day that John found her, she and her friend would both be dead, especially if she was with a man. Kate had expected to die at John's hand for so long that she could never really visualize a safe way out.

Any woman in hiding could identify with her; those who'd never felt that they'd been in mortal danger from a man they'd once loved probably couldn't understand.

As much as she worried for her own safety, Kate was still concerned for a woman who might have followed her as John Branden's obsessive "love" object, and she wanted desperately to warn her. Sometimes Kate thought about the conversation she could have with the nameless woman who might be in terrible trouble living with John, and she planned what she might say that would convince her to get out in time. But it could be any woman, anywhere, and Kate had no way of knowing who she was, although she was positive that, if John was alive, he would have to have a woman to depend on, to blame for all his failures, and to ensure he wasn't alone.

And, of course, she was right. Where before it had been Kate who'd sat at a typewriter or computer writing and typing John's projects, now it was Turi Bentley. He had found another woman who was a caretaker, who was kind and considerate, and, sadly, who had asked herself for a long time if it was *she* who was making his life so difficult. Like Kate, Turi had kept trying to please John, thinking there was a magic key to making him happy and serene, only to begin to believe that there wasn't.

Kate would be financially independent, if not wealthy, with her pension from American Airlines. She enjoyed her garden, and the jewelry she designed and made drew lots of customers. She thought about moving off-island. She missed the Oregon coast but feared it wouldn't be a safe place for her to live, and now she had new friends she hated to leave behind.

Her mother would have liked to have Kate move back to the San Diego area, but Kate didn't want to go back there. There were too many ghosts. And, indeed, she couldn't really move anywhere until she knew where John Branden was.

She kept waiting for something to happen.

By 2006, John had grown more erratic. Turi called Randall Nozawa often to come over and visit, just to lessen the tension a little. The three of them were still trying to get the Isagenix program off the ground, and they did fairly well when they discussed that—and the property in Idaho. John did leave Turi alone occasionally when they were visiting the Priest River property—which he now considered his— in Idaho, but that was because she had no place to go, didn't have access to a car, and was stuck in the middle of forty acres, thirty miles from the nearest town.

There was no telephone service until John and Andrew, a young contractor he'd hired, rigged an antenna; even then it still wasn't dependable. Turi could only use her wireless phone if the weather was cooperating and she found a spot on the property where the signal was strong enough.

John had started digging water and sewer lines, attempting to make the Idaho property self-sufficient. He was over sixty now, and even a man forty years younger in perfect physical condition wouldn't have been able to accomplish the task John had set for himself. He had never been talented at building, and he found that skilled workers wanted more money than he was prepared to pay. He kept querying Andrew about how many services he could put in the PVC pipes he planned to lay. Could he put electrical conduits inside? It was painfully clear he was in way over his head in terms of knowledge and experience. Andrew pointed out to him that even with a crew of men, it would take fifty years to install what John wanted, in order to change the wild land and harness power for easy living.

John was tackling it almost by himself, although he recruited Randall Nozawa as "slave labor" to work alongside him. Often the former dentist went along with Turi and John to the isolated Idaho property. Good-naturedly, Nozawa grabbed a shovel and dug ditches alongside John.

"He mentioned that I could have a little house up there," Randall told friends. "Not for my family—just for me, because he said men needed a private place of their own."

Nozawa wasn't interested, and he wondered how they were going to manage their Isagenix business from this wilderness in Idaho, where even their phones didn't work most of the time.

Turi again confided in Nozawa: "I'd be perfectly happy to stay in Gig Harbor, but John wants to live here, and I want him to be happy."

And there were times when John Williams seemed to be happy—or at least content—in Idaho. He would walk around the property with Randall Nozawa, pointing out the beauty of nature and the animals who lived on their forty acres. Despite setbacks and unrealistic expectations, John was convinced that this raw land would soon be the ideal place to live.

Priest River was about fifty-five miles northeast of Spokane, Washington, and forty miles north of Hayden Lake, Idaho, where Richard Butler had set up his Aryan Nations compound, a Nazi-like stronghold that drew racists. The area was also home to survivalists, aging hippies, those who wanted only to live a simple life in a paradisiacal setting, and just plain people. Former names from the headlines lived there, too: Bo Gritz lived in northern Idaho, and Los Angeles Police Department ex-detective Mark Fuhrman, who testified in the O. J. Simpson trial, did, too, commuting to Spokane for his radio show. In many ways, it was almost like the last frontier; those heading farther west into Washington State and Oregon found a lot more "civilization."

Most Idahoans hasten to disavow the less savory racist groups in their state. An actress on *ER* said, "I'm from Idaho—the potato part, not the white supremacist part."

Idaho is a beautiful state, and, all things being equal, Turi might have grown accustomed to living there—as long as she could have seen her family regularly. John might have told her that they would keep the Idaho property but not live in it full-time unless he saw that the world' as they knew it was coming to an end.

At any rate, Turi agreed to buy a prefab Lindal cedar home to be put up on the Priest River land. Lindal homes are expensive and attractive. As they waited for it to be delivered in late 2006, John, Andrew, and Randall did manage to get the concrete foundation for the cedar home poured. But bad weather and snow were just around the corner. When all the sections of the prefab arrived, Randall saw to it that they were protected from winter storms, covering them with tarps and other materials to keep them safe.

In the spring of 2007, they could start putting the house together.

*   *   *

John couldn't understand Turi's desire to be around people, to have friends. He had no friends—except for Randall Nozawa, whom he sometimes described as his best friend. And it was easy to see why he didn't have any other friends. "He was not easy to like," Randall said. "His language was terse. The things he said when Turi was in the room were terrible, and he showed her no respect. He was always shutting her up or trying to make her feel bad."

In early 2007, John planned a campaign for Isagenix, using Randall as their spokesman at the Gateway Fitness Center. He wanted to feature posters with Randall's face superimposed on Uncle Sam's body. He thought it was a brilliant idea, even though it had no relevance whatsoever to Isagenix, and Uncle Sam had been around for more than half a century. In fact, it was an incomprehensible and silly idea. Turi loyally commented that she thought it had possibilities and maybe they should suggest it to the corporate board of Isagenix. Taking his cue from Turi, Randall pretended to be impressed, too. In fact, if this was John's idea of a brave new world of advertising, it only showed that his mind was failing him.

For some reason, John thought that Turi and Randall were trying to take credit for the Uncle Sam campaign.

"That's *my* idea," he exploded, and he began to yell at Randall, calling him out to the garage, where he berated him for trying to steal his ideas. In truth, no one had so much as hinted that Uncle Sam wasn't John's idea—and all John's. Who would want to claim such a tired image?

But John was furious. He stalked to the farthest corner of the living room and sat there in the dark.

"He was pissed off," the former dentist said. "He was sitting there, pouting."

John was growing more and more volatile, and Turi called Randall often now, begging him to come over because he was the only one she knew who could calm John down. The little house on Lost Beach Road wasn't where Randall wanted to be, but he felt sorry for Turi, and he usually went—sometimes for meals, sometimes just to talk with John. He still held some hope for Isagenix, but John's moods could wear anyone out.

"I had to walk on eggshells," Randall recalled, "and be so careful what I said because you couldn't tell what might set him off. We had awkward, almost silent, conversations."

John was more on edge, and Randall was sometimes afraid to say *anything* at all for fear of upsetting him, so they simply sat in silence, with both Turi and Randall waiting for a cue from John before they spoke.

Turi tried once to tell Randall about the man he believed to be her husband. "There are certain things about John . . . ," she began, whispering. "Things you don't know—but I can't tell you—"

But Randall could sense she wanted to tell him. It never got further than that because John came back into the room and Turi stopped talking.

There were more port wine bottles hidden around the house, as there had been around the Idaho property before the snow closed in. But John never appeared to be drunk;

he was too tightly wound to seem drunk. He was, however, hyperalert.

There was something desperately wrong with John Branden/Williams's mind. He had apparently had OCD (obsessive-compulsive disorder) going back to his days as a superartistic lawn mower, but his bipolarity now zoomed up and down to extremes. Sometimes he felt he could do anything and was excited about all the possibilities that would finally allow him to make big money, but then he would crash into the deepest hollow of depression. Neither Turi nor Randall could predict when he would change gears. None of the mood spikes made him happy. He grew steadily more suspicious and more resentful, and he'd added frank paranoia to the mix in his turbulent mind.

He was convinced that the world was going to implode very soon. The necessity of procuring a safe hiding place for him and his daughters became an urgent mission. Bizarrely, at the same time, he was still frantically trying to build his fortune with Isagenix.

Chapter Twelve

In March 2007, John and Turi left for California, on one of their regular trips. They might have gone to see his daughters, or perhaps they had some business meetings. Maybe they only needed to get away from the steady rain and gray days of the Northwest in winter. It was too cold to start building their cedar home in Priest River, and it probably would be for at least two more months.

They passed through Oregon twice on this trip—going south and coming back. John preferred 101, the coastal route, and that meant they would have driven through Gold Beach. He called Randall several times from the road—as always from pay phones. The trip seemed to be going well, and Nozawa didn't sense any trouble.

They were due home on Thursday, March 29. John made his last call of the trip that day from a phone booth on the Tacoma Narrows Bridge, which was less than ten miles from Seascape Hills.

John said they'd had a very, very nice time in California, and everything was great. He said they were "searching for ways to be even closer," and he thought they'd made progress.

"Great!" Randall said.

But things weren't great now, apparently, as John continued, "We were doing so well, and then Turi said something as we crossed the bridge—and I'm very angry."

Whatever it was that Turi had allegedly said, circumstances would make it difficult for Randall Nozawa to remember. "But I remember thinking that it wasn't anything very much," he said. Still, John was going on and on about it."

"She ruined it," John went on. "Everything was fine, and she ruined it."

He asked Randall to come over to their house, and Randall said he would try to do that later.

It was almost midnight when Randall Nozawa got a call from Turi. She told him that she and John were still arguing and she had locked herself in the bedroom. She'd managed to find her cell phone to call him, and she asked Randall to come over as quickly as he could.

"Oh!" she said suddenly, before she could explain. "He's coming. I have to hang up—"

Randall started walking toward Seascape Hills. Because of the damage to his eyes, he had trouble seeing when headlights were aimed directly at him, and he compensated by looking away and judging how far away the cars were. On the way, Turi called him on his cell phone and said the argument was still going and they really needed him to hurry.

Nozawa picked up his pace. John met him at the front doorstep and told him Turi was inside. He didn't strike Randall as being in a violent mood. "He seemed more sad than angry," Randall said later.

"We can't finish the Idaho project," John blurted.

"Why?" Randall asked.

"Things just aren't working out." John appeared to be devastated.

The two men walked into the kitchen and Randall sat down at the table. John began to pace back and forth, stopping only to open a bottle of port wine. His words came in a steady stream, and they were all grievances about Turi.

"But he wasn't angry," Randall said. "He was just sad—and quiet."

They heard Turi unlocking the bedroom door, and John said with an eerie false brightness, "Look, it's Turi!"

He still wasn't angry. The table where Nozawa sat was close to the sliding glass doors, and Turi moved to stand beside him.

"You need to tell Randall the truth," Turi said.

"John got a look on his face like he was a kid who got caught with his hand in the cookie jar," the former dentist said. "Like it wasn't really a bad thing she was referring to, but, still, he seemed mortified. He kind of stuttered when he said, 'That's the kind of thing that guys talk about in private. Guys don't talk about that in front of people.' "

Randall Nozawa wondered what Turi Bentley had learned about John during their trip south, and he was almost embarrassed for him.

None of them moved for what seemed like a long time, then John walked out of the room.

Chapter Thirteen

It was 7:30 a.m. on Friday, March 30, 2007, when Detective Fred Douglas of the Gig Harbor Police Department was dispatched to the cul-de-sac in front of the little gray-and-white house on Lost Beach Road with a Man Down call. This was an unlikely neighborhood for such a call, and an unusual time—in the early morning hours. Still, there were many retired people living in Seascape Hills, and the person who had collapsed might be a resident who'd had a heart attack or a stroke. Douglas was at the address in four minutes.

There was no way for Detective Douglas to have prepared himself for what he found when he turned right into the little circular street, where the crocuses, daffodils, and cherry blossoms were just beginning to bloom. He had never worked a homicide in his ten years on the department, and he certainly wasn't expecting to find one.

A resident on the street—Ted Sanford, a retired headmaster of a private school—had heard someone calling for help when he'd come out to pick up his morning paper. It was then that he'd seen a terribly injured man, wrapped in a white blanket or a sleeping bag, now stained a mahogany red with dried blood. The injured man was on his feet, but just barely, near the carefully landscaped mound of earth in front of their houses. He was bleeding heavily from his mouth, and there was something wrong with his eyes.

"He kept saying, 'Help me . . . help me!' " Sanford said later. "I ran in my house and called 911, and then I came back out and stayed with him until the police arrived. It was very peculiar—nightmarish."

And, indeed, it was. The man's right eye was gone, and the wound still bled. His other eye appeared to be scarred, and he had injuries in his mouth, too. EMTs were summoned immediately, and he was able to say a few garbled words before he was rushed to the ER at Tacoma General Hospital, where he was admitted in critical condition and taken immediately up to surgery.

About all Douglas and Police Chief Mike Davis understood was that there had been some kind of domestic disturbance. It was amazing that the injured man could say that much; his eye was missing, his jaw was broken, several of his teeth were knocked out, and his tongue had nearly been shot off. It would take eight hours of surgery to even begin putting his face back together. Whether he would survive or not was up in the air.

The detectives were able to discern that there were supposed to be two people inside the house itself, but the victim didn't seem to know if they were dead or alive. Since Gig Harbor has a small police department, they called for an assist from the Pierce County sheriff's office, its detectives, and its SWAT team.

Quietly, officers from both departments cleared the street to avoid anyone else being injured if there should be more gunfire. They surrounded the house the injured man had come from. And then they called the phone in the house.

There was no response.

For hours, they attempted to raise anyone left in the small gray-and-white home, but the phone rang and rang, shrill but empty. It was the only sound inside.

There was a vehicle in the garage, suggesting no one had driven away. That, however, didn't mean that they hadn't. There might have been another car parked in the steep, short driveway. Neighbors had heard nothing alarming during the previous night, no screams, arguments, or gunshots. They said they hadn't really known the couple who lived there, but they had known the elderly woman who used to live there. Her name was Liv Lee, and they thought that the female half of the couple was Liv's daughter.

Public records indicated that the house was owned by Turid Lee Bentley. That was probably Liv Lee's daughter.

With so many hours of nonresponse, there was only one thing left to do—enter the house. It was 10:00 a.m. when the SWAT team went in. They were not met with any resistance. The house was as quiet as death, and they found only death inside.

"I can remember that scene," Fred Douglas said, "and I probably will for the rest of my life. It was shocking."

There were two people in the house, but they were both dead—the woman shot in the neck and head, and the man in the head. It looked like a murder-suicide.

The blond woman had to be Turi Bentley-Williams. Was the dead man Randall Nozawa or John Williams?

The mystery had just begun to uncoil.

Neighbors had seen enough of the couple who'd lived there to estimate they were both in their sixties, and police were quite sure that the deceased were in that age group. They had to be Turi Bentley and John Williams. The man in surgery had dark hair and looked to be about fifty. That would be Randall Nozawa. Becky Minton, a friend from the Gateway Fitness Center, who had waited outside during the long standoff, agreed tearfully. She told police that Turi and John were married, and were quite a bit older than Randall.

None of their names would be officially released to the media until families could be notified.

Becky Minton said Randall had spoken with one of the fitness club members just the night before, and he had told her that John Williams had seemed "disturbed" or "upset" about something, and that he thought he could help.

Becky couldn't believe that Turi and John were dead. "They were just back from a trip to California—on the coast—and having a great time. And [they] always had a smile in their voices whenever you talk[ed] with them. I just can't imagine . . ."

As the crime scene investigation began, Detective Todd Karr of the Pierce County Sheriff's Office's Major Crimes Unit joined the other law officers. They spread out over the property and house, looking for something—anything— that might help them get official identification of the shooter and the victims. As far as the motive for the triple shootings, they would probably have to wait until Randall Nozawa came out of surgery—if he ever did.

Fred Douglas found a bullet hole in the master bedroom. Ballistics would show that it didn't match the slugs and casings from the gun used to shoot Randall, Turi, and John, but it did match another of John Williams's guns found in the house. It must have been fired sometime earlier than the night before.

Douglas also found damage to the bedroom wall, where it looked as if a knee or an elbow had crashed almost through the drywall. A check of records showed no police calls to the house on Lost Beach Road, so if there had been domestic violence going on there, it had been kept private.

The wallet closest to the dead man's body had ID for John Williams, and the investigators believed that they knew who they were dealing with. At least they knew his name.

Or *one* of his names.

When they searched the attic in the house, they found a battered backpack hidden there. It contained many IDs—under several different names and birth dates. They were from Oregon, Florida, California, Washington, and other states. Several were from the British Virgin Islands. They might all have been fake, or there could have been one that was real: John W. Williams, John W. Hennings, John W. Jewell, John W. Branden, John W. Bentley, and John W. Howell. The Social Security cards in the backpack had two different series of numbers on them; two numbers had been transposed in about half of them.

Who was he. *Really?* The detectives from Pierce County sent Internet messages to law enforcement departments whose jurisdiction matched the addresses on the IDs. When they heard back from Detective Dave Gardiner in Curry County, Oregon, they knew that the most likely shooter wasn't John Williams at all; he was almost certainly the man listed on an Oregon driver's license in the backpack— John William Branden, DOB February 24, 1945, who had been a fugitive from Curry County since 1999. He had felony warrants out on him dating back to mid-1999, first locally and regionally, and eventually a federal warrant. They were all still in force.

His crimes in Gold Beach, Oregon, had been inflicted on a woman—his common-law wife, apparently.

And they had been crimes of violence: rape in the first degree, kidnapping in the first degree, attempted murder, attempted sodomy, menacing, and harrassment. His bail had been set at one million dollars.

He had been a fugitive ever since.

Ed Troyer, the sheriff's spokesman for Pierce County, kept a closemouthed stance with the media about that new information, saying only that the deceased suspect had a history of violence with a sheriff's office. It was not John and Turi with that history, and it wasn't Pierce County he was talking about; it was Curry County, and it was Kate Jewell whom John Branden had savagely attacked.

Gardiner told Pierce County detectives that he tried to keep in touch with Kate at least twice a year, and that he had a current address for her. But first, he wanted to call her and break the news of the tragedy in Gig Harbor to her.

"I believe I owe her that," he said.

What had happened to ignite John into causing the

bloodbath the police had found was a mystery to the Washington State investigators. Randall Nozawa couldn't tell them much; he was fighting for his life as his surgery stretched to eight hours.

And he was blind. He had lost the first eye in the automobile accident three years earlier, and now his remaining eye was gone, shot out at close range.

One had to wonder if John Branden—whom the newspapers were calling "The Mysterious Mr. Williams"—had deliberately aimed for his "best friend's" good eye, intending to blind him.

Those who knew and loved Turi Bentley were overwhelmed with grief. She was the last woman in the world anyone would ever expect to die violently. The shock waves rolled over Gig Harbor and then spread out. Grown women recalled how nice Turi had been to them when they were little girls. Church friends spoke about Turi's devout faith in God. A young woman who lived in Priest River recalled meeting Turi only once, but she said she had looked forward to living close to her in Idaho.

Turi's genetic heritage would have suggested that she would live into her nineties. Losing her at such a relatively young age was a bitter blow to hundreds of people and brought extreme pain to her children and grandchildren.

Chapter Fourteen

While most Gig Harbor and Pierce County police investigators were still asleep in the early morning hours of Saturday, March 31, 2007, and while Randall Nozawa was slowly regaining consciousness in one of the bedrooms of John and Turi's house, Kate Jewell was wide awake at 5:30 a.m. She realized that this day marked the one-year anniversary of her father's death at the age of eighty-three.

"I'm lying in bed," she remembered, "and thinking how much I miss him."

As she sometimes did, she talked silently to her father; it was half prayer, half communication with Harold Jewell: *Dad, I know you're in a better place. I often feel you looking out for me. I pray that from where you are you can help me put an end to this. I want to come out of hiding. I need to take my life back.*

It had been almost eight years in a peculiar kind of exile for Kate; she was caught in a space in time, on an island where she was still, essentially, living a lie—not to deceive anyone deliberately, but to survive.

Always a journal keeper, Kate would write down her thoughts later that morning:

I think back to last April, a few weeks after my dad's death. I'd been walking the beach in Florida, thinking about Dad and "talking" with him as I walked along the water's edge. I recalled hearing Dad say "I love you" just as I looked down to spy a heart-shaped piece of shell. I picked it up, marveled at this gift, and still treasure it today. Maybe when it's later, I'll take a walk on one of our gravel beaches and find another sign that Dad's still with me—possibly a heart-shaped rock.

My tear-filled lids close and I drift into restless sleep. Suddenly, I'm in my home in Oregon. I see John. He's chasing me with a knife. He's going to kill me! I must escape! I run the trackless steps of dreams, going nowhere, terror mounting. I try to wake myself up and find I'm paralyzed. Pain radiates in my chest. Panicked, I try to assess the situation as the pain on my right side subsides and deepens on my left.

My God, am I having a heart attack? No. I'm too healthy—heck, I swim a mile a day. I have to wake up and get out of this.

Suddenly, my heart seems to stop as I sense John just outside my bedroom door. My worst fear is realized; he's found me! But I still can't move. . . .

I then sense his anger, its intensity permeating my entire body with red-hot rage. Before I can formulate a thought of what to do, his anger passes, the pain eases, and I can move. I feel intense relief as I'm able to bring myself back to full consciousness.

And then Kate finishes her entry in her journal. "*John is dead.* My mind tells me that, and somehow, I *know* that he is!"

The dream was so powerful that Kate caught herself obsessing over it all weekend, vacillating between knowing it was true, dismissing it as crazy, believing in her intuition, and questioning her own sanity. She walked on the beach, but she didn't read newspapers or watch television news broadcasts. Even if she had, she wouldn't have realized the couple who'd died in Gig Harbor had anything to do with her. Over the weekend, their identities were listed only as "a married couple in their sixties."

On Monday, April 2, Kate's phone rang. She recognized the man's voice, although she hadn't talked to him for months. It was Detective Dave Gardiner of the Curry County Sheriff's Office in Oregon.

"Are you sitting down?" Gardiner asked.

"John's dead, isn't he?" Kate already knew.

Dave Gardiner was stunned, and he asked her who had told her.

"Nobody told me, Dave," Kate said. "I don't know how I know, but I do."

A torrent of emotions washed over Kate Jewell. She was free at last, but she felt horrible guilt because she hadn't been able to save a woman named Turi Bentley, a name Gardiner had just told her. Now, when it was too late, she knew the name of the woman who had come after her in John's life. If she had died on that May night in 1999,

John probably would have been caught and locked up, and Turi Bentley would be alive. Or maybe both of them would have been killed.

John was gone, but she thought about how sad it was that he couldn't have been the man she'd once admired. They had had the knowledge and opportunity to change so many lives for the good, and he had thrown it all away. He'd often told her that she had "ruined" many things for him, but it was he who had ruined them. His overweening focus on himself had destroyed hopes and dreams that other people had.

Kate had felt somewhat safer as eight years had passed, and it was shocking to hear that John had been so close, living in Gig Harbor. My God! She had considered moving there when she'd fled from Oregon. All this time, she had pictured John in California or Florida, or even in some other country.

And Kate was angry—perhaps irrationally angry—with John for dying before she knew what secrets he'd kept from her about his life in Florida. She had always thought that some day she would really know the man behind all the mystery, and that that would help her deal with the decade she'd spend living with him, and the eight years she'd lost hiding from him.

Now, she wasn't likely ever to know.

Local papers in Washington State and the wire services carried the story of "The Mysterious Mr. Williams." Reporters found Kate, and she agreed to give a few interviews, but her face on the television screen looked like a deer caught in the headlights. She was in shock, knowing her own story with John far too well but unsure about where he had been or what he had done since she'd last seen him. No, she didn't know Turi Lee Bentley. No, she couldn't say what his state of mind was in March 2007.

But she wanted to know, Kate admitted to herself.

When she talked with Pierce County Homicide Detective Todd Karr, Kate asked to see pictures of John—dead. She dreaded seeing them, but she still had an unreasoning fear that the body they had found on Lost Beach Road wasn't really John. Not John—who had always been so clever about escaping when his life got too uncomfortable for him. He had studied at the side of one of the greatest con men of all: Bill Thaw. John had once told Kate that nobody ever saw Bill Thaw's body after he committed suicide in Florida in 1987. There were no records of his burial or cremation. His body had disappeared. John had hinted that Thaw could be living in South America. Maybe John had managed to pull off the same feat, finding someone to stand in for him, to die for him. Maybe John was also on his way to South America.

Detective Todd Karr advised Kate not to view crime scene or autopsy photos; John had suffered a single head wound, and the stark police photos would be shocking to a layperson, especially someone who had known the deceased in life. He assured her that fingerprints verified that the dead man was, indeed, John Branden-Williams.

Dave Gardiner had seen John's postmortem photos, too. "It was him, all right," he said. "He was older, and balder, but I recognized him."

Kate hoped to talk to Randall Nozawa, the only survivor—so far—of the triple shooting in the early morning hours of March 30. For the moment, he was fighting for his life, and it would be a long time before anyone could talk much to him.

Despite all odds—multiple delicate surgeries, infections, and pneumonia—Randall Nozawa survived. He was totally blind. He'd lost his left eye in 2003 and his right eye on March 30, 2007. His tongue had been bisected by a bullet, but it was eventually reattached. His jaw had been broken, and he'd lost three teeth.

Although he sometimes wished he hadn't, he kept his memories of that tragic night.

"When John left the room, he seemed so calm that neither Turi nor I was afraid," Randall said, "but when he came back he had a gun in his hands. He stood by the refrigerator, pointing it at us."

They still didn't know if he was serious, but neither Randall nor Turi said anything, staring down at the kitchen table, afraid to speak. But then, John ordered Turi to kneel in front of him, and she complied. But suddenly her mind wasn't bending to his will any longer. She turned her head toward Randall and said, "He does this to make himself feel like a man."

"I didn't know what to say," Randall said, "and I just kept my head down and kept quiet. I thought maybe this was some ritual they practiced in their marriage. I mean, people have ways that they argue, but I'd never seen this before."

Randall was more embarrassed than he was frightened. He didn't want to be this close to someone else's private business, but he'd been drawn into it. Turi was kneeling close to the table, and he thought feverishly of some way to save her from John's icy anger.

"Tell him what happened in Oregon," Turi said. "Tell him what you did to her—"

Suddenly, John's gun boomed. Turi fell sideways without a sound.

Randall knew he shouldn't move from where he sat with his head down. But he *was* able to extend his arm beneath the table far enough to touch Turi's foot with his hand. He found no pulse there. She was gone without so much as a sigh.

"He shot me next," Randall said. "When someone is shooting at you, you don't hear a very loud noise. My ears rang, but I felt no pain at all—so I knew that Turi hadn't either. I was still looking down when he shot me, and then my sight went completely black. I went under the table—just kind of slid there. I was aware of bone chips and blood in my mouth, and I remember wondering how that happened, because he had shot me in my good eye. Later, I realized I'd been looking down at the table and he was standing over me, so the bullet must have gone in my eye at a downward angle, and it continued that path, splintering my jaw, and knocking out some of my teeth, and then cut my tongue in half before it exited."

Randall was surprised that he was still alive. He could hear John walking around the kitchen for at least five or ten minutes, but he couldn't see him any longer. He stayed motionless under the table, barely breathing and hoping John would think he was dead.

And then the gun sounded again, and he heard something or someone hit the floor. He could no longer hear John pacing or breathing.

Randall Nozawa waited a while longer, then stumbled to his feet and went into the bedroom, where he fell unconscious for several hours. When he came to, he found a phone, but he couldn't get a dial tone or a 911 call to go through. It was probably Turi's cell phone and the charge had seeped out of it, so it was useless.

He didn't know if it was day or night, but he somehow managed to find the front door and get to the street. And that's where Sanford found him.

"I don't know why I'm alive," Randall said a year later. "I guess I must have a very hard head."

He probably does. Thick bone growth is one of the reasons that some humans survive a shot to the head. Old ammunition is another. And once in a while it's just the angle of fire, when a bullet's path hits no vital organs or arteries.

Asked if he ever wondered if John Branden-Williams had deliberately shot him in his good eye, Randall paused. "Sometimes, I've thought about that," he admitted. "But then I think he really meant to kill me, so it probably didn't matter to him where he shot me—just so long as I died. I saw him shoot Turi, and he was also worried about what she had told me, so he couldn't let me live."

Somehow, Randall Nozawa did live, although whether he would remained questionable for weeks. As he slowly fought his way back through surgery and infections, he began to feel that he was meant to live—that he still had many things to do with his life.

Even completely blind now, he realized he could find ways he could work with people to find their own way back to health.

Sometimes he pondered on the irony of it. John, the health guru, had destroyed life and hope—but Randall himself felt he was meant to continue the work that John had only espoused in self-absorbed double-talk.

Randall still teaches yoga, Pilates, and physical fitness.

Chapter Fifteen

In essence, the homicide investigation was over, and Pierce County Detective Todd Karr told reporters that. There was a living witness to murder, and the prime suspect was dead by his own hand. There would, of course, be no trial.

The investigators kept John Williams's *real* identity secret for several days while they investigated possible charges against him in other states. Aside from the Curry County, Oregon, charges still extant in his attack on Kate, and his escape from deputies in Napa, California, they found none. The case was officially closed.

But it wasn't over for Kate. She was compelled to find out why John had left Florida hurriedly in 1986, and why he had been so hesitant to go back there. During their visit to the Mannatech executives who lived in Jupiter, Florida, John had been jumpy and irritable, and he hadn't been able to head back to the West Coast quickly enough. During the past eight years, Kate would have been foolhardy to ask questions of John's friends and associates, because he could have found her. Now, finally, she was able to search for answers.

Many people who had known John in the past failed to return her calls. She wanted to know when and where John had first met Turi, but even Turi's own family didn't know for sure. The Gig Harbor and Pierce County police investigators were convinced that Turi had had no idea about John's criminal background, had known very little about his life before she'd met him, and hadn't even known his real name. Kate felt that Turi's last trip with John, through Oregon, had apparently opened her eyes, and she'd wanted no part of him.

John's parents were dead, but in 2008, Kate read some letters that had been exchanged between John and the elder Brandens back in 1986. His mother begged him to tell them why he'd left, and she assured him that if they just knew the truth, they could help him. His father was ill with what seemed to be colitis—but it was in fact a metastasis of prostate cancer that would kill him within months.

"Dear Jack," his mother wrote, "we are very much upset, and things cannot continue like this much longer. The best thing for you to do is tell the truth and let us determine how serious these charges are against you. What you are doing is breaking up the whole family, and there is not much more we can take. All things must come to an end, and we could be reaching the breaking point."

John told his parents that he'd left because Florida health officials had been hounding him, trying to put him out of business—or perhaps even put him in jail—because they'd been trying to get rid of all those practicing alternative medicine. He said they'd been investigating some of the prescriptions he'd written. He assured them there was really nothing to the charges, and told them how much he loved them, and how happy he and Sue and the girls were in California.

Kate soon found another possible reason why John had left so hurriedly; some of the people she talked to said John had behaved inappropriately with a young female client who might even have been impregnated by him.

But Kate believed it had to be a lot more than either of those reasons. John referred to a "horrible" secret only when he was drunk, although he'd tiptoed around any details and shut up completely when she'd tried to ask questions. He told her that he'd made $30,000 in just one night and that the money was connected with his midnight escape from Florida. He never went further than that, though. How could he have made $30,000 in one night by impregnating a patient? Or by practicing naturopathy? No way. But there was Bill Thaw, whom John had idolized—Thaw, who was a con man's con man, and maybe a lot more than that. He either committed suicide or disappeared a year after John ran away from Florida. Maybe Thaw had been keeping horrible secrets, too.

When Kate wrote to Dwight and Susan Havener a year after John's death, she received only a short response. She hadn't told them that John was dead, but Dwight wrote back to say that they'd heard only "bits and pieces" about John and didn't care to know more, whatever he was doing in 2008. Kate couldn't blame him; John had never paid the Haveners the $1,500 he'd owed them, and he hadn't turned out to be the kind of "associate" they'd hoped for.

Actually, many of his former Mannatech associates may not have known that John is dead and will learn about it for the first time in this book.

Kate wondered where John had been between the middle of June 1999, when he'd escaped from deputies in Napa, California, and 2001 or 2002, when he'd resurfaced in Gig Harbor and Tacoma, Washington. Maybe he'd been in Bill Nichols's Mount Shasta home or in a monastery all that time? Hardly likely. He certainly managed to land on his feet, especially after he met Turi Bentley.

Kate still hadn't found out anything about his last days in Florida. She couldn't locate his older sister, whom John had accused of "turning him in." *Turning him in for what?*

After many false leads, Kate managed to find a phone number for Dr. Stanley Szabo, who had once been John's closest friend and, because of that, her apartment mate in Solana Beach. Stan had always been grateful to John for helping him out back in the late eighties; in return, according to Randall Nozawa, John had spoken of the now-retired dentist as someone he admired more than any other man. (He had long since stopped extolling the brilliance of Bill Thaw by the time he met Randall.)

After following numerous paths that led to slammed doors or no information, Kate found what she was looking for when she talked to Stan. After some hesitancy, he revealed that John had shown up at his house in Del Ray Beach, Florida, one day, walking in as if he'd only been away for an hour or so, when Szabo hadn't heard from him in at least two years.

"When was that?" Kate asked.

"Probably early 2001," Szabo guessed.

Dr. Szabo accompanied John to his hotel room, and they talked for six hours. John said he was "underground," after an unfortunate incident with Kate.

"I almost killed her," John said. "We'd been arguing all day, and I packed a 'getaway bag' just in case I had to leave in a hurry."

According to this latest version, John said he was holding a gun to Kate's head, and she managed to grab the phone and call 911. "I had the gun to her head and was ready to kill her when I heard the sheriff driving down to our house. I just grabbed my bag and ran."

He had rewritten the whole scenario. Maybe John really didn't remember the way he'd beaten and raped Kate; more likely, he had made himself sound tougher and portrayed Kate as a shrew, nagging and arguing with him all day until he could no longer control himself.

To Szabo's amazement, John asked him to leave behind his new family—which included his second wife and two teenagers—and go underground with him. John boasted that he had come upon a wonderful plan for a business that they could operate behind the scenes. The money would be amazing.

"I'll do all the legwork," he promised, "and you'll be the front man."

This was basically the same organizational plan that John would offer Randall Nozawa a few years later. John was disappointed when Stan Szabo refused his offer to leave his family and live on the edge of society with John Branden.

Kate asked Stan if John had spoken of a new woman in his life in 2001, but Stan couldn't recall John mentioning any female other than Kate. Maybe John hadn't met Turi yet. Although Stan Szabo couldn't recall the exact date that

John had shown up at his house, Kate got the impression that it was before September 11.

Szabo had no idea where John went after their long conversation in John's hotel room, and he never heard from him again. However, FBI special agents knocked on his door, asking about John. Stan didn't know if they *knew* John had been in Del Ray Beach, or if it was only a coincidence.

"I just promised John that I loved him like a brother," Stan Szabo told Kate. "And I did, too. I didn't think he ever really would have hurt you, and I couldn't bring myself to turn him in. Besides, I had no way of knowing where he was—other than [that] he was underground."

The FBI agents didn't question him again. Stan was suffering from an autoimmune disease that would eventually prove terminal, and he'd had to retire from his dental practice at a relatively young age. He told Kate that Detective Dave Gardiner from Curry County called him and questioned him about John's whereabouts shortly after Kate was attacked, but he had no idea where John might have been in 1999. Now it was nine years later, and, except for that one visit, he'd never known where John Branden had been.

Kate drew in a breath, wondering if she should ask Stan about what had happened more than two decades earlier to scare John enough to flee from Naples, Florida, in the middle of the night.

"He was 'training' with Bill Thaw back then."

"What do you mean 'training'?"

Szabo didn't answer her question directly. At one point,

he said, Bill Thaw, a chiropractor named Kirk Radovich,* and Szabo were working at the Cedars of Lebanon Hospital in Miami–Dade County, in various capacities. Thaw was working as a counselor or a therapist, although where—or if—he'd gotten his training for that no one knew. "He was one in a million," Stan Szabo said. "A devil and an angel. He could be humane, considerate, and helpful one minute, and then just the opposite, and could kill you for no reason. He was a classic, brilliant psychopath."

The retired dentist liked Thaw at times, but he was cautious around him because of his severe mood swings. "I had the most fun with Bill Thaw when he was 'on.' But he could turn on a dime, and he was a raging alcoholic."

This, Kate realized, was the man that John Branden had idolized, the man he had modeled himself after. It sounded as though John had been a "gofer" for Thaw, fascinated by Thaw's exciting life and charisma and seeking to escape from a humdrum life as a property assessor.

"Thaw had business ideas. When he broke away from Werner Erhard, he began the psi experience with me. We needed an investor with more money than we had, and I introduced Thaw to a man named Allen, who'd made his money in real estate. He was a millionaire. Our proposal was that we would have a presentation with Thaw doing the psi experience, and I would lecture on the nutrition part. Allen would supply the money until we got going. But at the last moment, Allen backed out. Instead, he introduced us to a banker friend of his. The bank loaned us thirty-five thousand dollars with Allen as the cosigner."

Stan said that he and Bill Thaw went to Miami to launch

their psi experience in style, and they did well for about a year. That was when Dr. Kirk Radovich entered the picture. He attended a psi training session and was impressed.

"Kirk invited Thaw and me to interact with his patients and do individual training in his office."

Kate waited patiently, hesitant to interrupt Szabo. So far, John didn't seem to be in the picture at all.

"What did John do?" she finally asked.

"We didn't know him yet," Stan said. "I met him when he came to one of my lectures. And he met Bill Thaw, too."

Once Szabo and Thaw hooked up with Dr. Radovich, they formed a new corporation, with the three of them cutting Allen out. The whole country was intrigued with things like est, psi, love beads, incense, and new "far-out" experiences, and Florida was the ideal place to be with the dynamic Thaw, Radovich's established practice, and Stan's well-grounded training and experience in doing hair and blood analysis. He was a dentist, but he had also studied in the field of blood analysis.

"Kirk didn't really understand the analysis I did," Stan told Kate. "If a patient asked a question about it, he would run down the hall and get an answer from me—but I was never allowed to actually see the patients. I got tired of that arrangement and went off and did my own lectures."

Bill Thaw was apparently helping patients with their psychological problems, which was a bleak joke—a sociopath acting as a counselor. "I've believed for a long time that we create our own reality," Szabo told Kate. "Once, I said to Bill, 'When *you* participate in a hurtful action against someone, you enjoy it.' Bill just laughed, and I knew he acknowledged that."

Stan explained that there was a balloon payment due on the $35,000 loan. He asked Bill what he should do, because he didn't have the money to pay it. Stan, Bill Thaw, and some "shyster lawyer" met in a Jacksonville hotel room with Dr. Kirk Radovich. Allen, the millionaire, was going to sue all four of them for defaulting on the loan he'd cosigned. Stan got on the phone with Allen and said, "You originally promised to put up the money, and you didn't. Then you cosigned for this loan. Now it's only right for you to pay it."

Bill Thaw grabbed the phone out of his hand and said roughly, "I'm only going to say this once. Pay the note off and be a good boy . . . or you're dead."

There was no question in Stan Szabo's mind that Thaw meant every word.

John Branden was on the fringe of the pseudo-medical group, learning to do blood analysis from Stan Szabo and learning darker things from Bill Thaw. It was Szabo's belief that Thaw was involved with organized crime and one step ahead of law enforcement.

"This was when John was living with him?" Kate asked. Finally, they were getting to the "horrible thing" that John mentioned only when he was very drunk. It was a thing that "tortured his soul."

"Yeah. One day, when Bill Thaw was beating up and torturing this . . . *person* . . . , John walked in and witnessed the murder that followed."

"Murder?"

"Yeah. Now Bill was in trouble. He was under pressure from the mob and from the police. The mob wanted Thaw dead because they didn't want him to snitch on them if the police picked him up—and they wanted John for the same reason."

So there it was.

Was this the night John made $30,000? Was the victim the mysterious Allen, whom Bill Thaw had threatened with death? Stan hadn't said if the victim was male or female; maybe he didn't know.

Kate tried to grapple with what really happened back in 1986: John had always either minimized or maximized the truth to fit whomever he was talking to. He had told his good friend Stan Szabo that he had witnessed Bill Thaw torturing and killing someone. Kate wondered if that was true.

And then she had a worse thought: Maybe John hadn't just walked in on a murder in progress; maybe John had been the real killer, and this had been part of his "training" with Thaw. Maybe Thaw had walked in on *him*? Or perhaps it had been an accident or John had been forced to commit murder by the man he idolized.

John was dead, and she could never ask him what had happened in Florida. But Kate herself had seen murder in his eyes, and he had demonstrated that it had been in his heart as he'd shot Turi and Randall.

Every day of his life after that night in Florida, he lived in hiding to lesser and greater degrees. Although he never opened up to her, Kate wondered if he confided in the psychiatrists he consulted with. He always boasted after those sessions that he knew so much more than they did that they weren't capable of helping him. Once, he went to see a female therapist, and he told Kate that he'd told the woman his "secret."

"She didn't show up for their next appointment," Kate recalled. "He wondered if he'd scared her away by dumping everything out on their first meeting."

Kate never really knew who John Branden was deep inside.

Probably no one did.

After John's final crimes appeared in the media—first in the Northwest, and, later, nationally—Kate was stunned to learn that even people who were close to her hadn't understood the true danger she'd lived with for more than eighteen years.

"The day after I told my sister, Connie, that John was dead and how he had died, she called me and said, 'I owe you an apology.' I asked her why, and she said, 'I never thought that John would actually kill you. I thought he was too much of a wimp.'"

Her own sister hadn't totally believed her, even though Kate had tried her best to open up to Connie, to let her see the fear hiding inside her. If her sister hadn't understood, why would anyone else have understood?

And then, a month or so later, a retired American Airlines pilot whom Kate had known in San Diego and who currently lived on Orcas Island approached her with another apology. "Kate, a lot of people thought you were just being overly dramatic when they heard your story. I guess we were wrong."

Suddenly she understood why too many women won't

talk about abuse or even grasp the fact that they are living in an abusive situation. No one will believe them, so what's the point of trying to escape? After her story became public, Kate heard from a number of women who had been living with domestic violence, although they admitted they'd always been afraid to talk about it. Studies show that most women attempt to leave eight times before they succeed in breaking patterns of abuse, fear, and guilt.

"Even worse is the attitude of women who have said to me, 'I just don't understand why the woman stays,'" Kate said ruefully. "Their tone suggests that *they* would never stay in such a situation. To them, I say, 'Don't judge me if you haven't walked in my shoes.' When you are a woman who gives her heart totally and makes a true commitment to a relationship—to honor that commitment and to remain loyal through good times and bad—it's almost impossible to believe that the situation will become too bad for you to fix.

"And there's also the dream factor. Most relationships are built on having common dreams and goals. I thought John and I shared that—helping people and making a positive impact on the world. I know Turi believed that, too. Letting go of that dream was excruciatingly painful. Sometimes it still is. Accepting that the dream is dead is an exceptionally hard thing to do. Accepting that *you can't fix it* is harder."

Afterword

There was something that Kate still needed to do, although many people might not understand it. She had wanted to warn John's next victim, but she'd never been able to find her. For eight years, she had thought of what she would say to save that woman. Now, she knew her name, but it was too late. She wrote to Turi Bentley anyway, hoping that Turi would somehow be able to hear her.

And hoping that women in similar danger *would* get the message and save themselves.

Here is Kate's letter:

Dear Turi,

Although I'll never know you, in many ways I feel I do. I know you were a kind and loving person who met a man who was warm, sensitive, tender, communicative, and appeared to be loving and supportive. He was very intelligent and you believed in his view of health and thought that he could reach his full potential with your love and support. You, who truly cared about people and wanted to help them to have better health, and, therefore, better lives, believed that the man you knew as John Williams had a gift. One that you embraced and wanted to help him share with the world.

I know these things because I too believed in John William Branden and nearly lost my life for doing so. How I wish I could have warned you. Would you have listened? How I wish you would not have challenged him that last night. Maybe if you had just stayed in your room, the outcome could have been different.

Yet I know how absurd, frustrating, aggravating and crazy-making John's insanity was. I know what it's like to look into the face of a man who has professed so very often to love you fully, unconditionally and forever, and then watch his lips form the words, 'I'm going to kill you.' I also know that you hear those words, look into his eyes and know he won't. If you can just survive the episode.

I also know that John could truly mean those words as when he told me, 'You're going to die tonight.' And his eyes said he was dead serious.

You cannot imagine the sorrow and guilt I've felt over your death. When I first heard of your tragic death, I felt guilty that I hadn't died, for then the authorities might have looked harder at John, you wouldn't have met him and would still be alive today, enjoying and being enjoyed by your children and grandchildren.

Your family is what I feel most guilty about. I have no children, no grandchildren. I so often wonder why I'm even still here and pray that I will figure out why, and use the rest of my life to give something good to the world.

I am heartsick that I could do nothing to change your outcome. I KNEW John WOULD KILL the next woman he was with, and still can't think of anything more I could have done. But how I wish there could have been something.

I probably know better than anyone what you went through that night, and the others when you locked yourself in the bedroom. Somewhere—and I think it began with the abuse from his sister (if any of that is true), and accelerated during his relationship with Bill Thaw, John's dark side evolved into creating his bipolar personality. His drinking, of course, led him deeper and deeper into his anger, paranoia, and psychosis. It wasn't YOUR job, or mine, to "fix" him, although I know we both tried our best to do so. We both sought to love and be loved, and thought at the outset that we'd found the perfect mate. We both were dead (and almost dead) wrong. I am sorry from the bottom of my soul that I could not help, that you were killed, and can only hope and believe that you are at peace in a better place. If you run into my dad, he can be a great comfort to you, as I truly believe he had a hand in John's turning the gun on himself. I only wish he could have gotten to John before John shot you and Randall.

We both know the good times shared with John. We both know the horrible. I ask now for your forgiveness, your understanding, and your insight. I am still on this planet, and like you, want to do some-

thing good for others. I would feel honored to ac-
complish something that you wanted to do in your
honor. Please let me know what that might be—and
how to begin.
   Sincerely,
   Kate

If this case seems all too familiar to you, if you are living in a domestic violence situation and need help, please use your own computer or one in a library and go to www.ndvh.com or call 1-800-799-SAFE (7233) or TTY 1-800-787-3224. You are not alone, and there are domestic violence shelters and centers in every state to help you. They will protect your privacy and security.

Get help now!

WRITTEN IN BLOOD

When I was much younger and far more naïve, I believed that almost any criminal could change, could become rehabilitated, and return to the free world without being a danger to anyone else. Counseling, understanding, and kindness could help them change their ways. I didn't understand the many personality disorders—and even mental illness—that entered into the equation. Men and women with sociopathic, narcissistic, histrionic, and borderline personality disorders seldom change, because they don't want to change.

I've often said that personality disorders are like rampant ivy: While it may be ripped out of one side of the brain, it's growing back on the other.

The people who possess these traits and entrenched reactions are the most important people in their own worlds, and they feel no empathy whatsoever for anyone else. In a way, it's better to be frankly psychotic—*crazy, insane.* Those suffering with a psychosis such as paranoia or schizophrenia cannot manage their lives and are often more amenable to treatment than sociopaths, who view themselves as managing very well, indeed.

Often—not always. Some psychotic individuals who are unwilling to accept treatment with drugs, therapy, or shock treatments, or who disobey their doctors' recommendations, can be extremely dangerous if they stop their therapy.

I don't know just where to place the killer in the following case on the mental-health scale. I do know he was incredibly dangerous, and those who lived around him in a small, quiet town had no idea of his background.

When the full story came out, a front-running 2008 presidential candidate was caught in the backlash of scandal. When I saw the killer's latest victims on the evening news, I felt an extra pang of sorrow. They'd had everything going for them and long lives ahead. They'd been newly married and in love.

And then someone had come knocking on their front door in the early morning darkness of a bleak November day.

Chapter One

November 17, 2007, was a Saturday, less than a week before Thanksgiving, and a day that promised to be full of rain. But that was to be expected in western Washington State in November, just as daylight barely lasts seven hours. In the summer, though, the sun shines and it's light out for eighteen hours. Most natives cheerfully accept the trade-off.

Graham is a very small town at the end of a multilane highway, and it sits in the shadow of towering and breathtaking Mt. Rainier. It's horse country. Acres of meadows are fenced in so horses have freedom to run for miles. The hamlet also has easy access to a number of pristine wilderness areas. Like the last case, this, too, took place in Pierce County, but it has a far different ambience from Tacoma or even Gig Harbor. Many of those who live in Graham commute to Seattle and Tacoma to work, but they look forward to coming home to the smell of freshly cut grass and alfalfa.

The building boom of the new century has spread to Graham, and in 2007, there were several five-acre parcels of land for sale on one side of 70th Avenue East at 305th, a gravel road. There were also new houses in various stages of completion, most of them unoccupied. A few houses along the road had families living in them, and there were also a number of trailers—some luxury double-wide mobile homes and some aged travel trailers, with shacklike structures built around them.

Local ordinances had not yet laid down all kinds of restrictions about land use and building permits. Basically, it was live and let live in this friendly town where almost everyone *did* know everyone else. There were some local taverns and, for those who didn't drink, grocery stores and the post office where they could catch up on the news.

One thing was certain. No one in Graham, Washington, knew that there was a savage killer living among them.

The call to 911 at the Pierce County Sheriff's Department dispatch center came in from a man named Jeff Freitas, who owned some prime acreage in Graham. He had halfway planned to take his neighbor, Brian Mauck, hunting that morning, but when he went by his house at 5:00 a.m., all the lights were out, and he figured Brian and his wife, Bev, were sleeping.

When Freitas returned from hunting at eleven that Saturday morning, he saw that one of the front panels of his friends' front door was knocked out. This wasn't particularly alarming, as he knew that the newly married couple sometimes forgot their house keys and resorted to removing the door section so they could reach in and turn the locks from the inside. Most of the neighbors knew that.

Brian kept intending to get extra keys and fix the door solidly, but other things got in the way.

When Jeff Freitas got to his modern double-wide mobile home nearby, he decided to call Brian and Beverly just to be sure everything was okay. Their habits were fairly predictable, and he usually saw them around their new gray and white ranch-style home with the three-car garage by this time of the morning. And the temperature outside was cold enough that he would have thought Brian would have fixed the door panel right after they got into the house.

There was no answer to his phone call. He tried both Brian and Bev's cell phones, and no one answered those either.

The Maucks' two vehicles were parked in their driveway, and this wasn't a neighborhood where people walked to the store. Why didn't they answer the phone?

Jeff Freitas told his wife and brother-in-law that he was going to walk down to the Maucks' house to check on them. Maybe their cell phones' batteries were dead, and the land line *could* have gone out, too. But the thought of the missing door panel kept bothering Freitas.

As he came up to the front door, he could hear a television playing loudly inside. He suddenly felt a dark sense of foreboding. He forced himself to kneel down and look through the space where the door panel should have been.

He wasn't quite sure what he was looking at, but it appeared that Brian—or maybe Bev—might have fallen asleep on the media room floor, and someone had covered them with a blanket or spread. He wasn't sure why they'd fallen asleep or what had happened. Probably they'd been out the night before; they usually went out on Friday nights, and maybe they had been tired enough to drift off in front of the TV.

Still, Freitas somehow knew the real explanation wasn't going to be good; he just tried to delay finding out why his nerves were jangling. As his eyes adjusted, he saw what might be spilled wine or catsup—his mind darted frantically so he wouldn't have to face the obvious source—or *blood* on the carpet.

Freitas was a logger, forty-two years old, six foot one, and 240 pounds. He was perfectly capable of taking care of himself, but he didn't want to go into the house. He backed away and called 911.

Pierce County Deputies Kent Mundell and Laura Wilson were dispatched at about two in the afternoon and met Detectives Brian Lund and Tom Catey from the Criminal Investigation Division, who arrived soon after. They checked the outside of the house and found no signs of a break-in. Actually, the front door still had a dead bolt in place, so whoever had kicked the door panel could conceivably have done so to reach inside and lock the door, rather than unlocking it. The door section still lay just inside.

Catey peeked through the door, just as Jeff Freitas had. He saw a blue fleece blanket and two blue and white flannel sheets spread out on the floor of the entrance hall and dining area, and he recognized that the dried red liquid at the edges of the bedding was almost certainly blood. In the great room just beyond there were two brown recliners and a matching couch, all placed so that viewers could see the large-screen television set. He thought he could make out a human form lying on the floor of that room, but most of it was blocked from his view by one of the recliners.

Deputy Laura Wilson walked rapidly around the perimeter of the house, checking for anything that seemed out of place and for other obvious points of entry. She came back shaking her head; she'd found nothing amiss outside the house.

Jeff Freitas had a key to the Maucks' residence, and he gave it to the Pierce County deputies.

It was time to go inside. As Lund and Catey entered the home to assess the scene, they stepped over a woman's black shoe that rested incongruously on the threshold. They saw more blood—this time blood spatter that had flown onto the walls from the floor of the dining room, leaving a large blank spot that was quite possibly the "phantom image" of a killer. The blood droplets appeared to be high velocity, as if they had come from a gunshot wound. In that case, the shooter and his clothing had probably trapped the blood spatter before it hit the wall.

Catey and Lund were apprehensive about what they would find farther inside. They saw bare hands and feet, and realized there were probably two bodies in the great room, both covered with blankets. Closer now, they could see a man's lower body clothed in jeans and with bare feet, and it looked as if a woman lay horizontally on top of his shoulders. Only her feet and one arm protruded from a blanket covering, but the two bodies formed the crude pattern of a cross.

The two deputies decided not disturb the scene. Instead, they would wait for Detective Sergeant Ben Benson, who would be in charge of this criminal investigation, before going further. He was on his way with forensic investigator Adam Anderson. Lieutenant Brent Bomkamp and Detectives Darren Moss and Jason Tate were on the property now. They spoke in hushed tones.

This was a crime that would shock even longtime law enforcement veterans, with some of the most totally unexpected twists and turns, and it had occurred in such a quiet and bucolic area. It was going to take some intense detective work to discern why it had happened and who had hated the victims enough to kill them.

During his more than two decades with the Pierce County Sheriff's Department, Ben Benson has worked everything from patrol to undercover drug investigation, and now he was a detective sergeant in CID who had seen his share of homicides. But none like this.

Benson, forty-seven, is tall and laconic, and never seems to get rattled. When he was just a high school student, he managed to get an interview with a local law enforcement chief who had been forced to retire in disgrace, a man who hadn't agreed to talk to any newspaper or television reporters from Seattle or Tacoma. Seventeen-year-old Benson's scoop, worthy of any metropolitan newspaper, was published in his high school paper. His interrogation skills had only improved in the three decades since. The average criminal was no match for him.

When he was just a rookie, Ben Benson was as mature as detectives twenty years older than he was. He owns a small plane, and he and his wife, Grace Kingman, a Pierce County deputy prosecutor, spend much of their time off flying over Puget Sound and the islands that dot it, taking photographs of the natural beauty that abounds in Washington State.

Benson is also one of the Sheriff's Department pilots. In July 2008, while he was flying over a suspected illegal narcotics operation with another pilot and two deputies, their Cessna 206's engine suddenly stopped. They dropped from 2,200 feet to within 500 feet of the ground in forty-five seconds, and they sent out a Mayday! call.

They looked down and saw they were over a large mall and a freeway, with no safe place to land. More dicey moments passed before Benson switched the fuel tanks back and forth, and the engine came back to life. In the air, in an emergency, he was totally calm—until afterward, when he thought about what *might* have happened.

No, nothing seems to alarm him, but even he was appalled by this scene of horror on a quiet country road.

As Benson arrived at the Maucks' house with Adam Anderson, Detective Lynelle Anderson drew up an affidavit for a search warrant. Lynelle Anderson had a special talent for organizing scores of details and creating comprehensive affidavits. The investigators had many buildings, trailers, mobile homes, and vehicles to search, and they needed the warrants ASAP.

At shortly after 2:00 p.m., the sun was already beginning to lower in the western sky, so while they waited for the warrant, Mary Lou Hanson-O'Brien, also a forensic investigator, took photographs of the exterior of the house, while Detective Tom Catey made a video recording as he walked around the house and surrounding area, describing what he saw.

Everyone arriving from the Sheriff's Department was an expert in his or her particular field. The familiar routines they followed helped a little to defuse their revulsion as they first encountered the crime scene.

But only a little.

Ed Troyer, a close friend of Ben Benson's who once worked with him when they were both road deputies and in the Narcotics Unit, has been the sheriff's media liaison for several years. Troyer is the first line of media defense, managing to juggle the people's right to know and the need for secrecy in many investigations. Now, he stationed himself between the investigators and the massive media response as word of a possible multiple murder was picked up from police radio calls.

Neither he nor the investigators knew just how bad the situation was, but Troyer told reporters as much as he could.

Jeff Freitas had said the house was completely dark at 5:00 a.m. when he passed it on his way hunting, but now both exterior lights were on. For some reason, Brian Mauck must have turned them on before it got light about eight. As Tom Catey walked around the outside of the house, he noted that all of the windows were securely locked: At the front door, he saw that someone inside could open the door when the push-button lock was set by turning the knob, but it could not be opened from the outside when the lock was set. If the dead bolt was shoved into its slot—as it was when the police arrived—the door could not be opened.

It would have taken a very, very thin person to enter through the missing panel's space, which was only twelve inches wide. No, it was more likely that Brian Mauck had heard something on the front porch, flipped on the outside lights, and admitted someone he either believed he could trust or someone pretending to be in distress.

Whoever had come to the Maucks' door should never, ever have been let in.

The bamboo floor of the dining room, just beyond the front door, was stained scarlet in many spots. These areas had been covered with the blue fleece blanket and matching sheets. Now that Benson was inside, he could see that something heavy had been dragged from the bloodied floor in the dining area, across a section of rug there, and then into the great room, where the television still droned on.

Benson moved into the great room, where he carefully removed the blankets covering the bodies. He found a white male, dressed in a gray T-shirt and jeans, wearing a black belt but no socks or shoes. He was in a prone position; the woman lay on her back, draped crosswise on top of him, over his shoulders. Rigor mortis was apparent; they had been dead for hours.

There was so much blood spatter—probably medium velocity (cast-off blood)—that it stained the walls red in two distinct patterns eight feet above the floor. The south wall had so much blood on it that it was hard to tell what color it had originally been painted.

Criminalists would determine that the killer or killers had swept a broom through the pools of blood on the floor, flinging it up on the wall. The broom had been dropped carelessly in the kitchen, as if whoever tried to sweep up the blood had realized it was a hopeless task.

Mary Lou Hanson-O'Brien used standard black fingerprint powder to process the exterior of the sliding glass door that opened off the great room and brought up latent prints from the sliding portion and door frame. They might be matched to the couple who lived here, or they might be the one key the investigators needed.

The blue blanket covering the female victim had hidden the fact that she was nude. She might have slept that way, or the killer's motive could have been a sexual attack. One bullet hole was obvious just above her nose near the corner of her right eye, almost certainly a fatal wound. After she was photographed, she was turned over, and a second wound now was visible in the back of her upper right arm. And then a third, in the back of her neck, just to the left of midline. She had probably been shot as she tried to run away from her killer.

She also had severe injuries to one elbow where she had fought her killer. Chances were that he—or she—would show bruises or cuts.

The video camera recorded sights and sounds; the photographer's words were terse and organized. Benson had to maintain a certain emotional distance as he looked down at a very young woman who had perished in an "overkill" by someone she was fleeing from. The only thing he could do for her now was to find her killer and put him (or her) behind bars.

The dead man was young, too. Freitas had said that Brian was thirty and Beverly was twenty-eight. This victim appeared to have two gunshot wounds in the back of his head and one in the right temple area—all fatal wounds. When the Pierce County medical examiner, Dr. Eric Kiesel, had finished his initial examination, his deputy ME, Bert Osborne, and Adam Anderson lifted the man to a litter. A gray cloth towel was revealed beneath where the victim's chest had been. It had blood on it—but it also had four bullet holes and gunshot residue on one corner. It might very well have been used as a silencer.

At this point early in the murder probe, the investigators had to consider the possibility that this could have been a murder-suicide after a quarrel—but then they realized that it was impossible that *both* victims had been shot in the back. Nobody's hands could bend and twist into a position that would allow that.

Almost all homicide detectives begin their investigation without knowing anything about the victims. When a superior detective winds up his case, he will know the dead better, perhaps, than he has known anyone in life. Ben Benson was fairly sure he knew the names of the people who had perished in this cozy home. An official identification lay ahead, but Jeff Freitas said they were Beverly and Brian Mauck, his neighbors and good friends.

The two vehicles parked outside belonged to them: a white Dodge 2500 Sprinter van that had EMERALD AIRE, INC. painted on both sides, and HEATING AND AIR CONDITIONING REFRIGERATION CONTROLS and a phone number beneath that. According to Freitas, Brian Mauck worked for that company as a technician. Beverly worked for Baydo's Chevrolet, and her vehicle, a gray Chevrolet Suburban, was parked next to Brian's van. Both vehicles were locked and didn't appear to have been tampered with.

Ben Benson knew now that the Maucks were familiar residents of the area, and that they had numerous ties to friends and family. He glanced around the home that they had shared in the first year of their marriage. Their house was neat, if a little cluttered. There were several movies around the television set, a few popular titles, some X-rated and untitled, three stuffed animals, some Seattle Seahawks memorabilia, plants, a cat scratching post—now tipped over—and two cats hiding from all the strangers, and between the brown recliners, a cheese knife and tray, coasters, and three TV remote controls.

Bev and Brian Mauck weren't teetotalers. The detectives had found champagne, raspberry coolers, and two six-packs of beer chilling on the rear porch. (They learned later that these were thank-you gifts for work Brian had done free for friends.) On an island in their kitchen, there was a nearly empty half gallon of vodka and a bottle of sour apple schnapps, the ingredients for an appletini. Two empty martini glasses rested on the island. There was a supply of liqueurs in a cabinet. Nevertheless, they didn't appear to be heavy imbibers.

They were obviously athletes. In the garage, Benson and his team of investigators found motorcycle helmets and boots, an exercycle, golf clubs, skis, hiking and camping equipment, twin Harley-Davidson motorcycles, a treadmill, two Ski-Doos with a trailer, and all manner of scuba-diving equipment from dive suits and swim fins to air tanks.

Benson surmised that Brian and Beverly Mauck had been attacked unawares before they had much time to defend themselves, although it looked as though Bev had

gotten in some good licks before her killer shot her between the eyes. The couple had to have been in top physical condition. They had also clearly been enjoying their
lives to the fullest. Probably they had been intimate the
night before; their undergarments were tossed aside in
their bedroom. He wondered if someone had been watching them through a window, someone overwhelmed with
lust, enough to break in.

If Beverly Mauck had been sexually attacked by the
killer, the postmortem examination and acid phosphotase
and DNA tests could determine that.

As Benson and Tom Catey moved from room to room,
they observed hundreds of articles. They would all be
listed on the voice recorder of the video camera. All told,
the detectives found six weapons: a .22 Beretta handgun
(unloaded but with a fully loaded magazine next to it), a
Buck knife, an aluminum baseball bat next to the bed in
the master bedroom, a Glock .40-caliber handgun, and two
rifles. Why hadn't Brian Mauck reached for one of them—
even the baseball bat—as he went to the door?

There were drops, smears, one fingerprint in blood, and
small pools of blood all over the house. Mary Lou Hanson-
O'Brien took samples of all of it. They could see that
someone had wiped down the light-switch plates with a
bloody cloth, making an effort to erase any fingerprints left
there.

There promised to be a lot of physical evidence; the
challenge was to connect the most telling evidence to a
suspect. In the end, the Pierce County investigators would
have 190 separate items of physical evidence, from bedding and blood samples to .22-caliber spent rounds (slugs)

and towels with gunshot residue burns to hairs and fibers and DVDs and underwear and apparently untouched ammunition.

Better to preserve too much than not enough.

When the forensic investigators lifted the bloodstained blankets and sheets from the entry hall so they could be dried and then tested in the police lab, Ben Benson saw more broom or drag marks beneath them. He caught his breath as he saw tread patterns from shoes in the midst of the streaks. They had come from both a large shoe—surely belonging to a male—and a much smaller shoe. The large print was well defined, with a sharp zigzag pattern; even the worn marks on the sole left a distinct imprint.

Who had left them there? The best physical evidence is a fingerprint left in blood; the bottom of a shoe in blood is almost as good. Beyond the pattern itself, there are signs of wear, cuts, and damage done by rocks and pebbles.

Any halfway intelligent killer would know that and throw away the shoes he'd worn as he committed his crime(s).

Ben Benson was hoping for a dumb murderer, or at least an overconfident one. But he knew that Brian Mauck himself could have left those marks if he'd been wearing shoes when he opened his front door to murder. And if he had lived long enough to walk a few feet through his own life's fluid.

But Brian was barefoot. It had to be his killer who left the prints.

It was close to two in the morning when Benson, the CID investigators, and the forensic criminalists cleared the murder scene. They carried with them innumerable containers and plastic baggies filled with what might be vital evidence, all sealed, dated, and initialed. They'd spent almost twelve hours processing it, and they had learned a great deal—but not enough.

The death house was locked and CRIME SCENE—DO NOT ENTER tape was posted.

Deputies would stand by to watch it overnight.

Chapter Two

Ben Benson and the criminalists were back the next morning—Sunday. This time, in the daylight, they could see vomit in the gravel portion of the driveway.

That, too, would be tested for DNA.

Twenty-four hours after Jeff Freitas's desperate call to 911, they had so far: photos of two shoe prints in blood and what appeared to be a fingerprint on a doorjamb, a fingerprint on the outside of a sliding glass door, some prints Hanson-O'Brien had lifted from a faucet in a bathroom sink, a broken front door, a mound of vomit, a towel that had been used as a silencer, and an initial sense of the makeup of the neighborhood where the Maucks had lived.

There would be all manner of forensic science tests ahead, autopsies, a canvass of the area for possible witnesses, and a search to determine if anyone had a grudge against the young couple.

The neighborhood along 70th Avenue East was home to all kinds of people, some well-to-do, some enjoying a comfortable living, and some barely making it. Beverly and Brian Mauck had had two salaries and no children yet;

they had intended to take just one more scuba-diving trip to Turks and Caicos before they concentrated on becoming parents. They weren't rich, but they had enough disposable income to buy all the "toys" that detectives had noted as they walked around their home. Anyone could have seen that this had been a happy couple who shared almost everything. There were *two* of all their sports equipment. Two cozy brown chairs in the great room. Benson and his crew would have to talk to many more people to verify their impression of this marriage, but it seemed to have been a good one, over far too soon.

On the day after the double murder, Mary Lou Hanson-O'Brien took digital images of more possible evidence: hairs and fibers, and other items that hadn't been visible in the darkness of the night before. She covered the door frame that had a bloody print on it with plastic while Lieutenant Brent Bomkamp sawed away that portion of the jamb. It might be an extremely valuable exhibit in a trial.

She collected the Buck knife, a digital camera that held photographs of Brian Mauck in the process of being tattooed, a bloodied paper towel, and a roll of paper towels.

Beverly had been very popular in high school at Mt. Rainier High in Des Moines, Washington. Some of her adventures were legendary among her peers. Bev was most memorable for falling out of the back of a truck in full clown makeup and costume. She loved to laugh and her sense of humor was infectious. She and Brian enjoyed popular comedians' CDs and Bev insisted that her friends and siblings listen to them when they were riding in her car. "Listen, *listen!*" she'd command her friend Jenny— who was as close as a sister—hitting her on the arm.

"I knew she'd heard it so many times before," Jenny recalled, "and she was funnier than any of the comedians she made us listen to."

Brian was mischievous and his voice could drown out anyone else in the room. His friends called him a "wild stallion," and he would try just about anything. He'd been fearless almost since he was born. When he was three, he slipped out of his house and headed for the 7-Eleven to buy candy. He got there, but it was almost a miracle because he had to cross two four-lane highways to reach the convenience store. Beverly was just as fearless, a tomboy who refused to wear dresses when she was a child and played on the boys' teams in high school. She'd grown up with two brothers, and she'd learned how to keep up with them.

If they had to die young, those who knew them would have expected it to be in a diving accident or a motorcycle crash.

Beverly Slater and Brian Mauck had known each other for years, and had dated steadily for four years before their wedding on May 5, 2006. And what a wedding it was. Held on Cinco de Mayo—the riotous Mexican holiday—it was fitting that they had chosen an island off Mexico for the ceremony. Their guests flew down to join them as they were married on a white sand beach. One of their neighbors said they had honeymooned on Turks and Caicos, their favorite spot for scuba diving.

Bev and Brian lived their lives full out; they worked hard and played harder. The young couple went bowling with old friends, and dancing, and usually went out on Friday nights, often to Ma's and Pa's Roundup, a restaurant/lounge/tavern near their home. When the University of Washington Huskies football team had a home game, they were there. Between the Huskies and the Seahawks, they had a lot of tailgate barbecues. Brian had season tickets to the Seattle Seahawks' games. All things being equal, he should have been sitting in his brown recliner watching the Huskies on the date of his incomprehensible death.

Brian was as strong as a young bull. On Friday he had carried a tall Christmas tree into the company where he worked so the staff could decorate it.

To someone looking on who didn't live the kind of life the Maucks did, jealousy was a possibility. It would have been easy for someone like that to dismiss how hard they worked and view them as privileged by fate and luck.

Word of the double murder quickly spread around Graham, and to friends in Tacoma. Everyone seemed to have a theory on the motivation for their deaths and some called the sheriff's office.

One of Beverly's coworkers at Baydo's Chevrolet contacted deputies to tell them that Beverly had been frightened by the nephew of a neighbor. He was in his early twenties, a huge man standing six foot three and weighing close to 300 pounds. Bev believed he was the one responsible for the theft a month ago when a number of things were stolen from her house, including her cell phone, some documents, and a .357 Magnum. "But she didn't want to report the gun theft because she and Brian hadn't gotten around to registering it. Later, she found the papers ripped up in her yard."

Even though the man no longer lived in the neighborhood, Beverly had become afraid lately to be alone in her house, and that wasn't like her. Her friends assumed that it was the man she believed was a burglar who still frightened her.

A male coworker at Baydo agreed. "Seven of us went out to eat at Mazatlan in Spanaway last Friday night—November ninth," he said, "and Bev didn't want to go home when we left at 10:00 p.m. Brian was gone all weekend to the NASCAR races, and the nearest house with anyone living in it was three hundred feet away; she just wasn't comfortable staying in her own house at night without him. She wanted us to drive her to her brother's house in Lynnwood, but that was over sixty miles away, and we'd been drinking during the evening. It just wasn't possible. We drove to her house instead, but she made us wait until a friend came to get her and take her to *her* house. Bev called me the next day to thank me for dinner. She said she was 'terrified' to be home by herself."

The car salesman didn't know exactly what—or who—was scaring her, and she hadn't said.

Those who loved them could not believe that Beverly and Brian were gone. They had been brimming over with life on Friday night when they met Brian's parents for dinner to celebrate his mother's birthday.

At a quarter to four on Saturday afternoon, after Ben Benson's crew of forensic investigators and detectives set to work on the crime scene inside the Maucks' home, Benson, Tom Catey, Bill Ruder, and Jason Tate talked to a few close neighbors of the two victims.

Among the have-nots in the Maucks' neighborhood were

Jeff Freitas's sister, Jennifer, thirty-seven, and her new husband, Daniel Tavares, forty-one. While Jeff and his wife lived in a large, modern mobile home, and Jeff and Jennifer's parents lived in a smaller—but very nice—mobile on Jeff's land, the Tavareses resided on Jeff's acreage in a very small travel trailer with no bathroom, a lean-to attached to it, and a Porta Potti or, as they called it, a "honey bucket."

Jennifer was a pretty but very overweight woman with long blond hair who resembled the late Anna Nicole Smith. She was rumored to have met Daniel through some kind of pen-pal connection, either on the computer or through ads in a tabloid. They had moved into the tiny trailer in July, four months earlier.

Tavares was apparently working with his brother-in-law as a logger. A powerfully built man at six feet and 225 pounds, he looked a good deal older than his age. It appeared that he and Jennifer might be the only ones who had any eyewitness observation of activity around the Maucks' home during the early morning hours of November 17.

Jennifer Tavares volunteered that she and Daniel knew Bev and Brian Mauck well. "They party a lot," she said, "and they usually play cards with my brother Jeff on Friday nights."

Jason Tate asked Jennifer about the man in his twenties whom Beverly was rumored to be afraid of. She nodded. "That's Billy Jack.* We're all related to him."

"Has he been around lately?" Tate asked.

"No," she said. "Several weeks ago he stopped by Bev and Brian's house to watch my husband give Brian a tattoo—Daniel's very talented—but Billy Jack only stayed for one drink, and he left right after."

"Any problems between the Maucks and Billy Jack?"

"Not that I know of. Someone stole Bev's cell phone, and maybe a gun, from them when they had a party last month. There were lots of suspects, I guess, but I don't know who. I really haven't spent much time with Brian and Bev in the last few months."

"Did you hear anything early this morning?" Tate asked. "Gunshots, screaming, anything like that?"

Jennifer told the detectives that she and Daniel were "fooling around" in bed about 7:00 a.m. and they'd heard a "pop" in the distance. They thought that it was probably a hunter, but then they had looked out the back window of their trailer and saw a "big guy with long hair."

Daniel had asked Jennifer who he was, but she hadn't recognized him. Immediately after that, they heard a vehicle's engine rev up and saw a small red truck driving northbound on 70th Avenue East. They hadn't been able to see inside the truck, however, and couldn't say who was driving it, or if there was a passenger.

Daniel Tavares's memory was more precise. He hastened to explain that he and Jennifer had been "trying to make a li'l one," that morning when they heard "several" gunshots and looked out to see a red Nissan pickup with a chrome roll bar and a chrome bumper in the Maucks' driveway. He described the driver as a fairly big man with shoulder-length hair pulled back into a ponytail. "He walked up to the door, but I couldn't see if he went in or not."

Tavares said another man, who appeared to be bald, was waiting in the red truck. The first man, who Tavares now recalled wore a red hat, returned to his truck in a couple of minutes, backed out of the driveway, and continued backing until he reached the next residence a block south. The truck stopped for a few seconds, then returned to the driveway of the Maucks' gray and white house. Thirty seconds later the driver put it into reverse and sped north on 70th Avenue.

"How many shots did you hear?"

"About five. . . . There was a pause of a few seconds after the first shot."

"How well do you know the victims?"

"I visit them often," Tavares said. "I met them through Jeff. I do tattoos as a sideline and I was doing a large one on Brian. I was almost finished with it. Just had to add color in a few spots."

The investigators noticed that Tavares had injuries on his face, including a bruised and swollen left eye and a cut through his right eyebrow.

Detective Jason Tate asked Daniel how he had received those cuts, bruises, and scratches.

"Jennifer's ex-boyfriend did it," Tavares said. "I was changing a flat tire at the Johnson's Corner Market, and he just drove up and started whaling away at me."

Tate and Ben Benson made a note to find the ex-boyfriend to check his version of any encounter, and, if there had been a fight, to determine if there were any witnesses to it.

The investigators had to consider that the Maucks had been the victims of home-invasion robbers, something that was becoming more prevalent all over the country. Maybe someone thought they had money or drugs, or had other reasons to break in.

Not drugs. Beverly's and Brian's families had come to the young couple's home and stood outside in shock and grief as detectives continued to work the crime scene. They were invited to the sheriff's office, but they didn't want to go there until all of their close family members had arrived. Brian Mauck's parents—Allen and Pamela—said that their son and daughter-in-law didn't use drugs, nor did they keep large amounts of money in their house. Their marriage was very happy, they had no financial problems, or any other problems, for that matter. As far as their close relatives knew, they had no enemies.

"We were with them just last night," Brian's mother said in disbelief. "It was my birthday."

Bev and Brian had gone out to dinner with his parents to celebrate Pamela's birthday. It had been a pleasant and uneventful evening. After dinner, they'd gone back to the elder Maucks' home and talked until Allen fell asleep. Paula had talked a little more with Brian and Beverly, and she'd offered them her old television set. Brian had carried it out to their car. He and Beverly were thinking about spending the night, but when Pamela too fell asleep, they had tiptoed out at some point and gone home to Graham.

From the look of their great room, they had apparently listened to music, watched a movie, and drunk appletinis as they wound down from a week's work.

Allen Mauck had called his son at 1:30 on Saturday afternoon and been surprised when he didn't answer; he expected to find him at home, watching the Huskies game on TV. At 5:00 p.m., he had received a call from the Slaters, Bev's parents, saying that Bev and Brian were dead—that they had been murdered.

It was the end of serenity for two extended families, just when they had all had happy endings. Bev had played cupid, introducing her divorced mother, Karen, to her soon-to-be stepfather. She and her mother were very close, as she was with her two brothers. Her brother Steve, particularly, adored Bev. Like everyone who loved the young couple, the shock of this tragedy had stunned both the Maucks and the Slaters. They had a difficult time believing it was true.

Were the younger Maucks afraid of anything? Allen Mauck said the only thing he could think of was the incident where Beverly's cell phone and a gun had disappeared during a party. He thought the phone had been found in a nearby field. Allen was the one who had given Brian the Glock handgun after that theft, to keep in the house for protection.

But he didn't think either Bev or Brian had been truly afraid; it was more that the area they lived in was somewhat isolated, and many of the newly constructed homes weren't occupied yet.

Odd. Daniel Tavares had mentioned the party, too. It was Brian Mauck's birthday party. Tavares thought he'd seen the suspicious Nissan truck parked outside their house during that party.

Detective Mark Merod talked with Beverly's best friend, Lisa. She and her husband and Bev and Brian were all best friends, and Lisa said that Beverly *had* been afraid of two men; one was a stranger Daniel Tavares had brought over one day, and the other was the nephew of a neighbor. "Bev was sure he was the one who took her cell phone—and Brian's handgun. She found her cell phone by calling her own number and listening for the ring. Someone had tossed it all the way across the road—not the driveway—to where it landed in a field over there. In fact, Bev had to get *three* new cell phones this year!

"There was something about those guys—especially Billy Mack—that scared Bev. That's why she wouldn't stay alone when Brian was out of town," Lisa continued. "She'd stay with us."

On the night of the party at Brian and Bev's where the thefts occurred, Lisa found that her new car had been deliberately keyed all the way along one side. Clearly, someone was jealous of the Maucks and their carefree friends.

"When was the last time you saw her?" Merod asked.

"Last Sunday. I'm pregnant and sick to my stomach. Bev worried about me, and she came over and cooked for us."

Everyone detectives talked to that first day—from relatives to friends who had known the Maucks for many, many years—mentioned how much they loved each other. Their biggest arguments weren't over anything more serious than who was going to take the garbage out. Did they have financial problems? detectives asked. No. In fact they were admired because they handled their money so well.

Everything had been perfect. But Beverly had been frightened of something . . . of *someone*.

When the news of Brian and Beverly Mauck's violent deaths circulated around Graham, many of their peers broke into tears. The shock was palpable.

There were more than two hundred mourners at their memorial service.

Chapter Three

Detective Sergeant Ben Benson read over Daniel Tavares's eyewitness description of the "killer or killers" and something jarred him: The distance from the travel trailer where Daniel and Jennifer lived was three hundred to four hundred yards from the Maucks' home. That was three or four times the length of a football field! He tested himself to see how much he could see at that distance, and it wasn't much more than vague shapes. How had the Tavarases—looking out of the little trailer window above their bed, in the darkness of a November morning—been able to describe the strangers in the Maucks' driveway so precisely?

Even if they had binoculars—which they hadn't mentioned—it was just too far between where they lived and where Beverly and Brian lived. And Daniel Tavares had gone so far as to describe the tires on the truck, and said the driver had had a "shady-looking face."

"Shady?" Tate asked.

"Kind of like . . . pockmarked."

"Pockmarked?"

"You know, when a face is all pocked up. Yeah."

"Okay."

"Yeah, and I mean, I can see. I got real good vision. So yeah. He kind of looked like he had an acne problem, like red on his face. No beard, no mustache, no hair . . . that I could see. But it was like red."

"Okay."

Tavares seemed to be waiting for a compliment on his excellent vision, but he got nothing more.

"Maybe the color wasn't red, but it was—certainly wasn't a white skin color."

Ben Benson didn't say anything either. When he read over the transcript of this first questioning of Daniel Tavares, he thought that Daniel must have Superman's amazing vision and marveled at the way he kept embroidering his story, adding a few more details than needed.

"We *knew* he could not have seen all that from his trailer," Benson said later, "but we let him talk."

Brian and Beverly hadn't gone to the Roundup on Friday night, but Daniel Tavares had been there, and he'd made quite an impression.

When detectives asked the night manager of the Roundup if there had been a fight or an attack on Tavares on Friday night, he shook his head. However, he recalled that Daniel had appeared to be either drunk or on drugs and was talking loudly about using meth and marijuana. He was annoying regular customers and "didn't fit in with the crowd." The manager had considered calling the sheriff or kicking him out of the nightspot, but Tavares had left on his own. When he came back after midnight, he was refused entry. The manager promised to make his security camera videotapes of the crowd the night before available to the detectives.

Jason Tate interviewed a man who had been with Daniel—or at least sitting at his table—on Friday night: Carl Rider.* Rider said he had been there with his girlfriend about 7:00 p.m., and since it was karaoke night, he'd consumed several shots of whiskey quickly to get up his nerve to sing. It was about nine when he became aware of Daniel Tavares.

"He was asking people if they wanted to buy drugs," and then he walked out the front door. Rider had walked out a short time later and seen Tavares in a red Ford Explorer (Jennifer's car) with Rider's girlfriend's son. They were smoking marijuana. His inhibitions lessened by the whiskey, Rider accepted some marijuana from Tavares and smoked it outside the Roundup. Then the party had continued after Tavares had asked Carl Rider if he wanted to "get high," and the three men had headed southbound on the Mountain Highway. "We were smoking marijuana *and* meth," Rider said.

Daniel Tavares had dropped Carl Rider off at Johnson's Corner, and he'd walked to where his fuming girlfriend was waiting for him. He himself was full of regret because he hadn't smoked meth in five or six years, and he had let Tavares talk him into it.

Whatever else he was, Daniel Tavares was a bad influence on those around him, a man seemingly without much moral fiber.

Rider was positive that Tavares hadn't had any cuts or bruises when he'd last seen him after midnight.

But deputies questioning him near four the next afternoon had seen injuries on his face. Where had he been between leaving the Roundup the previous night and when they interrogated him on Saturday?

The homicide investigation into the deaths of Beverly and Brian Mauck was just a little more than twenty-four hours old on this gloomy Sunday, November 18. As expected, a number of people called the Pierce County Sheriff's Department, with tips they thought might be important, or theories on the case.

A woman who worked at Baydo Chevrolet with Beverly called to say that Bev had been afraid of some man who had come to her home. "I don't know Brian, but she said he was getting a tattoo from someone, and the tattoo artist had brought along another man. That's the one who gave her the creeps."

The caller didn't know the name of either man. But Ben Benson thought the tattoo artist had to be Daniel Tavares, who was a living advertisement for the art of tattooing.

Ben Benson had been feeling more and more hinky about Daniel Tavares, and so had several of the other detectives. Tavares had a number of very professional tattoos on his body, many of them hidden by his clothing. Even in clothes, the tattoos on his neck showed—a snorting bull on the right side and "Jennifer Lynn" on the left. When he was bare from the waist up, Pegasus (the flying horse of Greek mythology), a clown wearing a hat, two angels lifting a chained body out of a hole in a brick wall, a baby on a cloud, a female face atop a prison tower wrapped in barbed wire and a pig head below, two masks—one happy and one sad—a castle with a mountain road, a genie coming out of a bottle, and some older, less expert ink tracings were visible.

Tavares even had a pig's head tattooed on his penis. Some of his tattoos seemed to have been designed to obliterate previous ones. Some were surely prison artwork by somewhat clumsy practitioners who had worked under less than optimal conditions.

They'd all noticed that Daniel Tavares was inordinately proud of his body enhancements and of his own skill as a tattoo artist. Apparently his bride had also been attracted to his illustrated skin.

Jeff Freitas thought that his sister had met Daniel Tavares through an online matchmaking service that hooked up convicts with women on the outside. There are many: Prison Pen Pals, Friends Behind the Walls, and the one Jennifer selected, Inmate.com. Freitas estimated that Jennifer had been writing to Daniel for two or three years before he was paroled.

Why so many women choose to find love with prisoners is a question difficult to answer. Some may not be able to attract men in the free world; some find dangerous men— "bad boys"—sexy. There are women who really don't *want* to live with a man or participate in sex, so a man locked behind bars in a prison with no conjugal visits is ideal. They can have a husband to talk about, but they don't have to be intimate. And there is the fame factor. While those convicted of major crimes net more infamy than fame, women with no particular accomplishments—good or bad—align themselves with men whose names have been in the headlines and on TV. It makes them feel important to be known as the love interest of an infamous criminal, and they bask in his reflected—if suspect—glory.

Possibly the most deluded prison sweethearts are those who convince themselves that all the man behind bars needs "to go straight" is the love of a good woman. And, of course, a woman with this delusion is sure that *she* will be the one person who can effect a complete change in a felon's personality. Oddly, it never seems to occur to these *rescuers* that they could become the next victims, or that they may be inviting chaos and disaster into their lives.

Jennifer Lynn Freitas had answered an ad that probably wouldn't appeal to most women. Daniel Tavares had listed his finer points: "Six-foot, 235 pound, Albino gorilla with over forty real nice tattoos. Can I get a li'l bit of love from a lonely female?"

She apparently found this description intriguing.

Her older brother, Jeff, wasn't very happy about her long-distance romance with a convict, although he gave her and her new husband a place to live and offered Daniel a job logging evergreen trees when he was paroled.

Now Jeff Freitas was a mighty nervous man the day after his neighbors were shot to death. He called Pierce County Deputy Bill Ruder, a longtime friend, to tell him that he was afraid of someone who was staying on his property and asked Ruder if he had "anything to worry about."

Ruder explained that he couldn't discuss the murder probe with him. They both knew they were talking about Daniel Tavares, who was the unknown quantity in the tight family group that lived on Jeff's property. His elderly parents lived there with an uncle, and so did his sister Jennifer, along with Jeff, his wife, Kristel, and their small children.

"What's your gut feeling about Daniel?" Ruder asked him.

"I feel like I have lots to be worried about," Freitas said. "Frankly, I'm scared to death of him."

He went on to say that Daniel had been acting bizarrely ever since the double murder was discovered. "He's just out of it," Freitas said, "and the more I think about his story, none of it makes any sense."

He had noticed the bruises on Daniel's face that made him look as though he'd taken a punch or two.

"He told me that he was driving home from picking up a printer at one of our cousins' house. He stopped at 304th and the Mountain Highway to check his lug nuts. He said when he bent over, a car stopped and two guys got out. He recognized one as Jennifer's old boyfriend, who ran up and kicked him in the head," Freitas said. "So he said he got that guy down on the ground and was punching him—and even broke his false teeth—and then the other guy took a pipe and began bashing Daniel with it."

The two men had slashed Tavares's vehicle's tires before they drove off.

"I asked him how he got home, and he said he drove home on the flat tires, going about two miles an hour—it's only a little over a mile."

It was eating at Jeff Freitas that when he'd left to go hunting at around 5:00 a.m. on Saturday, he'd glanced at Daniel and Jennifer's vehicle and it didn't seem to be leaning on one side. Of course he hadn't been looking at the tires—he hadn't heard Daniel's story of the assault at that point. But there were no marks or gouges in the gravel and dirt driveway. He was sure of that.

Jeff's wife, Kristel, had seen Daniel walking past their mobile home about 8:00 a.m., and he'd had a towel over his arm. When she opened her blinds, he'd been standing on the porch of the Freitases' mobile home. Shortly after that, he came to her door and asked if he could take a shower. She told him he could, but when he didn't come back in an hour, she told Jennifer Tavares that her husband would have to come back around ten—Kristel wanted to take a shower, and it would take that long for the water to heat up again for Daniel.

Asked if Daniel had a gun, Freitas hesitated. "Well, Jennifer had this twenty-two pistol that our mother had given her. With Daniel due to arrive this last summer, she told Jennifer she would have to get the gun out of the house before he got here because he was a convicted felon. I have no idea where that gun is now."

The Maucks had been shot with a .22-caliber gun.

Saturday, November 17, was a crazy and disjointed day. On the morning of the murder, Daniel had told Kristel Freitas that he needed to go down to Brian and Beverly's house and finish the tattoo he was doing for Brian, saying that he really needed the fifty dollars that Brian still owed him for the tattoo because he wanted to buy gas. But he didn't accompany Jeff when he headed down the slope to see why the Maucks hadn't responded to his knocks or his phone calls.

And then there had been the fire. Jeff was especially worried because he'd spotted flames near the rear of Daniel and Jennifer's fifth-wheel RV earlier Saturday morning. Daniel told him he'd been making repairs on it and a welding torch had accidentally ignited a rubber gasket.

Jeff said he'd wondered then if Daniel was on drugs. He didn't seem to grasp the urgency of getting the burning material out from under the fifth wheel before the whole thing went up. When Jeff ran for water, he shouted to Daniel, "Get a rake! Get a rake!"

Daniel had just stood there at first, and then complained that he didn't want to be "treated like a child." But he was acting like a child, or like someone who was in a drug stupor.

Motorists driving by had seen the smoke billowing, and they rushed up the road to Jeff's acreage to help. They were followed by the fire department and some Pierce County deputies' units. The fire had soon been put out completely.

With no thanks to Daniel Tavares.

It was then that Jeff Freitas had begun to worry in earnest about Brian and Bev. How could they have slept through all the commotion so close to their house?

To his sorrow, he'd found out that they weren't sleeping.

When Jeff came back after finding that his neighbors were dead, Tavares was still standing in his living room. "I didn't say a word to him about what I'd found, but it was like [he knew] and was expecting me to call 911. Just the expression on his face. When I told my wife what I'd just seen, Daniel acted shocked and kept saying, 'Oh my God,' over and over. That didn't sound like him, and I found it odd and phony."

Jeff Freitas now believed that his brother-in-law had murdered Beverly and Brian, and he was afraid for himself and his whole extended family. He said he was doing all he could not to let Daniel know he suspected him. He was afraid to leave his wife and children and his parents alone.

Deputy Ruder typed up a report of his phone conversation with Freitas and gave it to Sergeant Ben Benson.

Benson wondered if the motive for double murder could possibly be a paltry fifty-dollar debt. Freitas was correct that Daniel Tavares seemed to have many different explanations for his injuries, tailoring them to fit whomever he was talking to. He was blabbing continually, with first slight and then outlandish adjustments to his story.

Benson and his crew of investigators were gathering information and trying to lock in physical evidence. The fingerprint on the doorjamb in the Maucks' house proved not to be a fingerprint at all; it was a section of a palm print, caught in fresh, wet blood, and then it had dried. There wasn't much of the palm that had connected, and it had been natural that they thought it was a fingerprint.

"We need to get some palm prints," Benson told Mary Lou Hanson-O'Brien. "Let's contact Jennifer and Daniel and Jeff and his wife, and tell them we need to get clearer prints. When we get there, we'll find a way to get their palm prints, too."

Neither the Freitases nor the Tavareses objected to being fingerprinted. Mary Lou Hanson-O'Brien was matter-of-fact as she daubed ink from their fingertips up halfway to their elbows. The subjects didn't question her, and she and Ben Benson kept the conversation going, hoping they wouldn't notice what she was doing.

She pressed all of their fingertips to cards and labeled them. Then she pressed several sections of their palms to cards. Her eyes met Benson's and he nodded slightly.

Somewhere among those cards, Benson believed they had the print they needed to compare with the one on the doorjamb in the Maucks' house.

No one in the Freitas family seemed to know *exactly* what Jennifer's new husband had been in prison for, or how much time he'd served. Maybe Jennifer didn't really know. Daniel didn't seem eager to talk about it, but who could blame him for that? He'd come out west to a new wife and a new life, and he probably wanted to forget the past.

Although it was the weekend and many law enforcement records departments were closed, Benson contacted the Massachusetts State Police to check on what crime had sent Daniel Tavares to prison. He received word that it had been manslaughter in 1991. There was a warrant out for him for leaving New England without informing his parole officer or getting permission to cross state lines, but Massachusetts had declined to extradite him to their jurisdiction.

Manslaughter can mean a lot of things: He might have been responsible for a car crash that had caused a death. It might have been involuntary—an unplanned—manslaughter. For the moment, Daniel Tavares didn't come across as a dangerous felon.

One of the other possible suspects was the neighbor's nephew. But efforts to locate Billy Jack were fruitless. When detectives went to the last address given for him, they found that the building had been demolished. They eventually located him, jobless and living with his mother in a small town some miles away from Graham. He had an alibi for the early morning hours of November 17.

Ben Benson asked Jennifer and Daniel to come into the sheriff's offices to work with a police artist and attempt to come up with likenesses of the men they'd seen in the red truck. He would send an officer to pick them up. They agreed readily, saying they would be glad to help. Deputy Nick Hausner picked them up at their trailer at 8:00 p.m. on Sunday night.

Benson didn't believe there had been any strangers at the victim's house the morning they died, but the police artist request gave him a reason to bring the Tavareses in.

It was raining when Jason Tate followed Ben Benson and Daniel Tavares into the sheriff's office for further questioning, and they had to walk through puddles. As they stepped onto a covered cement walkway, Tate happened to look down. There, just in front of him, were the wet shoe prints from Tavares's shoes. All of the investigators who had seen the shoe prints in the victims' blood had memorized the distinctive zigzag pattern of the killer's shoes. Tate knew he was looking at the same pattern—not in blood, but in rainwater on a stretch of dry sidewalk.

Ben Benson immediately contacted Mary Lou Hanson-O'Brien and had her take digital photos of the prints Daniel Tavares had just made. It was essential to get clear photos before the ephemeral images dried and were lost.

She responded at once, adding those digital images to the piles of evidence they already had. She had seen the bloody footprints at the murder scene, and these prints in

rainwater looked the same to her, too. When she matched
up the two images, they were as close to identical in their
zigzag patterns as anything could be. She notified Ben
Benson.

Whatever Tavares had done in Massachusetts, he was
looking more and more like a good suspect in Washington.

Benson directed Daniel Tavares toward one interview
room and Jennifer to another. Tavares was calm and cooperative; he actually seemed to enjoy answering Benson's
questions during the first part of their interview.

Benson, with Detective Tom Catey looking on, began
by asking Daniel Tavares when he had moved to Washington. It had been July and he'd moved from Massachusetts
to meet Jennifer in person. "I met her online," he volunteered.

When they met in person, they had hit it off and were
married on July 31. Daniel said he'd gone to work for Jeff,
his new brother-in-law.

Asked how he met Brian and Bev, he said Jeff had introduced them. "They go to Jeff's house every Friday to play
cards—so every Friday we used to get together to play
cards. All of us—me, my wife, her brother, Jeff, and his
wife, Kristel—and then two more friends, which is Pat and
Marlene."

Tavares said that he and Jennifer did more than play
cards with their neighbors. He made it sound as if they
were close friends. They always stopped and talked when
they met on the private road between their residences, especially about Brian's motorcycles. "One time we went for
a Harley ride—me and him—for about an hour."

"How about the tattoo stuff?" Benson asked.

"He knew I was doing tattoos, and he wanted one . . . what do you call it? Your sign, like a Taurus, Scorpion— your *birth sign*—so he wanted a scorpion. I told him that I'd draw him up one, and if he liked my drawing and wanted it, I'd have no problem doing it for him. I did that for him."

"Did you just put one tattoo on him?"

Daniel Tavares nodded. "And his initials: B.A.M. Brian—I forgot his middle name, but it was a scorpion with 'B.A.M.' above it. That's the first tattoo he has, I think."

He said that Bev had shown interest in having a tattoo, too. She was drawing up an angelfish she wanted. " 'Cause they scuba dive."

Ben Benson noted that Daniel spoke of the dead couple as if they were still alive.

"So what was the agreement about the tattoo?" Benson asked. "Just doing it because you were a buddy of his?"

"Yeah, yeah."

"Or was he paying you to do it?"

"No, he paid me a hundred bucks to do it."

There was no money paid up front, according to Daniel, but he had been paid in full after he'd tattooed the whole outline and colored it in. He had wanted to "soup it up" a little by adding more red after it had healed enough, but Brian said he was happy the way it was. He'd finally agreed to have more color as Daniel recommended. That was to cost another fifty dollars.

"When was the last time you saw Bev or Brian, or both of them?"

"God, let me see—it's been a few days."

"Try and think for me," Benson urged. "See if you can pin it down."

Finally, Tavares said he thought it must have been in the middle of the preceding week. He and Brian had spoken as he turned into the driveway leading up to his trailer. "I asked him when he wanted to do the rest, but he told me he was so busy, had things to do. He was going to a birthday party, and maybe going hunting. He would call me and let me know."

Daniel said he hadn't seen Bev for more than a week.

Daniel Tavares was speaking in a more agitated way, his words tumbling over Ben Benson's before the detective sergeant could complete his questions.

Asked to describe the Maucks, he said, "Nice people. Good people. Good people. Good, good people. *Drunks*."

"They like their alcohol?" Benson asked, surprise in his voice.

"Oh, they love their alcohol."

Tavares paused, and with a sanctimonious expression on his face, he offered that Bev often started fights in taverns and could be wild. That didn't fit with what others had said about Bev Mauck.

With what the Pierce County investigators had learned so far about Tavares's drug and alcohol usage, he hardly seemed in a position to be painting the dead couple as "drunks" and worse. By now, the detectives had discovered that Tavares had bought at least four hits of meth within hours of the murders.

Still, Ben Benson said nothing, more than "um-humm." He could see that his subject believed that *he* was the one controlling the interview. That was fine with Benson.

"Did Bev ever flirt with you—or anything like that?"

"No . . . no." Tavares seemed taken aback by the question. He was in full saintly mode, but Benson wondered if he had had lustful feelings for the pretty bride.

Now Benson asked Tavares to go over his activities on Friday night, November 16. He had told other detectives that he and Jennifer were doing a puzzle together in their trailer. Yes, that was true, he said—but earlier on Friday evening they had been in Tacoma at a friend's house.

"Your wife was with you?" Ben Benson caught the disparity in Daniel's story. She hadn't been with him at the Roundup or when he took Carl Rider for a drive to smoke meth.

"Yeah, yeah," he lied now. "Well, she drives everywhere. I mean we are always together. So, yeah."

Tavares had talked his way into a dead end, and he struggled now to break out. He remembered that Jennifer wasn't with him on Friday night, but he'd had to call her on his cell phone to ask where the spare tire to her Ford Explorer was after he discovered a flat tire. He'd struggled with the lug nuts, and *that's* when he'd been attacked by her ex-boyfriend and another man, bruised and cut, and had another tire slashed.

He admitted he'd never seen his wife's ex-boyfriend before, but he knew his name was Eddie. He thought he would recognize a photo of Eddie. Now he added another person on the scene of the attack. Some young kid from a bar had come over to ask if he was okay.

"I'm like, 'No, I'm all set,' and he just got in his car and left."

His assailants had given him a message: *"It would be good advice for you to leave Jennifer."*

The more he talked, the more Daniel Tavares was making things worse for himself. He said he'd been attacked about eight to eight thirty, but Carl Rider had seen him last just after midnight on Friday night–Saturday morning and he had no bruises or cuts then. The details he kept inserting into his story warred with what he had told the sheriff's staff and his brother-in-law earlier.

Didn't he know that every time he gave a statement it had been preserved either on tape or in investigative notes?

Now, to add to the mysterious red truck, he recalled that a green and silver truck had been parked in the Maucks' driveway when he drove past, heading up the road to the Freitas property at 8:40 p.m. on Friday, inching along on two flattened tires. He told Ben Benson that he had replaced the tires but thought he could find the slashed and punctured tires somewhere on Jeff's acreage.

"Okay," Benson said. "This was about eight thirty. Did you leave again that night?"

"No. My wife told me, 'Look what I got,' and she showed me she picked up a puzzle at Goodwill. So we started, and it was like, 'Oh man, let's do this.' It was a real nice puzzle."

The puzzle that they'd allegedly worked on together was the image of a wolf. Except for the animal's penetrating and unfathomable yellow eyes, the rest of the evening sounded as benign and cozy as newlyweds at home could be.

Unless he was lying.

Nothing matched the facts *or* Daniel Tavares's earlier statements. He had said that the Mauck house was completely dark when he got home at 8:30 p.m., but both their cars were there so he knew they were home. Besides, the Freitas dogs always barked when someone outside the family drove up. And they hadn't barked.

Benson knew the Maucks weren't home; they'd been out to dinner with Brian's parents. Both of their vehicles could not have been there around 8:30 on Friday night.

Daniel said that he and Jennifer had worked on the puzzle for a few hours. A few minutes later, he estimated they had gone to bed at three or four in the morning. That was six or seven hours after he said he came home. Another slip.

Then he said they had had intercourse because they both wanted to have a baby. He'd gone to sleep about four and wakened shortly after seven when he heard the gunshots. One more slip. Both he and Jennifer had stated they were not asleep, but making love, when they heard the shots.

And this time, Daniel remembered that the dogs had "gone crazy" at the same time . . . and *that's* when he looked out and saw the "big, greasy-lookin' dude" down at Brian and Bev's.

Now he gave an even more exact description of the driver. He'd had on a red hat, but it was a baseball cap. He "walked kind of funny. His shoulders were hunched up so high that it looked like he didn't have a neck."

Daniel said he hadn't called the sheriff because he wasn't sure just where the gunshots were coming from, and Jennifer told him not to worry about it, that it was probably just duck hunters.

He had rolled over and gone back to sleep for a couple of hours.

Later that morning, he'd called the fire department because he'd had a fire under his fifth-wheel RV that was parked out in a nearby field. Daniel said he was repairing it for him and Jennifer to live in, and he'd accidentally set fire to the flashing near where part of the floor needed replacing. "I heated it a little too much, and it [the rubber flashing] caught on fire, and it dripped into the dry grass under the trailer. It just made a lot of smoke."

This was well before his brother-in-law had discovered the Maucks' murders. Benson and Catey wondered what else Tavares might have been burning. Bloodied clothing? A weapon?

Ben Benson asked about Daniel Tavares's prison time, and he said he was in for manslaughter. At least that was the truth.

"Somebody told me that they thought they saw that you'd been sentenced for fourteen years, but you served seventeen. So they thought maybe you had problems while you were in prison, 'cause your time had been extended?"

"Oh, yeah," Tavares said easily. "I lost good time. I lost statutory good time . . . for fighting."

Benson was just as casual. He knew Tavares had been inside the walls on a manslaughter charge, but he didn't know who the victim was yet—or the circumstances of that crime back in 1991. He was waiting for Tavares's complete case file to be sent from Massachusetts. Daniel volunteered that he'd lost his good time for assaulting a corrections officer.

"Now you're squared away—living a good life, huh?"

"Trying. I mean, I'm sure you must know what I was in prison for?"

"I just heard it was manslaughter," Benson said. "What *were* you in prison for?"

"I killed the person who molested my child."

"How'd you kill 'em?" Benson's voice was calmer than he felt, but he didn't want to put Tavares on guard.

"Stabbed 'em. It was a her. Family member."

"What kind of a family member?"

"My mother."

"*You killed your mother?*" For the moment, Ben Benson couldn't hide his shock. This casual and cooperative man in front of him had just admitted killing his own mother! Benson regained his composure before Tavares even noticed how astounded he was.

Daniel explained that he had killed his mother for molesting his daughter, back in 1991 in Massachusetts.

"Well, that's too bad," Benson said carefully. "That's not good for anyone to go through."

"Well, I made it through, you know. I made it."

He sounded as if he expected a medal for his bravery.

Detective Tom Catey had a few questions to ask Daniel. The tattooed parolee had made it sound as if he and Brian Mauck were close friends, and that he and Jennifer and Brian and Beverly had often mingled socially. But, under Catey's close questioning, he finally admitted that he had visited their home only three times—once when he and Jennifer were "invited down" to see the Maucks' house, once to start work on Brian's tattoo, and the third time when Brian asked him to ride motorcycles with him— lending one of his own bikes to Daniel.

These visits had begun in mid-October, only a month before. Tavares insisted that he and Jennifer had been invited to Brian's birthday party, but they'd had another engagement that night. All of the poker games had taken place at Jeff and Kristel Freitas's home.

Daniel and Jennifer lived in a cluttered, crowded little travel trailer with what looked like hand-me-down furniture, and they had to take showers at her brother's or her parents' mobile homes. Their only income was the hundred dollars a day that Jeff paid Daniel. Even though he didn't say it, it was obvious that the ex-prisoner from Massachusetts was envious of the home the Maucks shared and the life they lived.

But was it enough to spark murder?

There in the Pierce County Sheriff's Department interview room, the first tape ran out at a quarter to midnight. They took a break. Both Benson and Catey were stunned by the news that this seemingly easygoing man had stabbed his own mother to death. His affect and his attitude didn't jibe with what he had done.

If he could kill his mother, he probably was capable of killing neighbors he hardly knew.

They had the matching shoe prints. They had the palm print that matched the print in blood on the interior door at the Maucks' home. They had caught him in lie after lie, and they had witnesses who could refute his statements. In essence, they had *him*.

Their main question was *Why?* And what, if any, was Jennifer's part in the cruel crime? She appeared to be besotted with her tattooed bridegroom, and they suspected she would have done just about anything he asked of her.

Ben Benson put in a fresh tape and they continued.

"At this point," Benson said to the man across the table from him, "we've got evidence to arrest you for the murder of Brian and Beverly."

"*What?*" Daniel Tavares had thought he was doing so well, completely snowing the two detectives.

Benson continued. "And one of the reasons that we've talked to you kind of extensively here initially is because we know the answers to these questions that we've asked you, and we know that a lot of what you've told us are lies. Now, that being said, we've got some things here and hopefully you're gonna be man enough to stand up here and talk to us. Do some damage control. Here's what we think. . . ."

Benson told Daniel that he was going to be arrested for two murders, and, with his background, he was probably going to prison for the rest of his life.

"I'd just as soon not see Jennifer go down with you," he continued. "I think we've also got evidence that she was in the house—"

"We were all in the house," Daniel blurted. "That day when I tattooed—"

"Like I said, we've got evidence that you were in the house when the murders happened."

"That's impossible. I was in bed."

Chapter Four

Daniel Tavares protested that *he* had never kicked the door panel in, or done anything with the front door's locks. Then he added that he really *had* seen a red truck there, and he thought the occupants had kicked the door in. His next fantasy lie was that he'd met someone to whom he was to give the gun back, and that man had been driving a small white truck! That made a red truck, a white truck, and a green truck that were allegedly involved in the execution of the Maucks.

If it hadn't been so tragic, his rambling lies might have been funny. But the detectives knew far too much for Daniel Tavares to be a convincing liar. They had the tapes from Ma's and Pa's Roundup, showing him in the crowd. They knew he'd joined up with Carl Rider, and that they'd smoked marijuana and meth. They knew when the tires of Jennifer's Ford Explorer had been slashed, and they knew that there had never been any trucks with chrome roll bars in the Maucks' driveway.

*   *   *

It was Daniel Tavares's turn to be shocked. "Things are out of control here," he protested, as Benson and Catey pointed out the physical evidence they had that placed him inside the Maucks' home when they were killed.

Benson asked again if Jennifer was involved.

"She's not involved. Jennifer's not involved at all."

"Okay," Benson said. "Tell us what happened."

"It was a hired thing," Tavares said faintly.

"Who hired you?"

"Somebody that don't like them." Their subject was obviously scurrying frantically around his brain, trying to find something that would convince them he'd acted under duress, something that would save him from facing the death penalty. He insisted he couldn't tell them who had hired him to kill the Maucks. "My whole family would be killed. I can't do that."

Since his mother was already dead—thanks to him— the detectives wondered what family he was talking about. Jennifer? Jeff and Kristel Freitas, who were already scared to death of *him*?

He was slowly beginning to confess, but he couldn't recall when he'd gone over to the Maucks' house. He'd been high "on weed." He refused to discuss exactly what had happened, but he was adamant that Jennifer "didn't have nothing to do with it. Nothing."

"Does she know? Did you tell her what happened?"

Tavares refused to answer. He changed the subject to say he was supposed to get paid $20,000 to carry out the double murder.

"Did you get money up front?" Benson asked.

"No."

"What kind of hit man doesn't get something up front?"

"A stupid one," Tavares answered glumly. And he might have been right on target there. No, he hadn't taken any pictures of the bodies to show to the people who had hired him.

There had been two shoe prints in blood. One matched Daniel's shoes, and the other was a mystery. They thought it could be Jennifer's—but her husband kept insisting she'd never been to the death site. He was trying to protect her and to build on his story of being a gun for hire—but the people behind it all were the ones who gave him the gun and the ammunition. He couldn't recall what kind of gun it was, not even the caliber. No, he didn't know where Jennifer's .22 handgun was.

"We know you left after you shot Brian," Ben Benson said. "And that you came back at some point later on?"

He admitted that he'd been away from the Maucks' home for only five minutes—he'd gone up near the barn to wash his hands. But he'd always been alone. After the shooting, he said he'd given the gun back to those conspiring to kill Brian and Beverly Mauck.

The detectives had tended to believe that the young couple were killed sometime in the wee hours of Friday night–Saturday morning. But Daniel Tavares said he had gone to their house in the morning, after it was light out. Brian had been sitting on the couch, and Daniel said he'd told him what the "people" wanted him to say:

" 'Brian, listen,' I said. 'You owe a lot of money and this has to be done.' That was it. I shot him."

The confessed murderer said that he'd shot Brian in the

side of the head first, and then again when he slumped over and fell onto the floor.

Bev had come running from some room in the back of the house. He had shot her "at close range" as she ran toward the front door.

She had almost made it.

"Okay," Benson said evenly. "Did you physically grab her?"

"Yeah. By the hair."

"Did you rape her?"

"No."

" 'Cause you know, we're gonna find that out."

"No."

"There was no sexual assault?"

"No."

It was clear that Bev Mauck had tried desperately to get away from Daniel Tavares, to get outside where she could hide or scream for help. But she was a very small woman and he was the "gorilla." How many times he'd shot her, he didn't know. He remembered grabbing her by the foot—after he shot her—and dragging her over near Brian's body. He also recalled that she was nude. He didn't know why, but he'd covered them both up with the blue blankets.

Sometime later he had come back to the house to make sure that nothing was out of place.

Everything was out of place, and the two murder victims lay in their own blood. Benson thought he had covered them up so he wouldn't have to look at what he had done.

For some bizarre reason, Daniel said he had attempted to sweep up the blood. They already knew that.

"Were you trying to get rid of your shoe prints?"

"No," Tavares answered. "I didn't even know I left shoe prints."

The suspect said he'd felt as if he "wasn't really there." He blamed it on the antipsychotic meds that he'd just begun taking again: Buspar, Klonopin, Effexor, and Seroquel.

(Pill bottles with prescription labels would be found when a search warrant gave detectives permission to go into the Tavareses' small trailer. One was to treat seizures, and the rest were for anxiety, depression, and bipolar disorder.)

Add alcohol, marijuana, and meth, and the detectives saw why he might have felt as if he wasn't there. But that didn't make him innocent. Diminished capacity doesn't fly as a defense. Daniel Tavares had used illegal drugs along with prescribed antipsychotic drugs and alcohol of his own free will. And his brain had spun evil scenarios.

But *why*?

He still claimed he'd been hired to carry out two hits. Somehow, Jennifer had known what happened, but he couldn't remember how she knew.

Ben Benson pointed out that it didn't make him less guilty because he'd been hired to kill, and he agreed that he knew that. He hadn't returned the gun to the actual conspirators but had given it to a mutual friend. "I was told I'd be getting a call. And I haven't got no call—"

"I don't believe that happened," Benson interrupted. "You've been to prison. You've been around the block."

The detective sergeant suggested once again that "an obvious smart guy" like Tavares wouldn't carry out a hit without having some money up front and without getting a guarantee that he was going to get more money. "You're not gonna go kill two people and then sit around and wait for the phone to ring. . . . That doesn't make sense," Benson said. "I don't know if Brian owed you money for the tattoo and he didn't pay. What was the real reason?"

"I wouldn't do that for a hundred-dollar tattoo."

Daniel finally admitted that he had told Jennifer what he had done, and that she "kind of freaked out."

But she definitely hadn't helped him clean off his shoes or wash his clothing. He'd been wearing a gray hoodie with Sylvester, the cartoon cat, on it, and a pair of jeans. They wondered how he could have walked away from the Maucks' home without blood on his clothes or himself.

They didn't believe him. There was too much bloodshed in the house for him to have escaped getting it splashed on himself. But they hadn't located any bloody clothing. Somehow, he had to have gotten rid of it.

Tom Catey had some questions of his own, wondering just where Daniel had met the person who wanted Brian Mauck killed. Tavares continued to be cagey, insisting that he had shot Brian only because he owed "some guy" a lot of money over gambling. He'd met a *friend* of the real instigator at the Roundup; the arrangements for cold-blooded murder had all taken place through him.

The in-between man had recognized that Tavares had several prison tattoos and questioned him about his past. The stranger then mentioned that a man who owed big gambling debts lived close to Tavares. He named Brian

Mauck as the man who hadn't paid the loan shark. That had been about six weeks before.

"So that was about the time you were doing the tattoo [on Brian]?" Catey asked.

"Yes," Daniel answered, but he knew nothing about where Brian had gambled, how much he owed. In fact, he'd never discussed gambling with Brian. None of the other investigators he had talked to had mentioned that Brian Mauck had a gambling problem (which he did not).

"Okay," Catey said. "*Why* would you agree to do this?"

"For the money. To get a place to live."

It was obvious that Tavares was making things up as he went along. He'd already admitted to two murders, but he was trying to protect Jennifer. He insisted that he was hired to kill both of the Maucks for ten thousand dollars apiece, but Jennifer hadn't known about it.

"Did you use anything to muffle the sound of the gun going off?"

"Yeah, a towel." He believed he'd found it right there in his neighbors' house.

Brian had come to the door about seven and let him in. He hadn't been upset about having such an early visitor, Daniel said, and he hadn't argued with him. Tavares said he was totally focused on his mission to kill Brian, and he admitted he hadn't even tried to discuss ways Brian could pay the money he allegedly owed.

He'd simply carried out his orders, shooting Brian and then Beverly. He said he'd been "so med-ed out" that he was "in a fog." He told Tom Catey he didn't know why he had pulled Beverly over by Brian.

"How come you covered them up—took the time to put the blanket over them?" Catey asked the question again.

"Respect."

Both Ben Benson and Tom Catey were struck speechless for a moment. This was a man who seemed to have no empathy for others. He had taken two lives for no good reason they could see, and now he was talking about "respect."

He just didn't get it. It was almost like talking to a robot.

Lieutenant Brent Bomkamp walked into the interview room. He was a new factor in the dialogue. First, he complimented Tavares on being a stand-up guy who had basically told them the truth about the Maucks' murder. Tavares preened.

But then Bomkamp accused him of lying about part of his story.

"We know it, you know it, and what's gonna happen is these guys [who] have been working their asses off for the last two days are gonna have to go out and try to follow these little threads you're laying down. And you know they will end in nothing that fits with what you're telling us.

"These are smart guys," Bomkamp said, pointing to Ben Benson and Tom Catey. "These are my best guys. We've put you at the scene. We've got other physical evidence that's not matching what you're saying. You've shown you're willing to be a stand-up guy. You've been honest. Just tell the whole frickin' truth."

Tavares was off balance, going from Bomkamp's compliments to his accusations, and he protested weakly. Bomkamp assured him that his detectives would find out the whole truth, but they would have to search all of Tavares's property, question his wife, and it would take weeks before the case moved ahead.

"Nobody hired you to do this," Bomkamp asked flatly. "Did they?"

"No." Tavares admitted that he had lied to save face. He said that Brian Mauck had insulted him, calling him a "fucking punk," and that Bev had said even worse things about Jennifer Lynn, calling her the *c* word. Maybe Brian *was* mad because he'd gone down to his home so early in the morning to ask about the tattoo, Daniel allowed, but Brian's insults had just been too much for a man who'd spent so much time in prison. Being called a "fucking punk" had deeply insulted him.

Although the three detectives in the room doubted that either Brian or Bev Mauck had ever used those epithets, they didn't argue with Tavares.

Now, finally, he had told as much of the truth as he probably ever would. Transcribed, his lies and his slow revelation of what had really happened took a hundred and twenty-five pages.

The confession by Daniel Tavares proved once again that a well-trained and experienced detective knows he must avoid tunnel vision. Beverly Mauck had had reason to be afraid, but she'd been afraid of the wrong person. Billy Mack, who had probably stolen from their house more than once, had scared her, certainly, but this misfit neighbor she'd scarcely noticed, a man she had once fixed dinner for, who had left his mark on her husband's back, the man she and Brian tolerated because they felt kind of sorry for him, was far more dangerous than anyone in the neighborhood could have imagined.

It was very late on Sunday night, November 18, and Ben Benson next turned his attention to Jennifer Tavares. He was curious to find out if she truly knew her husband's background, and more curious to know if she had returned to the Maucks' house with him after the murder to help him "clean up." She might well have been an accomplice to murder before, during, or after the fact.

Benson was inclined to think that Jennifer had probably helped Daniel *after* the fact. She listened to her Miranda rights and was very concerned. She debated phoning an attorney but realized that might mean she would have to stay in jail overnight. When Benson mentioned that she might face time in prison, Jennifer was horrified. Apparently, that had never occurred to her. She wanted to go home, but Ben Benson explained that her trailer would have to be searched thoroughly, and she could not go home until that was done. She asked then if she could go home to her brother's mobile home.

That would depend on her attitude and her willingness to tell him the truth, Benson said. He explained that her husband had just confessed to killing Brian and Beverly.

"He actually said he did it?" she asked in disbelief.

"Yeah, he did. We knew he did it before we brought him in here; we had evidence that we collected from the house back there and that told us without a doubt that it was him. We didn't need him to talk to us, but he was man enough to do that, and that's good for him to do that—that's probably gonna help him out in the long run."

"I'm trying to protect myself here. I've never been through this before—"

"I need you to tell me what you know," Benson probed.

"I only know bits and pieces," Jennifer said.

Jennifer Tavares had been fascinated with a man in prison, a man whose description of his assets was an "Albino gorilla with over forty real nice tattoos."

"I met him on the Internet, about three years ago."

"Did you ever go see him while he was in prison?"

"No," she answered. "He was in Massachusetts."

Perhaps it had never occurred to her that she could have flown to the East Coast and met Tavares before she invited him into her life, into her family. She was either artless or cunning—or stupid.

"Do you know what he was in prison for?"

"He was supposed to have killed two people that molested his daughter. . . . He said [it was] his stepmother and her boyfriend, but I didn't think . . . he would, you know—somebody gets their daughter molested, you think, 'Yeah that's understandable,' you know."

Daniel had obviously lied about that to Jennifer Lynn. How she must have rationalized about everything she learned—which wasn't that much—about Daniel. She had married him without ever having met him before. He had walked out of prison and immediately flown to Washington. Within a day or so, they were married.

Jennifer seemed never even to have thought about it.

How could she have expected to find "the prince" with

only that information? She hadn't. She had aligned herself with evil, and now she was in danger of being sucked into the vortex of that evil.

Jennifer said that they had been very happy during the first few months. But things had started to go sour when Daniel went to a psychiatrist and walked away with prescriptions that changed him. Three days before the Maucks died, he'd been to his psychiatrist and received a new prescription.

Jennifer wasn't sure what it was, but the word she stumbled on sounded like Klonipin or Colotapins; she thought it was some kind of antianxiety med. "He started taking them and he was eating them like candy, and it was just making him act different—real different. I kept telling him, 'I don't like these pills—I want to throw them away.' "

That had made Daniel more agitated. "He turned into someone I don't even know, and he kept taking them and taking them."

Whether he had told his psychiatrist about all the other pills he was taking, only Daniel knew. He certainly hadn't confided about his alcohol and illegal drug use.

While her new husband had been a "real good" lover and companion right after they were married, he had become more "aggressive" and she felt he "manhandled" her the morning of the murders. Now she gave an accurate timetable.

Daniel hadn't slept at all on Friday night. And he hadn't come home at 8:30 either. He had called Jennifer to say he was on his way several times, but he hadn't come home until 1:00 a.m., "raging" about being attacked by two of her ex-boyfriends. And that was odd because she had broken up with Eddie twelve years earlier and almost as long ago with Todd.

She was angry with Daniel. He had promised to take her on Friday night to one of the many Indian casinos that abound in Washington.

Detective Mark Merod joined in the questioning of Jennifer Lynn Tavares. She was either being evasive or she had a terrible memory. At first she said she hadn't learned that Daniel had killed Bev and Brian until later on Saturday. She didn't know if she'd heard gunshots, but she'd heard "something" and peeked out her window around 7:00 a.m.

"I just looked and I didn't see nothin'."

"See Daniel?"

"Didn't see Daniel, no," she said. "I just kinda had this feeling, but then I was scared 'cause I met him when he was in prison, and I didn't know what he was gonna be like. I believed he was a good person, didn't think anything was gonna happen. And now this. I was scared. I was pretty much told by him not to say anything. I was afraid it would happen to me—like *them*."

Daniel hadn't told her what he had done—he'd said only that the Maucks were "gone." She said she'd had no idea beforehand what he had planned to do. When he left their trailer just as the winter sun was giving off pale light at about 7:00 a.m., he'd said he was going out to use the "honey bucket." He'd been gone awhile, but she hadn't heard the door of the outhouse squeaking as it usually did.

"When he came back," Jennifer said, "he acted real agitated and kinda freaky."

She estimated he'd been gone for twenty minutes.

Jennifer recalled her husband saying something like, "They were running their mouths" and "They won't do that anymore." Then he had warned her not to call the cops on him, threatening her with reprisal if she did.

"All I could think of was, 'Oh, my God, my whole family's here; I can't have something happen to them. My little nephews and everything, because I'm the stupid fucker that met him. And I believed he was so great . . . ' "

Jennifer was either totally afraid of Daniel or pretending to be. She was definitely in shock to find herself at the sheriff's office. When Ben Benson asked her why she hadn't told the deputies or detectives what she knew on Saturday, she explained she knew Daniel could break out of jail and overcome cops.

He had threatened her and her family if she told anyone. Gradually, Jennifer modified her memories of Saturday, November 17. She admitted that she knew the Maucks were dead within fifteen minutes of the murders.

Daniel had been eager to leave the Freitas property. They couldn't drive her red Ford Explorer because two tires on one side were flat, so they borrowed a car from Jeff and Kristel and drove to Point Defiance Park, along Five Mile Drive. They had been married there four months earlier in the summer sunshine in a sylvan setting at one of the turnoffs. That was a much happier day.

Point Defiance extends high above the Tacoma Narrows and Commencement Bay, and the cliffs are steep there. She was driving and followed his directions to turn into the spot where they'd promised to love and cherish each other. On this day, there was no sunshine, no romance, and the wind carried sheets of rain over the cliffs. Daniel had told her that he needed to walk down a path to urinate. She watched as he disappeared into a thicket of evergreens. He was back within minutes and had seemed a little calmer.

Before going home, they'd gone shopping at Big Lots, a discount store, and eaten at a Mexican restaurant.

The two Pierce County detectives refused to believe that Jennifer had no idea what Daniel was doing when he walked down the trail to the cliffs. She finally said she had asked him if he had a gun with him, and he'd kept telling her not to worry about it.

"That told me that he did have a gun with him."

It had also been very important to Daniel that the water far below was salt water. She didn't know why, but the detectives did: If Tavares had thrown the death weapon into the sea, he would have hoped the metal would corrode rapidly.

Asked about what guns were in the travel trailer, Jennifer said she didn't know where her .22 handgun was; she thought her mother had it. Daniel had owned an assault rifle until a few days before the double murder. She thought he'd sold it.

Benson and Merod shuddered at the thought of what a man like Daniel Tavares might have intended to do with an assault rifle. He could have taken out everyone in the neighborhood.

Now Ben Benson led Jennifer's focus back to the murder site. He showed her photographs of fingerprints and palm prints in blood, and the ridges of shoes etched in the dried blood. One was Daniel's; the other was from a smaller foot. She was adamant that she had not been in the

Maucks' home with him. As Jennifer grew more anxious, her language became less than ladylike. She had an extensive vocabulary of four-letter words.

She accused Daniel of taking one of her shoes down to the murder site and deliberately making a bloody print with it—just to involve her in homicides she had no part in. The person who had vomited in the Maucks' driveway had probably been Jennifer, but she stubbornly insisted that she had never, ever, walked down to their house—particularly not on the morning they were killed. If DNA tests linked that to her, it was because she'd gotten sick in her own trailer Friday night—into a paper bag—and Daniel must have taken it down there to try to make it look like she was there.

She had known some things, yes. She knew Daniel had been smoking meth on Friday night and admitted that she had joined him. She had had a problem with drugs sometime back, but she'd been clean for a while.

Jennifer said she was doing anything she could to calm her husband down. She'd kept working on her wolf puzzle, and they were having a "heart-to-heart talk." That had led to sex—not in the morning but sometime in the middle of the night.

The detectives didn't think she had accompanied her husband on his killing visit to Beverly and Brian Mauck's home, but they did believe she had gone back there with him a short time later at his insistence that she help him clean up the death house. Maybe it had been Jennifer who tried to sweep up the pools of blood, only to become violently ill at the smell of it.

The short honeymoon of the convict and the farm girl from Graham, Washington, seemed to be over.

Despite her protestations, Jennifer Lynn Tavares was charged with rendering criminal assistance and booked into the Pierce County Jail at around 2:00 a.m. on Monday, November 19.

Chapter Five

Convinced that they had the Maucks' killer locked safely in jail, the investigators continued to assemble new information about Daniel Tavares's behavior after the crimes and to learn more about his background.

Jeff Freitas had learned that Tavares had told a few people he was angry that Jeff had found the victims so soon after they were killed.

"Why was he angry?" Tom Catey asked Jeff.

"I guess he thought no one would check up on Brian and Bev until Monday, and he supposedly had planned to go down there and set their house on fire—destroy any evidence—before they were found."

But Freitas wasn't sure who had heard that information in the first few days after the murders. He thought that his mother had overheard it, and told his wife, Kristel. It was one of those rumors that seemed to make sense, and yet it was very difficult to track it back to its source.

An older uncle who lived on Freitas's land reported that Daniel Tavares had come to his home and asked for some bleach. He had then poured bleach over some jeans he carried. But detectives hadn't found any bloody or bleach-stained clothing in the fire that occurred shortly after the murders. They had seen the phantom blank spot image on the dining room wall and believed that the clothes Tavares wore during the shootings had to be speckled with back-spatter blood from his victims' wounds.

But they hadn't been able to find them.

On Monday morning, Ben Benson received an over-night package from the Massachusetts State Police. A mug shot included in the file was of a much younger Daniel Tavares. He appeared to be in his early twenties and had only one tattoo—the one of Pegasus, with "Danny" written above it. His facial expression was one of anxiety, even fear. It was the same man, all right—but the young Daniel had been fairly attractive at six feet tall and 180 pounds; now he weighed sixty pounds more than that, and he had aged significantly. At forty-one, he looked well over fifty.

As Benson perused the file, he saw that Daniel had in-deed killed his mother, forty-six-year-old Ann Tavares, in their home in Somerset, Massachusetts—just a stone's throw from Fall River, the city where Lizzie Borden had gone on trial for the murder of her father and stepmother ninety-nine years earlier.

Lizzie resided at 92 Second Street and Daniel at 31 Winslow. Both crimes happened on blistering hot days; August 4, 1892, for the Borden hatchet murders, and July 11, 1991, for Ann Tavares's homicide by kitchen knife. Most people believe that Lizzie, twenty-four, was found guilty, but she wasn't. She was acquitted after a sensational trial and died at age sixty-seven in 1927.

Ann Tavares's crime scene was just as full of scarlet

liquid as the Borden bloodbath. Or, Benson thought, as the Maucks' home.

Daniel Tavares was the youngest child of four born to Ann and Daniel Tavares Sr., joining three older sisters. He was spoiled and indulged by his mother, a Laundromat manager, who doted on him, particularly after she and her husband split up when Danny was less than two years old. In his early twenties, he often found work as a disc jockey at local clubs and for weddings and other festive occasions. He was a minor local celebrity.

He was also a drug addict and a mental patient who mixed alcohol with physician-prescribed antipsychotics, mood elevators, and even drugs to help with some of the side effects of the former. He added cocaine, Valium, and almost anything else he could get his hands on. He took Prolixin, an antipsychotic drug designed for bipolar patients; doxepin, an antidepressive; and Artane, to alleviate uncontrollable trembling caused by the other two drugs.

Given that, it was difficult to know which came first: his bizarre behavior after ingesting drugs or his mental illness, which he compromised by his illegal drug addictions and heavy drinking.

He apparently hadn't changed his dangerous ways in two decades. And it was almost impossible to know whether to believe *any* of his wild stories. Even so, he hadn't had much trouble getting dates, as rude as he could sometimes be, or as peculiar as his behavior was. There were young women in Massachusetts who had found him exciting.

*   *   *

On Thursday, July 11, 1991, Somerset, Massachusetts, smelled of honeysuckle, melting asphalt, and the sea wind that blew off the bays, rivers, and ponds that snaked from the Atlantic Ocean to the southeast corner of the state. As the sun began to set, shade trees would become cooling canopies, and weathermen promised the temperature would drop to the upper sixties and clouds would overcast the area by midnight.

Daniel Tavares asked two sisters who shared his surname—but to whom he was not related—to go to the Kokomo Club in Tiverton, Rhode Island, just across the state line. Stephanie and Heather Tavares agreed to go with him. Stephanie had known him for two months, but she'd dated him for only a week before she heard that he had two children by two different young women. Stephanie thought a romantic relationship with Danny would be too complicated so they'd agreed to remain only friends.

When Daniel arrived at Heather's apartment, her babysitter, Joey Lynn, noticed that "he didn't look good." Heather snatched off his sunglasses and saw that his eyes were red and the pupils were dilated.

"What's wrong with you?" she asked.

"I've been drinking and I took nine Valiums," he said, "because Tracy [an ex-girlfriend] is taking me to court, and I won't be able to see my son anymore."

The sisters noted that he was acting strange and that he wasn't "walking right."

At least he wasn't driving—Danny didn't drive. He said a friend was picking them up.

While Heather and Stephanie were in the bathroom fixing their hair and putting the final touches on their makeup,

Joey Lynn watched Danny reach into Stephanie's and Heather's purses and count out money from their wallets, and then stick it into various sections of his own billfold. When the Tavares sisters checked, Stephanie found that nine dollars was gone, and Heather was missing thirteen dollars.

They were angry and decided not to go to the club. Danny lied and said he hadn't taken the money; the babysitter had. "We suspected he'd taken it, but what were we going to do?" Stephanie asked. "We decided to go and have a good time—Danny said he'd pay for us."

They arrived at Kokomo at ten minutes after nine, and Danny bought them each a beer and two for himself before he left them at the bar and started shooting pool.

"We kept watching Danny," Stephanie said, "because he'd taken the 'V's' and we had no money to buy drinks or anything. He came over to our table around eleven, bought us each another beer, and danced one fast song with Heather. Not too long after that, we noticed he was gone."

As far as she knew, Danny drank just two beers in the ninety minutes he was at the Kokomo. She had no idea how many he'd had before he arrived at her sister's apartment.

Heather said Danny had spent only ten or fifteen minutes with them all evening. They were stuck without a ride home, and with no money. He'd bailed on them a few weeks before, too, and they were chagrined that they had trusted him again.

Ben Benson read on. Danny Tavares and his mother had had an unusual living situation: Ann Tavares, her current boyfriend of seven years, and her former boyfriend each owned a third interest in the house on Winslow. Apparently there were no bad feelings between the men in Ann's life.

John Latsis,* the former lover, lived in a basement apartment, Ann and Kristos Lilles* lived on the main floor, and Danny had his own attic apartment.

Sometime after eleven on Thursday night, July 11, Danny Tavares had called his mother and told her that someone had put three tablets of LSD in a White Russian he was drinking, and he was afraid of the effect it might have on him. Since he didn't drive, his mother was used to picking him up from one club or another. She and Kristos drove to the Kokomo to get him, and the three of them got home about midnight.

What happened after that was almost inexplicable. Kristos was tired and went to bed. After driving Danny and the two young women to the Kokomo earlier that night, John Latsis had returned home. When Ann, Kristos, and Daniel returned, he and a male friend were visiting in the lower apartment when they heard screaming and shouting from somewhere upstairs. With Latsis in the lead, they sprinted up the steps. They saw an out-of-control Danny Tavares with a large butcher knife in his hand, and Kristos Lilles struggling with him.

They had no idea what had happened but were relieved when Kristos managed to disarm Danny. Told to calm down, Danny yelled, "Get back or I'll fucking kill you!"

John shouted at his friend, "Run downstairs and call 911. Ann needs help!"

John Latsis was bleeding from the right side of his

chest. Danny Tavares banged his own head so hard against the wall that it burst through the attic ceiling, as he cried, "Mama! Mama!"

At nine minutes after midnight, Somerset patrol officers W. E. Caravallo and Peter Massa were dispatched to the house on Winslow by radio: "Domestic dispute—involving a mental party. Possible stabbing."

As they ran up the stairs, they observed Sergeant John Solomito leading a zombielike handcuffed prisoner down. There was such chaos in the house that it was impossible to tell what had happened.

They were stunned to see how bad it was in Danny Tavares's room. An attractive woman in blue shorts and a white T-shirt lay on her back in the center of the room, bleeding profusely from her chest, belly, and face. The two officers knelt to administer first aid and CPR to the victim. It was all in vain. Caravallo tried one compression on her sternum and saw blood squirting out of her left side. Somerset Fire Department EMTs had entered the room, and after four compressions, they touched Caravallo on the shoulder and shook their heads.

Ann Tavares was dead. It would take an autopsy to determine how many times she had suffered what were obviously deep penetrating wounds.

John Latsis was hospitalized for his chest wound; he couldn't remember whether Danny had stabbed him deliberately or if it happened during the struggle to get him off of his dying mother.

Kristos was in shock and baffled. The ride home from the Kokomo had been completely uneventful, and the three of them had carried on a friendly conversation. He'd had no concern about Ann's going upstairs to talk to her son.

Massachusetts State Police Sergeant Bruce Jillson processed the crime scene. It began on the stairs leading up to Danny's room, where he found a hypodermic needle on a step. In the room itself, he found signs of a struggle. Plants were overturned, a stuffed raccoon had been knocked from its mounting, furniture was out of place, and there were holes in the plasterboard. A spoon with white powder residue and a plastic baggie with a small amount of the same powder and the missing top of the syringe on the stairway rested on a wicker love seat.

There was an empty six-pack of ale, a bottle of mezcal, and a wood-handled carving knife with a twelve-inch blade. It was smeared with blood.

Ann Tavares's body still lay spread-eagled in the middle of the room in her own blood. Dr. William Zane arrived just before Jillson pronounced her dead. The two men counted approximately fifteen separate wounds to her neck, face, arm, abdomen, and back.

Chapter Six

Detective Sergeant John O'Neil of the Somerset Police Department and Detective Lorraine Levy of the Massachusetts State Police joined forces to try to find some motive for Danny Tavares to kill his mother.

Surprisingly, he was calm and cooperative as he was questioned shortly after 1:00 a.m., although he breathed, "Oh, God," when he was told his mother was dead.

The Massachusetts investigators learned he had recently been a patient at the Corrigan Mental Health Center and that he was taking many drugs—both legal and illegal. He claimed to have heard voices in his head, telling him to kill. He thought that had happened because Heather Tavares had told him that her sister, Stephanie, had dropped three hits of LSD into his White Russian. "Halfway home, I lost it," he said. "I just started flipping out."

Asked why, Danny said he had been sexually abused by his mother and both of her lovers, beginning when he was eleven, and that he just couldn't take it any longer.

"I was being raped constantly, constantly."

"Who was raping you?" O'Neil asked.

"John Latsis. It went on for a long time, till I moved to

California in eighty-eight. I stayed out there for almost one year and moved back and it started happening again. Then my mom met this new boyfriend—Kristos—and he was making me have sex with my mom and him.

"He said, 'Go upstairs, I have a surprise for you for your birthday.' My mom was tied on my bed, and he pulled out a gun and told me that if I don't do her, he was going to shoot us both. And I was scared—so I did."

"Okay," O'Neil said. "You lost it tonight when you got home. How did you lose it?"

"I walked in the house and I went up to my room and my mom came upstairs and said, 'Kristos wants us downstairs, so come down and get undressed,' and I said, 'For what?' She said, 'What do you think?' and I said, 'He's got the gun out, doesn't he?' and she said, 'Yes.'

"So I knew what was going to happen. It flipped me out. I couldn't take it anymore. I couldn't take it, [so] I stabbed her up."

Neither of the two detectives believed him, particularly when he moved easily to the familiar excuse many murderers use: "I blacked out."

Blacking out at the peak moment of a homicide is a ploy that rarely convinces detectives, jurors, or judges.

Danny Tavares said he had started a blank audiotape going when he arrived home from the Kokomo. He needed it for his job as a DJ. So he was sure that all of that conversation about weird sex with his mother and her lover would be found on the tape.

Despite his instructions, detectives would never locate that tape, if, indeed, there ever was one.

Danny said he'd slit his wrists in a recent suicide attempt and that he had no control over his thoughts. He might be fine one minute and then a voice would tell him to jump off a bridge the next. He admitted that he was a "recovered addict" who had used cocaine and lots of Valium.

O'Neil tended to believe the "addict" part but not the "recovered."

The prisoner's tales of kinky sex continued and became more bizarre. He tripped himself up often. Even though John O'Neil and Lorraine Levy told him that a blood test could substantiate his story of being slipped acid, he refused many times.

Finally, he agreed to urine and blood tests.

There was no LSD in his system at all.

There were traces of cocaine, but not enough to have impaired most subjects' judgment. He seemed obsessed with sex and drugs, but the rest of his conversation was normal enough.

Twenty-five-year-old Danny Tavares was charged with murder (matricide) and attempted murder and booked into jail.

Detectives O'Neil and Levy talked with Stephanie and Heather Tavares and asked about Danny's allegations that Stephanie had slipped LSD into his White Russian.

"No way!" Stephanie said. "We were friends. Why would I want to do that?"

"Maybe you were angry because he stole money from your wallet?" O'Neil asked.

"No way! I don't do drugs—I don't believe in them."

"Did you see Danny drinking a White Russian?"

"I only saw him drinking a beer."

Heather chimed in. "I *never* told him that Stephanie put anything in his drink. He's lying."

The Somerset cop and the Massachusetts State Police trooper talked next with John Latsis, the victim's former lover. He admitted that he was bisexual, although he had had a number of heterosexual relationships, including one with Ann Tavares.

"Danny told us that you raped him," O'Neil said.

"I don't believe he brought that up!" Latsis said. "Are you kidding me? That was ten years ago. It happened around 1980. I 'raped' him twice, but it wasn't rape—it was 'fondling.'"

"What do you mean by 'fondling'?" Lorraine Levy asked.

"I was just rubbing his penis. Danny's never mentioned it since."

John Latsis said he had pleaded guilty to two counts of indecent assault and battery to save Danny from embarrassment and served forty days in Bridgewater Hospital/ Prison.

As Latsis casually explained the household setup, it certainly didn't sound like *Father Knows Best*.

"We're all as close as family," he said. "We have all always stayed close friends. In fact, Ann, Kristos, and I have lived together for eight or ten years. The three of us bought the house together.

"It was cocaine that made Danny do this. He's been off it for a while, but I guarantee he's shooting coke."

When Sergeant O'Neil asked Latsis if, to his knowledge, Danny ever participated in sexual acts with his mother and Kristos, Latsis suddenly erupted. "Oh, my

ANN RULE

God," he burst out, "he said *that* about Kristos and his mother? I'll never forgive him. That woman was not promiscuous; she could go twenty years without sex."

Apparently, she hadn't, but O'Neil made no comment. The entire household was one of the most bizarre he'd ever encountered.

John Latsis also denied that there were any guns in the house, and he had never seen Kristos Lilles with a gun.

Although Latsis admitted that he had molested teenage Danny, how much damage he had done was an open question. Latsis himself tried to slough it off as almost "normal."

A dozen years later, it would appear that Danny was spouting his own fantasies about sex, and that they had little basis in reality. Psychiatrists had ventured that it was quite probable that Danny had an Oedipus complex, a sexual fixation on his mother. She had raised him alone and spoiled him since he was a toddler.

Theirs had, indeed, been an unusual household, but apparently it had limped along for a decade. Whether Danny Tavares's claims of parental abuse were true was questionable. The Massachusetts investigators already had a lot of medical background on him that indicated he was addicted to cocaine and perhaps other illegally obtained drugs. Bruce Jillson had gathered up fourteen vials of psychiatric medications as he processed Danny's attic "apartment."

Bristol County District Attorney Paul Walsh Jr. felt that the State could not prove that Danny Tavares, at age twenty-five, had a "sound mind." Therefore, his charges were reduced to manslaughter, and he was allowed to plead guilty

288

to that. He was sentenced to seventeen to twenty years in prison and moved to MCI–Cedar Junction in Walpole, Massachusetts's maximum-security prison.

He was not the prison staff's favorite inmate. He quickly gravitated to the white supremacist group, and one of the corrections officers referred to Tavares as a "cell warrior," who was always making trouble from behind the bars of his cell. Full of hate, he spat at guards who walked by his cell and threw his urine and even feces on them. He made violent threats.

He wrote threatening letters to public officials and his own family members. The Massachusetts State Police investigated Daniel Tavares's intimidating letters to his father in Florida. He hated the older man. "He threatened to kill me," Tavares Sr. said. "He said he'd come down here when he got out and break all my ribs and maim me."

Finally, Daniel Tavares was placed in Cedar Junction's Departmental Disciplinary Unit, a prison enclosed within another prison. He was housed there longer than any other inmate—more than seven years. And he lost "good time" again and again because of his refusal to abide by prison rules. In the end, he spent more time in isolation than all but a few convicts at Cedar Junction and lost a thousand hours of good time. He could have been released almost three years earlier than he was.

But there was an instance when Daniel Tavares *did* cooperate with Massachusetts authorities. Ben Benson's eyes widened as he read about another connection between Tavares and violent death.

*   *   *

Two decades ago—in 1988—still unsolved cases of serial murder had occurred in and around New Bedford, Massachusetts. On July 3, a woman who had stopped to pick wildflowers along Route 140 stumbled over a skeleton in a woodland clearing. The desiccated remains were later identified as Debra Medeiros, twenty-nine, of Fall River. Over the next nine months, the bodies of eight more women were found alongside Bristol County highways. The serial murders became known as "the Highway Killings."

Like many other vulnerable targets who fall victim to serial killers, the dead women had all spent time in Weld Square, a section of New Bedford known for prostitution. Reportedly, they were all dependent upon illegal drugs.

There have been a few prime suspects; one committed suicide three years after the first body was discovered, and another was charged with murder, but the charges were eventually dropped.

Although the Highway Killings were never connected directly to Danny Tavares, the victims lived in the same area and shared the same addiction to drugs.

Another unsolved murder case in the Fall River–New Bedford area in 1988 has so many connections to Tavares that it is almost incomprehensible that he was not charged with murder.

On October 27, 1988, pretty, dark-eyed Gayle Botelho, thirty-two, vanished from her home. Hers was the kind of disappearance that couldn't have happened—and yet it did.

Gayle lived at 114 Prospect Street in Fall River with her fiancé and one of her three children. At 4:30 p.m., she answered a knock on the door of their second-floor apartment and called back to her boyfriend that she was leaving to talk to someone (a man) and she'd be gone about five minutes.

She didn't come back.

Seeing that she had left behind her purse, money, all of her sweaters and jackets, her fiancé was concerned. It was close to Halloween, and the weather was chilly at night. When she didn't return for several hours, he called the police. Everyone in the Fall River area was jittery because of the Highway Killer's victims, and although Gayle really didn't fit the victim profile, her case was treated seriously from the beginning.

Gayle was the middle child among seven sisters and two brothers in a family that had lived in Fall River for generations, and they missed her dearly. Waiting year after year for Gayle or her body to be found was agonizing for them.

Danny Tavares had been in prison for nine years in early September 2000, when he sent a kite (a prison note) to the Massachusetts State Police telling them that he could locate Gayle Botelho's body. It was probably a ruse, or possibly he was planning an escape once he got outside the walls.

Nevertheless, the state police paid attention.

In mid-October, Gayle's onetime neighbors noticed police detectives going in and out of the basement of a large two-story house across from her old apartment. They were there for hours, and when they left quietly, they carried a number of articles. That didn't seem like prime gossip, but what happened next did.

The residents on Prospect Street watched curiously as

state troopers and deputies from the state medical examiner's office erected a tent in the backyard of the two-story house at 314 June Street. Although the houses fronted on different streets, the tent where the troopers were digging was directly across the street from the apartment where Gayle Botelho had last been seen.

The crew from the state police had a dog with them—a necrosearch dog trained to sniff out human remains.

What no one knew at the time was the identity of the tipster who had told the troopers where to dig: Daniel Tavares. Furthermore, in 1988, the house on June Street had been the home of Ann and Danny Tavares, and Kristos Lilles. This was where they lived just before they bought the house with John Latsis in Somerset. Gayle vanished almost exactly three years before Danny stabbed his mother to death.

With the necrosearch dog's signals, they focused their digging next to a brick outdoor barbecue that was built against a wall that separated the Tavareses' former backyard from the driveway of the house next door.

They were extremely careful as they dug. It had been a dozen years, and they used small tools, their gloved hands, and brushes to remove soil. If Gayle lay near the outdoor hearth, her body would have long since gone back to earth, leaving only delicate bones. They hoped to find other items and artifacts in the ground, too—perhaps some they could connect to a killer.

She was there, not far at all below the surface. For all those icy Northeast winters and simmering summers, Gayle Botelho had lain within seventy feet of where her fiancé waited for her to come home.

An autopsy and X-rays officially identified her body. The cause of death? Stab wounds. There were enough defects on her bones to indicate where a knife had plunged in, even though her soft tissue had disappeared many years earlier.

At the time Gayle's fate was discovered, Bristol County District Attorney Paul Walsh—the DA who had accepted Danny's plea bargain to have his mother's stabbing death lowered from murder to manslaughter—did not reveal who the tipster was.

Danny told investigators that he, Gayle, and two "acquaintances" of his had attended "some wild party." He said the other two men had stabbed Gayle to death, while he was only an observer.

At the time, he would have been twenty-one or twenty-two, and he already had a history of drug use and theft.

Given his tendency to embroider the truth, most detectives would have suspected Tavares of Gayle's murder, as well as those of the other nine victims of the Highway Killer *and* two subsequent suspicious deaths of similar female victims that had come to light.

Massachusetts state detectives located the two men that Danny Tavares had named but refused to comment on what, if anything, they had learned from them.

Indeed, the public had no idea that a convicted killer had led troopers to Gayle Botelho's body seven years before he murdered Brian and Beverly Mauck. When the Tavares connection to Gayle's murder hit the media in Massachusetts, Washington, and the wire services and the Internet, her family was outraged. They had never heard of Danny Tavares and had known only that a "prisoner" had led police to their sister's body. And now he was out of prison and he'd killed two more people.

Lori Fielding, one of Gayle's sisters, spoke for her family. "I can tell you after nineteen years, it still hurts. A little healing is allowed to take place, and then it starts again. Gayle mattered, and she was somebody's sister and daughter and mother in spite of the problems she might have had. But she didn't seem to matter to anyone else."

Ann Tavares's fiancé, Kristos Lilles, had his doubts about Danny, and with the news that he had been charged with double murder in Washington, Lilles talked to the media, telling them he believed that the young man who was like a son to him for many years might very well be the Highway Killer.

"He kept talking about them," Lilles told the *Free Republic*, "and saying, 'I know that one.' One was found buried in the yard."

Lilles recalled the night in October 1988 when Gayle Botelho went missing, even though it had been nineteen years earlier. He and Ann had been at a party, and they came home to find Danny staring out the window at a police cruiser outside Gayle's apartment.

"They're looking for Gayle," Danny said.

"I said, 'How do you know? Did you talk to the police?'"

"No," was all Danny said.

Lilles wondered how Danny would know that Gayle was missing if he hadn't talked to the police. He himself hadn't known the missing woman. The conclusions Kristos Lilles came to were too horrifying to deal with.

He never asked Danny about Gayle Botelho again. Shortly after that, he, Ann, and John Latsis had purchased their home in Somerset and left the June Street house. And twelve years later, Gayle's remains were found in the backyard of their former home.

Three years later, corrections officers at Walpole Prison found a kite that Danny Tavares sent to an official regarding his inmate account. It was written on June 18, 2003, and it was one of his threatening letters:

Mrs. B.

I know you purposely made an issue out [of] that punk $100. It never made it into my account. I'm getting sick of everybody trying to jack me over. Charlie said you told him you already sent it to me and to check with the treasurer's office. I shouldn't have to! I'm the last person you will ever jack over 'cause when I get out, I will do shit to you and your daughters that you can't imagine! And trust me when I tell you that I have experience with women . . . just ask Nancy or Debbie or Mary or Sandy or Chris or a few others. Oh, we can't forget about my favorite . . . Gayle. Oh ya, if you can bring them back to life, then ask them. I want my money!

He had blatantly listed the first names of some of the Highway Killer's victims, and of Gayle Botelho. Was he lying or was he bragging? Ben Benson saw how vicious Tavares could be when he believed someone was holding money back from him. Tavares had first signed the kite but then scribbled over his name.

*   *   *

With the tragedy in Graham, Washington, Daniel Tavares suddenly became bad news for a number of politicians, and Massachusetts voters wondered why a roving monster like Tavares had been released from prison at all.

Paul Walsh, who had just been unseated after sixteen years as district attorney, insisted there was not just cause to charge Tavares with Gayle Botelho's murder: "The mere knowledge that this guy knew where she was buried can lead you to all sorts of conjecture, but at the end of the day, you need some evidence."

Perhaps. Any prosecutor hopes for hard physical evidence. It is unwise for a prosecutor to go ahead with a case where there are no fingerprints, no blood or fluid DNA transfers, no suspicious hairs and fibers, no bullets or casings or a gun to compare them to, no tool marks, no car tire imprints, or other evidence to show to a jury. Most prosecutors who face election every four years try to keep their conviction percentages well over 90 percent and prefer not to risk not guilty verdicts. And if a homicide defendant is acquitted, double jeopardy will attach, and he cannot be tried again for that crime.

A number of convictions have been won, however, where there was overwhelming circumstantial evidence and where crimes were committed in a similar pattern.

Despite all the "good time" he lost, Daniel Tavares became eligible for parole in the summer of 2007, after serving over sixteen years in Walpole. However, he had two charges pending—one for spitting on a corrections officer, and the second for smashing another guard with a heavy cast that had been applied after Tavares had wrist surgery. Bail on those attacks was $50,000 apiece, and he faced ten more years in prison if he was convicted.·

Tavares had sent letters threatening the lives of Governor Mitt Romney and Massachusetts Attorney General Tom Reilly. His father in Florida considered him "pure evil," although he had tried to get his son off drugs when he was a teenager. The elder Daniel Tavares was even more terrified when he allegedly received a phone call from Jennifer Lynn, his future daughter-in-law, telling him that Daniel would soon be on his way to break his legs and kill him. Daniel's father was sleeping with a gun under his pillow.

In the summer of 2007, Mitt Romney was no longer the governor of Massachusetts; he was among the top candidates for the Republican presidential nomination. One of the appointments Romney had made during his governorship was that of Superior Court Judge Kathe Tuttman. Critics said he had named Tuttman for purely political reasons—to appeal to female voters. She was among a quartet of women appointed to the judiciary in April 2006. Until then, out of forty-two judicial appointments made by Governor Romney, only thirteen had been female.

Tuttman had a good reputation as a former assistant district attorney and as a strong advocate for victims' rights. She had been awarded many honors as head of the Essex County District Attorney's Family Crime and Sexual Assault Unit. Many sources called her a "brilliant lawyer."

On the advice of others, Mitt Romney gave Kathe Tuttman a judgeship. He would live to regret it.

As fate would have it, Daniel Tavares and Judge Tuttman met for the first time on July 16, 2007, at the Worcester Superior Court. She knew little of his past beyond the fact that he had served his complete sentence for the manslaughter charges, and that this was a bail hearing on the two assault charges involving the corrections officers in Walpole Prison—one in 2005 and one in 2006.

Tavares's attorney, Barry Dynice, pooh-poohed the charges of any attacks on guards. He pointed out that the Massachusetts Department of Corrections had waited until the very last moment—when his client had been practically walking out of prison—to bring up those charges. He argued that Daniel Tavares had paid the price for his crimes and deserved to be released on his own personal recognizance.

Dynice said Daniel wasn't a flight risk. He had a twenty-four-year-old daughter, he'd worked hard to earn his GED (high school equivalency), and he was totally amenable to pretrial probation. "He has requested that he be placed on some kind of monitoring system," Dynice said, "if there's any concern about this." (Tavares's "son" wasn't mentioned.)

Daniel Tavares was fully capable of putting on a good face and a calm attitude to get what he wanted. He was no longer a wild-eyed, muscular man in his twenties. His hair was gray, and his physique was portly. He had dark circles beneath his eyes and the pasty greenish-yellow prison pallor.

He didn't look dangerous.

Prosecutor William Loughin tried his best to point out Tavares's long history. All of his crimes had involved violence, and he had even "committed crimes of violence while he was serving time for a crime of violence."

But this was only a bail hearing, not a murder trial.

Judge Tuttman looked at the man she'd just met and mistook him for someone who had paid for the horrible crime he'd committed, who wanted only the chance for a new life, someone who was safe to let out on the streets. Although his fiancée was in Washington, she didn't think he would leave Massachusetts. She didn't even think it was necessary to have him wear an electronic bracelet or anklet so he could be tracked if he left the jurisdiction.

And he promised to show up for all of his scheduled three-times-a-week probation appointments, to live with one of his sisters, and to find a job.

Judge Tuttman released him on his personal recognizance. He showed up for two of his probation appointments, but he failed to appear on July 23.

And then he was gone. He was on his way to Washington.

A warrant for his arrest was issued, although there was no promise that Massachusetts would extradite him from other states. And, despite the fact that Massachusetts authorities knew about Jennifer Lynn Freitas and had her address, there were no warnings or requests to locate sent to the Pierce County Sheriff's Department. Ed Troyer, their media spokesman, commented on what an egregious oversight that had been. It was like letting a mad dog out of his cage while he frothed at the mouth and growled. If only the sheriff's office in Washington had known who had sidled quietly into their midst, into a small town where nobody worried about locked doors.

"But they didn't tell us—"

Granted, almost any state would have preferred to see a

man like Tavares outside their jurisdiction. The Freitases, the Maucks, and anyone else who encountered him had no warning at all of who was headed their way.

Mitt Romney, with his rugged good looks, deep voice, and charisma, in the summer of 2007 became the center of a national media firestorm, his reputation sullied—perhaps fatally—by a vicious "punk" he'd never heard of before.

Chapter Seven

Ironically, Mitt Romney was in Washington State on the campaign trail when Brian and Beverly Mauck were murdered. Even while the Pierce County detectives continued their investigation, the word of Daniel Tavares's latest act of violence had spread to Massachusetts—and to New York City.

Rudy Giuliani, then Romney's chief rival for the presidential nomination, seized upon the story and used it to cast doubt on his leadership qualities. "The governor is going to have to explain his appointment," Giuliani told the Associated Press, "and the judge is going to have to explain her decision—but it's not an isolated situation. Governor Romney did not have a good record in dealing with violent crime."

Mitt Romney called for Judge Tuttman to resign and attempted to put as much distance between himself and his appointee as he could. He said he'd never really known her.

Romney's spokesman managed to put a spin on the devastating results of Daniel Tavares's release. He cited the Tavares case as a reason for states that had abolished the death penalty to bring it back. "This is a dangerous man who killed his own mother," Eric Fehrnstrom said. "He should have been held on bail, given his violent record, attacks on correction officers and a history of threats against public officials, including Governor Romney. It is because of monsters like Daniel Tavares that we need the death penalty."

Fingers were pointing in every direction, and no one involved, even in the slightest way, let any blame stick to him or her. Kathe Tuttman perhaps got the most abuse—even though she had been tough on violent criminals in the past. In a poll posted by the *Boston Herald*, asking if Judge Tuttman should resign, 85 percent of readers voted yes, 11 percent voted no, and only 4 percent were undecided.

Darrel Slater, Bev Mauck's father, was bitter and blamed Mitt Romney: "He was the governor—he picked the judge. He should be answering for what happened."

But Romney did not apologize or accept any blame. Either way, the kiss of political death marked his cheek. The killings in tiny Graham, Washington, may very well have been a deciding factor for the former governor to drop out of the presidential race.

He still, however, had a chance to be nominated for vice president, depending on whom the Republicans chose as their presidential nominee. Almost to the time of the convention in St. Paul, Romney's name remained on the short list. In the end, he could not lose the specter of Daniel Tavares, who clung to his coattails like a burr.

John McCain bypassed Romney and chose Sarah Palin, a virtually unknown governor from the state of Alaska.

Nothing is less forgiven than political missteps.

* * *

Back in Pierce County, Sergeant Ben Benson and his team were tying up the ends of their tragic case. Daniel Tavares had confessed to murder, but Jennifer Lynn still insisted she had had nothing to do with the Maucks' murders, before, during, or after. She had admitted that she suspected her husband of getting rid of a gun by throwing it off a cliff along Five Mile Drive and seemed willing to go with detectives to look for it.

On Monday morning, November 19, Detective Elizabeth Lindt and Lieutenant Brent Bomkamp visited Jennifer in the Pierce County Jail and asked her if she would show them where she believed Daniel had disposed of the gun used in the murders—somewhere in Point Defiance Park. She agreed to accompany them.

When they reached the park, Jennifer directed them to the area where she and Daniel had been married. It was gray November now, Thanksgiving week, and the sunshine of late July was long gone.

"Daniel walked down this trail from the parking lot"—Jennifer pointed—"until he disappeared. He was gone for at least five minutes. He told me he went to a ledge over the water, and he threw the gun in. He told me that he was afraid the gun hadn't made it to the water."

The parking lot where they stood started at the Vashon Island Viewpoint, and the northernmost trail, close by Commencement Bay, passed by a clearing. Beyond that a cliff overlooks Commencement Bay. About fifty feet down, there was a thick cluster of brushy vegetation before the land dropped off some forty feet into the bay.

Lindt and Bomkamp scrambled down the path to the greenery that seemed to get its energy from the air itself; there was precious little dirt there. But they couldn't find the gun. It might have been hidden among the Scotch broom and blackberry bushes, or it could have been on the bottom of the bay.

Or maybe Tavares hadn't thrown the weapon at all but only wanted Jennifer to think he had?

Under the M'Naughton Rule, a killer who has made an effort to cover up his crime is deemed to be sane and cognizant of the difference between right and wrong. For the sadistic sociopath, the delineation between the two is perfectly clear; it just doesn't matter to him because he answers only to himself. Daniel Tavares, who was fully aware that he had a history of reacting violently to heedless combinations of drugs and alcohol, might have seemed totally insane after he used them, but he knew full well that he was doing wrong. He made several attempts to cover up his vicious acts. He had always blamed others for making him do what he did, or he denied committing his crimes at all. He blamed his mother for sexually molesting both himself and his daughter, although no one else was ever aware of that. He denied any guilt in the murder of Gayle Botelho, and he said Brian Mauck had insulted him and refused to pay him the fifty dollars he allegedly owed for a tattoo. And he attempted to cover up his crime in the deaths of Bev and Brian Mauck.

Although his crimes and alleged crimes were horrific and seemed to have no logical motivation, Daniel Tavares wasn't insane under the law, or even medically. His own father called him "evil." And maybe he was.

There was more evidence that Tavares had attempted to cover up the murders of his neighbors. On December 16, Jeff Freitas called the sheriff's office to report that he had made a startling discovery when he moved his riding lawn mower out of his shed and began to dump the grass clippings out of the grass catcher. Some clothing dropped out, too: a pair of pants and a pillowcase, both of which had dried bloodstains on them. The jeans were splotched white where Tavares had poured bleach over them. Detectives finally located a burn pile near the Tavares trailer. It had a partially burned blue shirt tangled in it.

Although he had denied it, Tavares *had* changed his clothes and hidden them to keep the investigators from finding his victims' bloodstains there. He had gotten rid of the gun. He had made up a wildly untrue story to explain his facial injuries. He had told Jennifer exactly what to say to back up his story. He had lied and lied and lied.

Although he avoided the death penalty, it is unlikely that Daniel Tavares will ever again see the world outside prison walls. For her part in helping him cover up the Mauck murders, Jennifer Lynn Tavares is serving a year in the Pierce County Jail.

It wasn't until after Tavares pleaded guilty to the Maucks' murders, and received his life sentences, that Detective Sergeant Ben Benson glimpsed the rage that others had described. Benson and Tom Catey had spent many hours interviewing Tavares the Sunday after the homicides were discovered. And through it all, the suspect had been remarkably civil.

"After he confessed," Benson recalled, "Daniel sat back and smiled. He didn't even seem angry or upset."

But Benson had Tavares brought to his office after his sentencing.

"I asked him if there was anything more he wanted to tell me. He was evasive, and he lied about having a fistfight with Brian Mauck. I corrected him, telling him I knew that wasn't the truth.

"He came out of his chair in a complete rage, headed right for me. Finally, I saw the monster that his victims must have seen. It was shocking—more so than any reaction I've ever witnessed. That, I believe, was the *real* Daniel Tavares."

It's only natural to wonder if things could have been different. If time could be rewound, and if information had been shared and red flags given proper attention, are there many lives that would not have ended so soon, and many careers that would not be blemished?

Karen Slater, Bev Mauck's mother, takes some comfort in her belief that her small but feisty daughter did some damage to her killer. "He had to shoot her between the eyes to stop her," Karen says. "I know in my heart that it was Bev who gave him that black eye and left bruises and cuts on his face with her elbow. Somehow, that makes me feel a little better."

Back in Massachusetts, Danny Tavares was allowed to plead guilty to lesser charges of manslaughter and attempted manslaughter in the savage murder of his mother and the attack on George Latsis, and he was never charged with Gayle Botelho's murder.

Many citizens of Bristol County, were horrified when they learned that Daniel Tavares had known all along where Gayle's body was.

If only he had been arrested in 1988, his mother might still be alive.

If only he hadn't been released from prison—despite his disruptive behavior—the Maucks might be alive.

If he is, indeed, the Highway Killer of New Bedford—which is a more remote possibility—some of the eleven young women tossed away in the bushes and wild grass beside the roads might have survived.

That is, of course, hindsight.

The current district attorney of Bristol County, Sam Sutter, has reopened the investigation into the Highway Murders and the death of Gayle Botelho.

And so the story of Daniel Tavares may be far from over.

Pierce County Sheriff's Office Detective Lieutenant Brent Bomkamp (*left*) and Detective Sergeant Ben Benson (*right*) rushed to the multiple murder scene in tiny Graham, Washington. Bomkamp later explained to Daniel Tavares that Benson and Detective Tom Catey were two of his best investigators, and they could always ferret out the truth. So there was no good reason for Tavares to lie.

Detective Sergeant Ben Benson faced one of the most convoluted cases of his long career as he was assigned to head the probe into a double-homicide investigation.

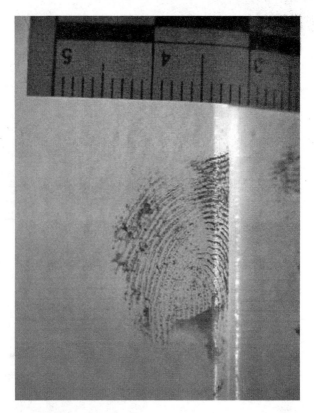

Ben Benson and Brent Bomkamp thought at first that they had located a fingerprint in blood on an interior door of the Maucks' home. Bomkamp sawed the section out, but experts in the crime lab reported that it was a portion of a palm print instead. Benson took criminalist Marylou Hanson-O'Brien to swab four subjects' arms almost to the elbow for identification purposes. They didn't object, but perhaps they should have.

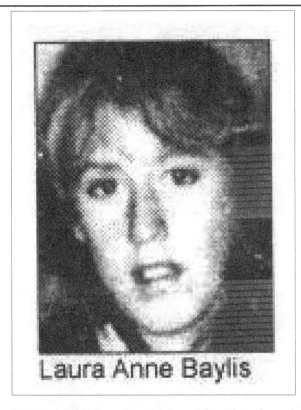

Laura Anne Baylis

Julie Costello aka Laura Baylis led a carefree life on the road, and believed she could handle any situation. Sadly, she was overpowered by an evil presence too big for her to fight. She will always be the young woman in this photo.

7-Eleven all-night clerk Laura Baylis is filmed by the security camera she triggered as she opened the cash register. An unknown male stands to her right.

The camera clicks on mindlessly as Laura bends to scoop money out of the till.

The stranger, wearing a billed cap, protective glasses, and a khaki jacket, appears to hold a knife to Laura Baylis's back as she puts the money into a bag. These would be the last photos taken of Laura alive.

Clarence Williams (*right*) stands in a police lineup. He is wearing clothes identical to the robber/abductor of Laura Baylis as seen in security camera frames. Even so, he denied that he bore any resemblance to "the stranger."

Robbery Detective Larry Stewart joined homicide detectives in the investigation into the disappearance of Laura Baylis, and talked to dozens of neighbors and possible witnesses.

Robbery Unit Lieutenant Bob Holter's crew were the first ones to investigate the 7-Eleven abduction. It didn't appear to be a homicide in the beginning, and there was an avalanche of murders in Seattle in the summer of 1978. Holter's men kept running into blank walls.

Seattle Homicide Detective Hank Gruber shook his head in disbelief when Clarence Williams insisted he wasn't the man in the 7-Eleven photos, even though Gruber glanced from the security camera shots of the man himself—and found them identical.

Mike Tando was a young homicide detective in 1978 when he was assigned to the murder investigation in the death of fifteen-year-old Sara Beth Lundquist. Although he worked around the clock for days, talking to Sara Beth's friends and relatives and dozens of tipsters, the identity of her killer remained obscure. When it was finally solved, Tando had reached retirement age.

Sara Beth Lundquist got off a bus at midnight and walked into the darkness—forever. Although it took three decades to find her killer in a case long gone cold, she was never forgotten—not by her family, her friends, nor Seattle detectives.

Mike Tando points to blood stains on the interior door of the ladies' room of a deserted gas station. Sara Beth was found inside, stabbed repeatedly.

A construction worker, remodeling the service station, could not open the white door on the right. Sara Beth's body was blocking the door.

Seattle Police detectives, patrol officers, and crime lab experts gather evidence of an inexplicable murder on a Sunday morning in July 1978. It was one of the saddest cases any of them had ever worked on.

Seattle Police Detective Mike Ciesynski was just out of high school
in Chicago when Sara Beth died in 1978. Now, he *is* the Cold Case
Unit of the department. At her brother's request, Ciesynski vowed to
solve Sara Beth's murder. And he did.

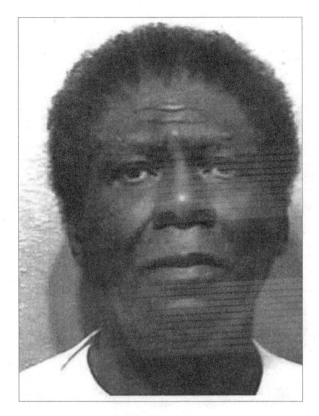

Clarence Edward Williams, now sixty-four, agreed to talk to Mike Ciesynski in a Minnesota prison. But his mind was full of denial. Would he ever tell the Cold Case detective enough to tie up loose ends in *two* murders?

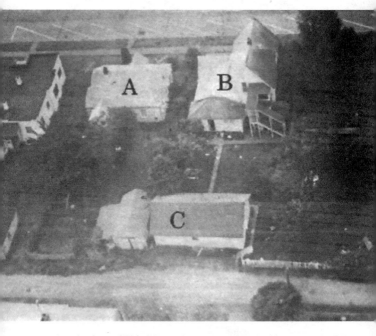

An air view of Third Street in Marysville, Washington, a "safe" small town. Traia Carr lived in house A, a widowed mother lived in house B with her teenage children, and building C was a washhouse that held shocking evidence of murder.

Marysville Detective Jarl Gunderson, who knew almost everyone in town, searched Traia Carr's house and yard. He found that the flowers beneath her windows were crushed by someone who had watched her and stalked her. Traia was afraid, but she had no idea *who* the male stalking her was.

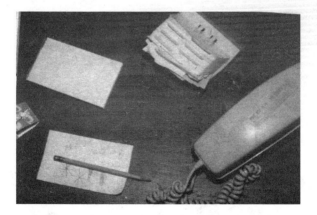

Traia Carr's phone line had been cut, her jewelry was stolen, and she herself had vanished into the night of July Fourth as fireworks blazed in the sky. It would be a long time before anyone knew where she was.

Snohomish County Sheriff's Detective Bruce Whitman, and his partner, Detective Dick Taylor, came to Marysville on another case, but returned to join Jarl Gunderson in the search for Traia Carr.

Dick Taylor was one of the three detective who were determined to find out who had been stalking Traia Carr. They worked tirelessly to find her. Had she been abducted by an obsessed "admirer," her fiancé, or had she left home suddenly for her own reasons?

Detective Bruce Whitman stands in a dense forest on an Indian reservation. At last, they had physical evidence leading to Traia Carr.

Third Street in Marysville, Washington. Ironically, in the end, all the answers to the disappearance of Traia Carr could be found along this street in a family neighborhood.

IF *I* CAN'T
HAVE YOU . . .

It has been said—and often—that hell hath no fury like a woman scorned. I suspect there is a fury that far exceeds that of a woman rejected by her man, and that is the rage of a cuckolded male, or one who *believes* that his mate has been unfaithful. Every day I get at least one e-mail from a woman somewhere in the world who is struggling to be free of her "prison of love."

Most days, I get three or four.

As we've seen in the first case in this book, it is far easier to fall in love than it is to abandon a love that is not what it seemed to be. Many men still consider that a woman, once pledged to him, is his personal property, his chattel and possession forever. He would rather see her dead—violently dead—than picture her making love with someone else.

In one Seattle homicide, a fifty-three-year-old man proved once again that some men cannot let go gracefully. His name was Melvin, and his former wife, Kathryn, was fifteen years younger than he was. He'd always believed that she would leave him one day, and it was a self-fulfilling prophecy. His jealousy and suspicion ruined his marriage. Kathryn had tired of him long before their divorce decree was final.

She moved forward in her life, and some months later, she had a new love whom she hoped to marry. Melvin was enraged when he learned that.

In the fall of 1976, he lay in wait and shot and wounded Kathryn's lover. The wounds weren't critical, and Melvin received little more than a slap on the hand and a suspended sentence from the judge. Although Kathryn was still afraid of him, no one else involved—except for her lover—believed that Melvin would act out violently again.

Within days of his release from jail, Melvin decided to break up Kathryn's romance in a most final way.

On February 5, 1977, he loaded his shotgun and carried it stealthily up the alley behind his ex-wife's home. He then dragged a garbage can beneath the kitchen window so he could look inside. What he saw seared an unforgettable image in his brain. Why his wife and her lover weren't more afraid is puzzling. They should have moved into a bedroom, or at least pulled the blinds—but they didn't.

Unaware that they were being watched, his wife and her lover were making love on top of the dining room table.

Melvin leveled his weapon on the windowsill and called out, "Move—and you're dead!"

Involuntarily, the lover drew back and Melvin's slender, beautiful ex-wife started to sit up. Had she remained still, she might have lived.

The shotgun blast reverberated throughout the house, its full force piercing the helpless woman in one breast and tearing completely through her body, taking out her heart and both her lungs in its lethal course. She was dead instantly, senselessly, forever.

Seattle homicide detectives had no trouble locating Melvin; neighbors who ran out of their homes at the sound of the shotgun had spotted his car license as he drove away. And, of course, many of them recognized him and his vehicle.

Booked into jail, Melvin had very little to say. He seemed oddly satisfied that Kathryn was dead and no longer in the arms of another man. If he thought at all of their three children who were now virtually orphaned, he didn't comment on it to the detectives. In his mind, Kathryn had been his to do with as he saw fit, and he saw fit to destroy her.

But he also destroyed what was left of his own life. Tried and convicted, Melvin was sentenced to serve a hundred years in prison for murder in the first degree, plus another twenty years for assault against his rival, who lived.

Melvin's motivation was not unlike that behind another tragedy brought about by suspicion, jealousy, and a sense of possession of another human being. This murder occurred four months after Melvin shot his ex-wife's boyfriend, and eight months before he killed the woman he swore he loved more than anything.

Although it's been thirty-two years since I first wrote about the case of Amelia Jager, her story is one of a small percentage that refuses to leave my conscious memory. Cruel fate somehow brought the principals together, and it was a sorry thing that they ever met at all.

Amelia Jager, twenty-seven, was a flowerlike Eurasian woman, a small and fragile brunette with lovely eyes whose beauty combined the best of both the East and West. She weighed barely 100 pounds and stood about five foot two. She was stronger than she looked, but she was no match for a man, especially for an irrational stalker.

Ironically, Amelia had never loved anyone with the intensity she felt for the·man who would eventually destroy her; she had never been unfaithful to him, and she had left him only because she feared his dark side. Nothing in her former life had prepared her for the sudden waves of blackness and hate that washed over him, mercurial emotions she neither foresaw nor understood.

Except for the unpredictable vicissitudes of fate or karma or whatever it can be called, Amelia would never have met Heinz Jager at all. She grew up a world, an ocean, many continents away from the native of Bern, Switzerland. Amelia had never known anything but a peaceful, loving family life with her parents and her sisters and brother.

Amelia had no prejudices against anyone. Her parents'

marriage had shown her that different cultures and different racial backgrounds could blend into a strong, fine union. She and her siblings had been blessed with beauty and brains, and there were real bonds among them. Their home in one of Seattle's finest suburbs was charming and gracious. That was all Amelia had ever known. Perhaps if she had been brought up in turmoil, she might have recognized the danger signs sooner.

Amelia was a teacher in California. Her summers belonged to her after she'd completed her mandatory "fifth-year" postgraduate courses in education, and she was free to travel during her vacation time. In 1973, she embarked on a tour of Europe. Although she enjoyed the whole trip, it was Switzerland that attracted her the most. That was probably because of the man she met there: Heinz Jager. Heinz was a tall, handsome Swiss with startling clear blue eyes, thick brown hair, and a beard. He was a theatrical engineer, successful and much admired for his work. He towered over Amelia's petite frame and made her feel safe and protected.

Although they had some language difficulties, Heinz seemed to know what she felt and what she thought, and she believed she understood him, too. Although her family and friends back home called her Amy, Heinz liked the more formal Amelia; he said it suited her.

When Amy reluctantly returned to California to honor her teaching contract in the fall, she missed Heinz, far more than she had expected. Their correspondence became increasingly frequent and intimate. It was only natural that she go back to Switzerland the next summer to be with him.

This time, in 1974, Amy's sister Jill went along with her, intrigued by her sister's glowing reports of Switzerland. Jill was younger than Amy, but taller and stronger, a statuesque woman, very attractive in her own way. She took a job as a waitress and bartender in Bern and both sisters had a wonderful summer.

Amy and Heinz communicated in French, although her native language was English and his German. They both became more fluent in French, and their second summer together convinced Amy that this was the man she had dreamed of all her life.

He was eight years older than she was and had been married once before, but that didn't matter to Amy. Many men learned from the mistakes of a first marriage, and it often made their second marriages stronger. When she and Jill left Switzerland, Amy knew that she would be back again. She hoped that the next time they were together, she might never have to leave Heinz again.

No one could say that they rushed into a committed relationship. They'd grown to know each other not just in person but also through hundreds of letters.

When Amy returned to Bern in the summer of 1975, her love for Heinz had not diminished; it had grown. She wrote happily to her family and friends in America that she would not be coming home in the fall because she and Heinz were to be married in October. She planned to give up teaching and work hard to adapt completely to her new country. And to her marriage.

It was difficult for her family to think of their daughter so very far away, but, as always, they wanted her happiness. That that happiness meant they would see Amy rarely, and probably that their grandchildren would be born and grow up in Switzerland, was bittersweet.

And Amy *was* happy, but only for a short time. As her lover and suitor, Heinz had been considerate and nothing she'd done ever seemed to annoy him. But Heinz appeared to change on their wedding day. It was almost as if someone had flicked off a light switch. Everything was different now that they were married, and Amy was stunned. As long as Amy remained at home, catering to Heinz's every need, she pleased him.

She thought he would be happy when she signed up to take German lessons. She wanted to become a real part of his homeland, and to do that, she would have to learn to speak the language. And their own communication would be so much better if she was able to speak his native language. Perhaps there were shadings of meaning, slang terms, vocabulary that meant something other than Amy thought they did, and that was causing their difficulties.

But something was wrong. Heinz didn't want Amy to go to class. He didn't like the idea of Amelia having friends other than himself. He frowned when she told him of the new friends she was making at school. He became sullen, then jealous, if he saw her talking even casually to other men. She tried to tell him that they were only students at the school who meant nothing to her except as acquaintances.

She assured Heinz that she had never loved anyone but him and that she never could love any other man.

He appeared not to hear and turned away from her, pouting like an angry child.

During the weeks before their first Christmas, Amelia

stopped being puzzled at Heinz's actions. She became afraid. If she hoped to remain in his good graces, she realized that she would have to stay in their home, a virtual recluse. She wouldn't be able to speak to anyone at all, or have any friends.

The man she had married was gone. The "new" Heinz was terrifying in his alternating jealous rages and coldness. To her horror, Amy discovered that he kept a collection of knives and swords, as if to ward off everyone in the world outside their home. And now he threatened her, accusing her of liaisons and treachery—ugly things she had never done, or even dreamed of doing.

But Amy was a proud woman and, despite everything, one who still tried to be optimistic about the future. She didn't write home about her situation; she had loved this man for years, had chosen to turn her back on the United States, to make a marriage and a home for him. She still hoped that somehow she could make it work, and she could not bear to tell anyone of her marital troubles. That would be a betrayal of Heinz and an admission that she had made a dreadful mistake.

In January 1976—after only three months of marriage— Heinz's behavior and his erratic mood swings became untenable, and Amy sought medical help for her husband. The doctors who examined him agreed that he was not rational. He was admitted to the Bern Psychiatric Hospital because of his volatile behavior and his threats to Amy. It broke her heart to see him locked in a mental hospital, but, if possible, she still hoped to save her marriage. They were barely out of what should have been the honeymoon stage. She visited him faithfully, did what the psychiatrists suggested, and avoided discussing anything that seemed to upset him.

Treatment didn't help him at all. He resisted all efforts to medicate him and would not talk to the therapists who tried to reach him. Heinz Jager's pathological obsessions about Amy had gone much too far. She wondered how he could have maintained such a normal façade during the summer months they were together and then become Mr. Hyde to the warm Dr. Jekyll she had fallen in love with.

Amy didn't know his history yet, possibly because of the language barriers and because Heinz had forbidden her to make friends, but he had always taken this approach to women. Once he had taken lovers, they became trapped like butterflies in a glass jar, beating their wings hopelessly as they tried to escape.

In April 1976, Amelia Jager accepted that her dreams of happiness were doomed to failure. She still cared for Heinz in a way, but not as she had once loved him. She was too frightened by his strange moods and his collection of sharp weapons. She hurriedly packed a few possessions and then slipped away from their house while he was out.

Her note of April 9 displays the compassion she still felt for him and also her sadness:

Dear Heinz,

I wanted to say "Goodbye" in person, but I thought it would be too emotional a scene.

I feel so sad and empty that our marriage didn't work. I always loved you more than anyone. You were my "dream man."

It seems that everything in our marriage has gone

downhill instead of improving and it's really better to stop now instead of fighting a losing battle. I will be filing for divorce in America.

I really liked Switzerland and thought being married to a foreigner would enrich both our lives. But you beat me down in my attempt to adjust to life here. Simply trying to learn German turned out to be a major catastrophe. Police, attorneys, running away, were never a part of my life and I have really lost self-respect in facing these situations weekly.

I think that counseling and therapy would have been our only chance but when you're threatening me and irregular about it, I even lost faith in that.

I hate leaving our apartment garden and good times together, but I can't take any more horrible scenes with knives, swords, yelling, and screaming. Saying "I'm sorry" and repeating the same things doesn't help.

I hope you will not do anything drastic because of my leaving. Your new job sounds like a good start in the right direction.

Please don't hope I'm coming back. I will be starting a new life for myself in America.

Love,
Amy

P.S. I put some clothes in the yellow sack in the kitchen that might fit Sonia [a Swiss friend].

It was the farewell letter of a rational woman who had taken all she could bear. A rational man might have accepted her decision. But Amy Jager was not dealing with a rational man. She realized that, but even she could not guess the lengths to which Heinz would go to keep what he considered his. She allowed herself to feel somewhat safe after she talked with officials at the American embassy in Switzerland and begged them not to give him a visa—on the slight chance he would attempt to follow her.

They assured her they would not. Anyway, Heinz had no money; she felt he would not leave Bern. In time, she thought, he would come to accept what had to be.

Amy Jager came home to her family. She couldn't find a teaching job in Washington in the middle of the school year so she obtained a position as a secretary. She took back her maiden name and made preparations for filing for divorce. After a few weeks, she began to smile again. She was only twenty-seven; her life wasn't over, and there could be better days and years ahead. Letters to friends showed that she was once more becoming the optimist she had been before her marriage.

She had seen the love of her life turn into ashes, but she did not burden those around her with her sorrow. She was determined to go on with her life.

On May 11, 1976, the doorbell rang at Amy's family home. It had been only a month since she'd left Switzerland, and she'd assured her relatives that Heinz wouldn't be able to get a visa to follow her.

But he had. They were shocked to find Heinz Jager standing there. Somehow, some way, he had obtained a visa and enough money to fly to Seattle.

He had come, he said, to convince Amelia that they should continue their marriage. They were meant to be together, and Heinz was insistent that Amelia would understand that if he just had a chance to talk with her alone.

They feared him and the chaos he might cause, but he wouldn't leave, and it took a call to local police to persuade him that he could not stay with Amy's family. They found him a motel room, paid for it, and waited anxiously to see what he would do next. They didn't want to see him on the street, and they felt compassion toward him. They also felt apprehensive.

They were a gentle family and could not understand this man who had flown halfway around the world to seize the woman he had married and take her away again.

Amy understood him, though, and she was very afraid.

On May 18, Amy wrote to Senator Henry Jackson and demanded to know why Heinz had been given a visa to America. She said it would not expire until June 21, more than a month away. In the meantime, she and her family felt like hostages to a madman. She asked that he never be given a future visa.

What Amy didn't know was that Heinz Jager had no intention of leaving America—ever. He had disposed of all his possessions in Switzerland and arrived with the few belongings he had left, only his skis and some clothes.

He had a knife, too, but the family didn't know about that. The year 1976 was long before airport security teams made thorough checks for weapons in luggage.

As they waited out what they thought would be thirty-three days, Amy's family guarded her, shepherding her to work and protecting her in their home at night. They tried to be as gracious to Jager as they could, taking him on a well-chaperoned sightseeing trip to the mountains of Washington. Because they were kind, they hoped that Heinz would have good memories of his last visit to see his about-to-be-ex-wife and leave them alone once he was back in Switzerland.

Heinz made no preparations to leave the United States. He seemed to have no plans beyond the day.

After a few weeks, Heinz said he was going to California to visit a friend. He seemed calmer, and the family dared to hope that he would return to Europe and leave Amy alone. His friend in California welcomed Jager and assumed that he was accepting the fact that his marriage was over. He encouraged Heinz to make a new start.

But Jager had plans. He returned to Seattle on June 5, a Saturday, and surprised Amy's sister Jill at work. He said he'd just arrived by bus from California and needed a place to stay. Jill arranged for him to go to the YMCA and surreptitiously listened on a phone extension as he placed a call to Amy.

She heard Amy explain to Heinz that she had purchased a plane ticket for him and made reservations for him to fly out of Sea-Tac Airport the next day. His destination would be his home in Switzerland.

Jill was at a disadvantage because she could not understand the language Heinz spoke as he talked to Amy. But she could discern easily that he was angry and upset. Still, he left to stay at the Y without commenting to Jill about his phone call with Amy.

Amy and her family spent the night with ambivalent feelings—anxiety mixed with relief that Jager's visit was almost over. They agreed that Amy, Jill, and the girls' brother, who was a golf pro at a local country club, would all go to the airport with Jager. That should prevent a terribly emotional good-bye. Even so, Amy's brother—who had never owned a gun in his life—was worried; he arranged to borrow a small handgun, a .32 automatic, and placed it under the driver's seat of the family's green 1973 Fiat station wagon just in case, although he prayed he would have no reason to use it.

Heinz's moods were like clouds sweeping across the Alps. Amy had explained to her family that he was always like this—sunny, cloudy, stormy, calm, bleak, and back to sunny again. She herself had come to a point where she didn't really know who he was, but the doctors in Switzerland had diagnosed him as bipolar and manic-depressive.

Sunday morning, June 6, dawned bright and clear. By 8:30 a.m., the green Fiat, loaded down with Jager's skis and belongings, stopped to pick up Jill for the trip to Sea-Tac Airport fifteen miles south of Seattle. Amy sat in front next to her brother, and Jill climbed in the backseat with Heinz. She could see that he was very upset and had been crying. As they backed out of the driveway, he continued to plead with Amy, saying that he could not go back without her or everything would go "kaput."

That word Jill understood and it frightened her.

Heinz asked Amy to switch places with Jill and come sit in the back with him, but she refused, giving him one excuse after another. They didn't have time to stop and change seats because they'd left a little late. As they neared the airport, Heinz became more and more agitated.

Sea-Tac Airport is a huge complex that sprawls over

hundreds and hundreds of acres in the South King County area. With its shops and restaurants, and with the thousands of travelers who pass through its gates every day, it is a small city in itself. The Port of Seattle Police Department had ninety-six officers in 1976 and was the fourth-largest municipal police department in the state of Washington. It was the law enforcement agency responsible not only for the airport but also for the shipping docks along Puget Sound and Elliott Bay. Then headed by Chief Neil Moloney, onetime assistant chief of the Seattle Police Department, the Port of Seattle Police Department was kept busy with cases much like those of any big-city police department: burglaries, forgeries, stolen cars, narcotics, sex crimes.

Even in the midseventies, the Port of Seattle Police Department didn't handle the minimal airport security that existed then; that was the province of private airport security firms hired by the airlines, although, in case of trouble, Port of Seattle officers assisted.

The role of police officers at Sea-Tac had evolved from what had once been essentially "tour guides" to full-time law enforcement work. Homicide, however, wasn't something anyone expected to encounter in the airport.

On this Sunday morning in early June, the airport was alive with travelers and airline personnel, and every few minutes or so a huge jet taxied down one of the runways and took off for Portland, Los Angeles, Honolulu, Juneau, Denver, Chicago, Houston, Atlanta, and other hubs of the major airlines.

At the passenger drop-off area just in front of the revolving doors to the Northwest Airlines ticket counter,

Amy's brother maneuvered carefully into a spot next to the curb. He pulled on his parking brake, grabbed one of Heinz's bags and his skis, and headed into the airport. Annoyingly, Heinz followed him, snatched his bag back, and took it to the car, placing it just inside the open tailgate window.

The two sisters had quickly exited the Fiat and remained outside the car. Amy looked beautiful, clad in light slacks, a sheer blouse tied at the midriff, and platform sandals, with her dark chestnut hair flowing over her shoulders. Jill wore a similar outfit. Both young women were nervous but were determined to carry off the good-byes with a minimum of emotion.

Frustrated by all of Heinz's delaying tactics, Amy's brother discovered to his chagrin that he had been successful in making them arrive too late to board his scheduled flight to London.

The jet's doors were closed, the steps rolled away, and it was already taxiing out toward the runway. The ticket agent explained firmly that they could not call it back at this point.

Amy's brother stepped to another desk to try to get Heinz on one of the next flights that would end up in Switzerland. There would probably be several hours' wait, and he worried that his determined brother-in-law might leave the airport and make his way back to their home, looking for Amy. He didn't want that to happen. If need be, he would wait at the airport with Heinz, after sending his sisters someplace safe.

*   *   *

At two minutes after 9:00 a.m., the dispatch switchboard in the Port of Seattle Police headquarters at the airport began to light up. The first call came from a maintenance man who said someone had yelled, "Help! Attempted murder!" The man was so excited that he failed to give a location.

One minute later, a Northwest Airlines ticket agent called the radio dispatcher to say that there was "a fire" right in front of the building and requested an ambulance.

The profusion of calls tumbled one after the other—all requesting either an aid team or an ambulance to respond to the area just outside the Northwest Airlines entrance.

The dispatcher requested that Sergeant L. L. Quein and officers J. E. Baertschiger and D. G. Krows respond to the scene of a "possible fire." They arrived in two minutes, expecting to find a car fire. There was no smoke visible, or even flames. Instead, they saw two men struggling to pin a third man to the pavement in the middle of the five-lane passenger loading road. One of the men said that the subject on the ground had just "stabbed someone."

The tall, bearded man on the ground was still struggling as the officers separated the tangle of arms and legs. He wore a light jacket, soaked with bright red fluid, and they recognized the metallic smell of blood. He did not appear to understand English, and he didn't stop fighting them until the officers had handcuffed him.

Officer Krows looked toward the railing near the curb. He gasped as he saw a pretty young woman sitting there, half doubled over, holding her abdomen. Her breasts and midsection were stained crimson. Nearby, a taller woman held tight to her own left hand, which Krows saw was almost cut in two.

It was difficult to take it all in—they had come to fight a fire and instead found two terribly injured young women and a battling foreigner who seemed unable to understand what they said to him.

The bearded man, whom many bystanders insisted was the attacker, was taken to a holding cell. The officers on the scene were given a large bloodstained Buck knife by Sergeant Quein, which they bagged into evidence.

There was no time to find out just what had happened; the witnesses assured the officers they would wait in the squad room until the victims had been rushed to the hospital.

Baertschiger and Krows rode with the ambulance carrying Amy and Jill. Valley General Hospital in nearby Kent had already been alerted that a red-blanket case was coming in, and Jill ignored her own wounds to try to comfort her sister. The ambulance crew administered lactated Ringer's solution to Amy to keep her veins open, but they silently shook their heads. She had no blood pressure and a fluttering rapid pulse. Her pupils were already beginning to dilate.

By the time Amy Jager arrived at the emergency room, she was in severe shock, near death, and she no longer had any pulse at all. She was breathing only in sporadic gasps. She had no heart sounds. ER doctors inserted an airway and tried everything in their power to bring Amy back, but their efforts were in vain.

Five minutes later, Amelia Jager was pronounced dead at the age of twenty-seven.

Jill, who was left-handed, had suffered lacerated tendons in that hand. Her cuts were so deep that she could not flex her fingers. She would require extensive surgery to try to bring her hand back to any kind of normal functioning.

The Port of Seattle Police Department had four detectives, and Detective Sergeant Dave Hart was on call that Sunday morning. Hart, who retired as a lieutenant from the Seattle Police Department to join the Washington State Patrol Drug Control Assistance Unit, came to Chief Moloney's department with a wealth of experience. Now he would try to piece together the events leading to the incredible stabbing that had left one woman dead and another terribly injured.

He talked to an airport shuttle driver who had seen a tall, bearded man struggling with Amy. Before this witness could react, the attacker had suddenly stepped behind the dark-haired woman and placed his left arm around her neck while he grasped a large knife in his right hand. Pulling her tightly against him as the shuttle driver watched, horrified, he had made a sweeping left-to-right movement across her stomach and the driver saw blood gushing out. The driver had leaped from the bus and called for help on his walkie-talkie as he raced to stop the awful struggle. By the time he reached them, the woman was down on the pavement, while the man still held her around the neck.

"He was kneeling, still trying to hurt her," the driver recalled. "I jumped on his back but I couldn't get a good grip. I grabbed his left arm and we both fell backward. I pinned his left arm and pinioned his legs with mine. Then a soldier ran out to help us and he started choking the guy. Both of us together couldn't get him off her."

Heinz Jager had continued to fight them, and the soldier had growled, "Knock it off!"

There had been no lack of good Samaritans trying to save Amy Jager. The soldier was Sergeant John Dimsdale of North Carolina, who had been sitting inside with Sergeant Leonard Tatum of Georgia. Dimsdale told Dave Hart that he had watched the silent tableau through the window.

The women standing there were both pretty, both dressed in slacks and light blouses. "I saw the man try to kiss the smaller woman, and she stepped back away from him.

"He grabbed her by the shoulders and pushed her toward the car. The other woman came to help and both women tried to push him away. He hit the little one with the flat of his hand. When I rushed out, I saw the knife had blood on it. The shuttle driver ran to help and I grabbed the guy's throat and held him till the police came."

Sergeant Tatum had somehow managed to extricate Amy from the struggle and had led her to the sidewalk. She could walk at that point, but he'd seen the blood just above her navel and between her breasts.

"Another guy grabbed the knife," Tatum said, "and threw it out into the middle of the road."

Amy's brother told Dave Hart of his sister's attempt to escape her life with her jealous husband.

"We all went to the airport to protect Amy. Heinz was talking to her in French. He was crying and pleading with Amy, grabbing her by the shoulders and begging her to go with him, saying he couldn't live without her.

"I was afraid to leave Amy with him near the car but there were so many people around that I chanced it."

He had made what seemed to be the best decision, and

he agonized that he hadn't stayed with his sister to protect her. But he was trying to get Jager on another plane and out of their lives for good. Suddenly, he'd heard the screams and had run out to see Amy and Jill and Heinz grappling on the pavement.

"Amy was on her back and Heinz was choking her while she tried to pull his hands away. I helped the others to pry Jager's hands off Amy's neck."

Heinz had seemed to have the strength of three men. Crazy strength, as he was determined to destroy Amy if she wouldn't go with him.

Finally, Amy and Jill had been helped to their feet and walked over to the curb, where passersby tried to comfort them. He was unaware that his sisters were grievously injured.

"I talked to Amy but she didn't respond, although her eyes were open."

Dave Hart interviewed Jill at Valley General Hospital as she awaited surgery. The brave woman knew Amy was dead, but she had tried with all her might to save her. She told Hart that, as soon as their brother was inside, Jager had tried to drag Amy back into the car. He had reached into the bag he had grabbed from their brother.

"He pulled out a long silver knife. He knew exactly where it was. He was sort of standing alongside Amy and holding her with one hand. He stabbed her in the stomach. We both started to scream. I grabbed for the knife with my left hand and held on as hard as I could. He moved the knife back and forth to get it out of my grasp—"

Jill had clamped her bare hand around the razor-sharp blade to try to save Amy, and Jager had deliberately sliced the tendons in her hand in his frenzy to kill the woman he professed to love.

Detective Dave Hart found the red zipper bag in the back of the Fiat wagon. A black leather knife sheath stood upright in the bag. Jager had only to reach in and pull out the knife. He had to have planned that ahead of time, a last-ditch effort if his pleading didn't convince Amy to leave with him.

Booked into the King County Jail, Heinz Jager was provided with interpreters from the Seattle Language Bank to inform him once again of his Miranda rights and to ask him questions. He refused to talk to the police or anyone else—he said his attorney was in Switzerland. He whined, however, that he'd been injured by the bystanders who had pulled him off of his dying wife and complained that the jail doctors would not treat his injuries properly.

In truth, Jager had been taken to a hospital for treatment of his scratches and bruises, which were minor. He insisted that he wasn't satisfied with the treatment he'd received and complained, "Someone kicked me in the ribs at the airport." He also said that he was hungry and hadn't been given anything to eat.

When he was asked about Amy, he said, "*Who* is dead? Is she dead? I don't know if she is dead. I had the knife in my hand. I stabbed blindly. I don't know how many times. I was blind with rage. I took my knife and hit her many times. Is my wife dead?"

Amy was, of course, dead. And Jill was undergoing four hours of surgery to repair her injured hand. Their whole family was in despair because all of their efforts to protect their beloved Amy had failed.

Amy Jager's autopsy showed that she had suffered eight stab wounds, one of which had perforated her liver and left lung. She had died from massive internal bleeding. For all intents and purposes, the slender teacher who had flown across the world to save herself from just such a fate was dead from the moment of the first vicious knife thrust. Even if paramedics had been there seconds later, they probably couldn't have saved her from bleeding to death.

After examining Heinz Jager, psychiatrists declared him mentally fit to stand trial. His trial began in late October 1976. Doug Whalley and Janet George, deputy King County prosecutors, would speak for the State; Carl Hultman, the public defender, would represent Jager.

Through an interpreter, Jager was made fully aware of all the testimony given.

Hultman pointed out that Jager had had a disturbed childhood; that he had been abused and had a history of mental problems. He claimed that Jager was abnormal at times and couldn't stand stressful situations created by problems with women.

The handsome Swiss had once told a psychiatrist that his wife was his possession, that she belonged to him, and that if he could not have her, no one else ever would either.

Defense attorney Hultman explained to the eight-man, four-woman jury that his client was totally dependent upon maintaining the relationships he had started with women.

There was no argument about his obsessions. Hultman said that Jager always behaved strangely when he feared those relationships were threatened.

There was no question that he was a stalker, following his love object, spying, and then falsely accusing the woman of being unfaithful until the relationship fell apart.

His first marriage had ended in divorce; he could not face another parting.

But was that an adequate defense for murder?

Prosecutors Whalley and George did not dispute that Heinz Jager was mentally ill; what they did dispute was that he was insane to the degree that he was not responsible for his actions when Amy was killed. Under the M'Naughton Rule, the accused must know the difference between right and wrong at the time of his crime. But it's almost impossible to determine what state of mind someone was in at a particular time. Jager had clearly placed the knife in his bag where he could grab it. He had wrestled that bag out of Amy's brother's hand and carried it back to the open rear window.

The prosecutors called Jager's California friend as a witness. He testified that the defendant had seemed sane and rational during his visit just prior to the killing. The State called psychiatrists, who pointed out that Jager had not only prepared for the killing by placing the Buck knife where he had easy access to it but also had acted with complete rationality after the killing, mostly complaining about his own pain and the way he was being treated.

Prosecutor Janet George was particularly adept at questioning the psychiatric experts. In addition to her law degree, she had a master's degree in public health and once taught psychiatric nursing at the University of Washington. Intrigued by the interaction between the law and mental health, she left nursing to study law. She was no neophyte as she led the professional witnesses through the finer points of madness.

Insanity is a handy plea for a murder defendant because the mass of humanity does not think something as violent as killing another person is the act of a sane person. Even so, the insanity defense rarely convinces a jury.

To kill what one cannot have, just to prevent the victim from ever having another relationship, is an act of consummate selfishness and of inexplicable brutality.

The photographs of the mortally wounded Amy Jager sickened the jury.

The fact that Amy had truly loved Heinz Jager with single-minded devotion disturbed them.

They understood that Amy had done everything in her power to hold the fledgling marriage together. Her loyalty to the defendant permeated the case. The man at the defense table had had the whole world in his grasp, and he had destroyed it with his green-eyed ravings. When he lost it, he hadn't rested until he destroyed Amy, too.

On November 4, the jury began its deliberations. Although the defense held that Heinz Jager was insane, the jurors kept returning to one point: The knife was there. It wasn't buried deep in his luggage. The knife was ready. Jager had held it out as his last method of keeping Amy with him. And he had used it cruelly—again, again, and again.

At 11:30 p.m. on that very first night of deliberation, the

jury signaled that it was ready with a verdict. They found Heinz Jager guilty as charged.

A sad Christmas passed. On January 10, 1977, King County Superior Court Judge Earl Horswill sentenced Heinz Jager to a term of up to life in prison. Under Washington statute at the time, he had to serve a minimum sentence of thirteen years, four months—*plus* five more years for the use of a deadly weapon in committing his crime—before he became eligible for parole.

He could have been released from prison in about 1996, but my research has failed to find him. He may have returned to Switzerland, either by choice or by deportation. Now Heinz Jager would be close to seventy—if he is alive—no longer the silver-tongued and attractive Swiss who could lure and then terrorize hapless women who had the great misfortune to fall in love with him.

There is one piece of the puzzle still unexplained. Perhaps it is a warning that Amy Jager failed to heed, a warning that this man she was about to marry was not all he seemed to be. Perhaps it was only a lovers' pledge that they would live and die together. It is a short note, found among Jager's possessions, dated August 5, 1975, and signed by Amy. Amy cannot say what she meant and Heinz would not discuss it.

Two months after she wrote it, Amy married Heinz, so she probably was more in love than she was afraid.

Or was she living in terror even then? I will always wonder if Heinz forced her to write it and also forced her to marry him.

In effect, Amy had written her own epitaph:

> *I will rest in Switzerland the rest of my life, under-*
> *ground, if I don't write this letter, with Heinz Jager.*
> *Amy*

But Amelia Jager does not rest in Switzerland. She was able to come home to rest in her own country, and in the hearts and memories of her beloved family.

THIRTY YEARS
LATER

> Where there is no vision, the people perish.
> But he that keepeth the law—
> Happy is he.
>
> —Proverbs 29:18

I cannot count how many times I stepped over this bronze plaque set in concrete just outside the east entrance to the Seattle Public Safety Building (police HQ) as I researched hundreds of homicide cases to write about. Unconsciously, it imprinted its adage on my brain, just like the poem I memorized—and then forgot when it counted—for my third-grade play. I remember that, too.

Over the thirty-plus years I've been writing true crime, I've come across a few homicide cases that I never expected to see solved. Most of these were committed by serial killers whose crimes almost always evolve from stranger-to-stranger encounters. Two people who have never met before cross paths, a tragedy occurs, and the one who is left behind can no longer tell what happened. The other disappears, leaving precious few clues.

Unless a fingerprint is on file with AFIS (Automated Fingerprint Identification System) computers, or there is a known suspect, there is no way to link it to anyone. Today DNA evidence can usually be absolutely matched, but before the 1990s, body fluids and hair follicles were only rarely preserved because no one knew everything that DNA could tell us then. But DNA can sometimes be found even on decades-old evidence, a propitious accident.

The cases I've hoped to see successfully closed tend to be those most difficult to unravel. Families are left to mourn but have no answers about why someone they loved very much was killed, and they may never know who the murderer was. It is galling to think of a brutal killer having the last laugh on detectives. But it happens.

The following cases are true, of course, but they surprised at least two generations of detectives who passed through their assignment to the Crimes Against Persons Unit of the Seattle Police Department. And it certainly surprised me. Many of the detectives retired with a sense of frustration that they hadn't been able to find out more about the second murder, and, worse, that they had never located the person who killed the first victim.

Usually, there are patterns of behavior and similarities in victim types that help investigators connect a suspect to different crimes. But not this time.

I could never have imagined the denouement that came after three decades and made headlines in 2008.

Unless we live in sprawling apartment complexes or thick-walled condos, most of us think we know our neighbors pretty well. But can we ever be sure? If we were truly able to see inside the convoluted pathways of someone else's brain, to know all there is to know about his or her inner life, his or her *real* life, we might realize how mistaken our first perceptions were.

Julie Costello was one of those people who lived a secret life far removed from her origins: the attractive young woman's very name wasn't even her own. If a predator hadn't ended the world she'd built for herself, her carefully constructed masquerade might never have been revealed. She wasn't a wanted felon or a fugitive. Not really. She'd harmed no one: She did only what she felt she had to, and her life was happy until a tragic encounter on a warm September night.

Julie Costello had the great misfortune to be in the wrong place at the wrong time, and, because she *was* there, she became prey to a killer.

She wasn't really Julie Costello at all, but her abductor didn't know that, nor did the detectives who carried out the investigation into her fate know—at least, not for a long time.

The twenty-three-year-old blond woman's Seattle acquaintances knew her as Julie Costello. She worked as a clerk at a 7-Eleven on Beacon Hill, one of Seattle's oldest neighborhoods, where families of myriad ethnic heritages live—usually in harmony.

Julie worked the graveyard shift, alone, from 11:00 p.m. until 6:00 a.m. Clerking in a small neighborhood wasn't considered very dangerous, but that all changed with the advent of stores that were open around the clock. 7-Elevens and other chains open twenty-four hours soon became tempting targets for armed robbers. Since they are usually the only businesses open in the wee hours of the morning, and they usually have a lone clerk on duty, robbers find them vulnerable and easy targets.

The corporation that owns the 7-Eleven where Julie Costello worked has taken steps to avert attacks on their clerks. I don't want to lay out a blueprint of security systems for those plotting to steal from all-night markets. I will say only that those steps have proved very effective.

Julie took the bus to work from her apartment on Capitol Hill, and it was full dark at 11:00 p.m. when she began her shift. During the winter months, the sun didn't rise until hours after she headed for home. She wasn't afraid. She was, at heart, an adventuress, and she had been in any number of situations more perilous than traveling across the city in the hours of darkness or working alone all night when most people were asleep. She knew a lot of her customers, and the police patrolmen working Beacon Hill during Third Watch often stopped in for coffee.

But on Monday morning, September 25, 1978, none of the security measures helped Julie. When the store manager, Rita Longaard,* arrived to relieve her shortly after 6:00 a.m., she was startled to find the front door locked, the lights out, and no one on the premises. The store was supposed to be open, and Julie should have been on duty.

Because the store was never empty, the changing of the guard didn't necessitate having a key. Rita Longaard hadn't brought one with her, so she went first to the home of her assistant manager to see if she knew anything about what was going on. She didn't.

The two women drove to Julie's home on Capitol Hill. Maybe she'd gotten sick during the night and just locked up and gone home. That wasn't like her; she was very dependable and would have called one of them, but they avoided talking about what might have happened.

Rita had been puzzled at first, and then a little angry with Julie, but now she was alarmed. There was no answer to their knocks on her apartment door.

There was nothing left to do but go back to the store and call a locksmith to open the front door. When they gained entrance, the women switched on the lights and carefully walked up and down the aisles. They were all empty. The only sound was the buzzing of the neon lights. At the checkout counter, they found that the cash register's drawers were open—and empty.

Yet when they walked toward the back of the store, they found an envelope stuffed with cash on a counter. That was where it was usually left while clerks worked the combination on the lock of the floor safe, preparing to deposit their shift's receipts into it. Why hadn't Julie finished hiding the money in the safe?

The safe hadn't been tampered with. As the two women moved nervously into the back storeroom, they saw Julie's purse in the spot where she always left it during work hours. Everything was basically normal.

Except that Julie was missing.

Rita Longaard checked the hidden surveillance camera. If clerks were concerned, they could trigger it surreptitiously. In the event of a robbery, the thieves' photos would show up on the film. Rita wasn't positive, but she thought the camera had been activated.

She called 911.

Detective J. D. "Jimmy" Nicholson arrived first. Nicholson's special area of expertise was security cameras. They had proved invaluable to police in store and bank robberies. He verified that the camera had indeed been set off, and he retrieved the film and marked it carefully for evidence. If something had gone wrong during the night, the investigators might just be fortunate enough to find it recorded on film.

Lieutenant Robert Holter, commander of the Robbery Unit, and his detectives—Sergeant Joe Sanford, Larry Stewart, and Jerry Trettevik—arrived shortly after Nicholson. It appeared that they were dealing with a possible robbery-kidnapping. The investigators glanced around the store. Nothing was out of place or knocked over. There were no signs of a fight, no blood spots anywhere. Either Julie Costello was somehow involved in the theft from the cash register, or she'd been frightened enough that an intruder hadn't had to subdue her to get her out of the store.

Two bags of salted sunflower seeds were lying on the counter. They were wrapped in cellophane, and that was a good surface for fingerprints. The detectives also took Julie Costello's brown leather purse.

Larry Stewart rushed the film from the camera to the photo lab for immediate processing.

Bob Holter and Jimmy Nicholson drove to Julie's apartment, but they didn't find anyone home either. A neighbor told them that Julie's live-in boyfriend, Jack Atkins,* worked at a restaurant nearby. "It's right across from Group Health Hospital," the woman said. "The one that serves foreign food—and [has] a really good bakery. The docs from Group Health eat there often."

The two detectives found Atkins at work. He seemed as mystified as everyone else that Julie was missing. He was also very worried.

"I walked her to the bus stop last night about ten—I always do—and saw her off to work. I haven't heard from her since, but then I haven't expected to. Sometimes, we're like ships passing in the night. I usually leave for my job before she gets home from the store in the morning."

"Was Julie afraid of anyone?" Holter asked. "Had she said anything to you about trouble at work?"

"Yeah," Jack Atkins said, after thinking about it. "There's some teenager who's been pestering her. He's a big kid, she said, and he's been coming into the store. I think he has a crush on her, because he keeps slipping her notes. I've got one of them here."

Holter and Nicholson took the note, carefully preserving it for fingerprint testing. It appeared to be a simple, badly spelled love note. It was signed "Bubba."

The investigators asked Rita Longaard if she knew of a teenager named Bubba who had been bothering Julie.

"Oh, Bubba," Rita said, rolling her eyes. "Yes. I've had to kick him out of the store for bothering clerks. He's only sixteen, and his name is Bubba Baker.* He has the biggest crush on Julie."

Rita described Bubba as over six feet tall and weighing about 250. He was a light-skinned black teenager who was really more of a lovesick nuisance than anyone they'd been afraid of.

A check of juvenile records showed that a Bradford "Bubba" Baker lived about five blocks from the 7-Eleven. He had a short juvenile rap sheet for minor offenses but nothing violent. At this point in the probe, he seemed the most likely suspect in Julie's disappearance. But that was because he was the *only* suspect.

Patrol officers from the Georgetown Precinct were sent out to canvass the neighborhood surrounding the store in the hope that they might turn up witnesses to any unusual events during the night of September 24–25.

They didn't find anyone who had heard screams, shouts, or cars gunning their motors. Nothing. Whatever had happened had been silent and swift.

Julie was still missing the next afternoon when Jack Atkins came to headquarters to give a complete statement to the detectives.

Jack had some startling admissions of his own. Detective Maury Erickson was astounded when Atkins told him that he'd lied about being twenty-one.

"I'm really only fifteen," he admitted.

That was hard to believe, but Erickson waited for Jack to say more.

Jack Atkins said he was a native of Philadelphia, and he'd been raised there. "But I've been 'on the road' for more than a year now."

Jack was short and wiry, and he might possibly have been any age between fifteen and twenty-two, but when the detectives stared at him more closely, and looked at his *true* ID, they realized he probably *was* only fifteen. Still, he had an adult, responsible mien about him. At the moment, he was very concerned about his missing girlfriend.

"I have thought and thought about it," he said, "and I've decided that I have to tell you the complete truth about Julie."

Was he about to confess? It sounded like it, but they couldn't read the emotion on his face. He had tears in his eyes. They didn't know if these were guilty tears or worried tears.

They waited.

"I met Julie at the Carpinteria State Beach in California— it's between Ventura and Santa Barbara."

"When did you hook up with her?" Erickson asked.

"It was on July 28, 1977, more than a year ago," Jack said. "And her name isn't really Julie Costello; it's Laura Baylis."

The robbery detectives realized that this case was getting more and more complicated.

"Laura's from England," Jack continued, "and there was something about her passport or her visa running out, so she had to get some different ID so the authorities wouldn't send her back. And so she took the Julie name."

As unlikely a liaison as it might seem, Laura and Jack had found that they shared a love for travel, and they soon shared a love for each other—despite the eight-year difference in their ages.

"We teamed up on the beach in California and we began to see the country," Jack said. "We went to Springfield, Missouri, in the beginning of September 1977, and we stayed there until New Year's Day. She worked at a café and I worked for a wrecking company while we were in Missouri. Laura became pretty good friends with a girl named Julie Costello at the restaurant, and Julie gave Laura some of her ID papers so Laura wouldn't have to get deported."

Jack said he had lied to Laura's Missouri employers, telling them that she had run off with another man and left him. Then he had met her at a prearranged spot, and they'd left Springfield together.

"We hitchhiked to Kansas City and stayed there until May 1978. From Kansas, we went to New England, and then Wyoming, and then we went back to California again."

Jack Atkins said they had enjoyed hiking in each state's mountains, and they'd had enough money because they took odd jobs. They shared their finances and always had enough for food and a place to stay if the weather made it impossible to camp out.

Jack said his parents knew he was with Laura. "They figured she was dependable and they knew they couldn't stop my wanderlust. They felt like she was taking good care of me—but it was mutual. We make a good team—"

"When did you get to Seattle?" Erickson asked.

"August tenth, this year. We both got jobs, rented our apartment, and we opened up a joint savings account. We have about three hundred and fifty dollars saved in the bank."

"You two ever have arguments?" Erickson asked.

The youth shook his head. "Not really. Oh, sometimes about money. We've decided to get separate checking accounts, so if either of us wants to buy something, we can use our own money. We thought that might be more fair."

"Do you feel"—Maury Erickson chose his words as tactfully as he could—"that maybe Laura might have just gotten tired of the situation and left?"

"Not Laura. She's very responsible, and she would never leave me like this. We really get along."

The detectives exchanged glances. Jack Atkins was very earnest and sure of Laura/Julie's love for him, but they knew there was always the chance that a fifteen-year-old boy was simply naïve. Laura could have met a man her own age. They could have robbed her store and simply taken off together.

It was obvious that Jack Atkins didn't know that much about Laura's background before they'd joined up to hitch-hike across the country fourteen months earlier.

He knew that Laura had relatives in England, and perhaps in Missouri, but he didn't know any of their addresses. The peripatetic couple had lived in the moment, and he'd never asked Laura for specific names and addresses of her family.

"What was Laura wearing when you walked her to the bus Sunday night?"

He answered quickly. "Tight blue Bullitt jeans, a blue parka with a red lining, reddish-brown shoes—kind of like earth shoes—two thin gold necklaces. One was plain, and one had a small star, and she has pierced ears with small gold loop earrings."

Nothing that Jack Atkins was saying served to explain why Laura Baylis might suddenly have decided to clean out the cash register where she worked and run away. Rather, everyone they had talked to said that Laura was a very stable young woman.

Although he was only fifteen, Jack seemed older, and he clearly loved the missing woman. And she seemed to have loved him. The detectives could not see him as a viable suspect. Nor could they picture her as a thief.

Besides, if Laura had decided to cut and run, taking the money from the cash register, why hadn't she taken the envelope full of large-denomination bills from the back shelf? There was a lot more in there than in the till. (Rita Longaard said that they were all trained to periodically take the "big money" out of the till and put it in a safe place.)

No, Lieutenant Bob Holter and his crew felt that something had happened to Laura. She hadn't come back to her young lover because she *couldn't* come back.

Neither Laura nor Jack had a record of felonies in any state; their only contact with police had been two stops for hitchhiking in states where it was forbidden.

Jack Atkins said he didn't know anything about Laura's reasons for leaving her home in England. "We don't talk about the past," he said softly. "We are our relationship. Our relationship is now."

The robbery detectives didn't have the heart to remind him that "now" might be gone forever.

Jack pulled out a picture of Laura Baylis. It showed a pretty girl with large blue eyes, a shy smile, and masses of curly blond hair.

The detectives had seen her before. They'd gone over the film from the security camera in the 7-Eleven with a magnifying glass. This was the same girl they had seen in those photos.

But, in those pictures, Laura wasn't alone. Laura, dressed in blue jeans and a navy blue shirt, was at the cash register, and she held a brown paper bag in her left hand. Her expression was deadly serious.

There was a man in the later photos. He was a tall black male dressed in an olive green jacket, and he wore a blue billed cap and glasses. As the film frames moved forward, the man appeared from the back and from the side—as if he were glancing around to see if anyone was approaching. He had a mustache and a scraggly beard. It was impossible to tell if they were real or stuck on with spirit gum.

If he held a weapon, it was hidden.

"Is that Laura in the picture?" Larry Stewart asked Jack Atkins.

"Yes. I think it's her," Jack said, his voice trembling. "It's not real clear—but it has to be her."

The bags of sunflower seeds were on the counter in the picture, but there was also a small bottle of orange juice. The bottle had been gone when police arrived.

The man in the picture was clearly not Bubba Baker. He

was older and bigger. Holter and his men felt a chill as they perused those pictures. They sensed that they might be seeing Laura Baylis during the last few moments of her life. The pictures flipped rapidly as the mindless camera had clicked every few seconds, until they became *almost* "moving pictures."

The men watching experienced an eerie feeling, as if what they were seeing was happening in the present, right in front of them. They watched Laura Baylis as she obeyed the man standing behind her. She had obviously cooperated with him and given him the money in the cash register.

But where was she now?

The detectives took on the tedious task of searching through 911 calls for Sunday night. Buried in hundreds of calls, they found a brief report of trouble at the Beacon Hill 7-Eleven at 11:30 p.m. But it wasn't Laura Baylis who had made the call; the clerk who worked the shift just before hers had called Seattle Police to report a shoplifter. The thief wasn't a tall black male. Not at all. It was a teenage girl who'd tried to make off with a large jug of wine.

Detectives Al "Beans" Lima and Myrle Carner interviewed the clerk in the shoplifting incident. That had been fairly routine, but she was still in shock over Julie/Laura's disappearance and tried to remember anything that might help the detectives.

"Julie came in for work at eleven p.m. She wore blue jeans, blue shirt, her blue ski parka. Everything was normal," the clerk said. "She was in a good mood. She almost always was. All I know about her was that she lived with Jack, and she traveled back and forth between England and the U.S."

Eventually, the Seattle detectives would talk to all of the missing woman's coworkers. Of course, they all knew Laura Baylis as Julie Costello. They were aware that Bubba Baker had been annoying her, but they'd felt she could handle him.

"He's a little off upstairs," the four-to-eleven checker said. "But he's more inclined to shoplift and get goofy crushes on the younger girls here. I've never thought of him as capable of harming anyone."

Bob Holter's team tried to pinpoint just when the robbery had occurred. The liquor cabinets were supposed to be locked, by Washington State law, at 2:00 a.m. They had been locked when Rita Longaard arrived. The store's two clocks had been stopped at between 3:40 a.m. and 4:13 a.m. They were electric clocks and they had stopped because someone had tripped the sixteen-circuit breaker.

It would appear that Laura Baylis had been taken from the 7-Eleven around 4:00 a.m. Myrle Carner and Al Lima dusted the circuit breaker box for prints, then removed the clocks to put them into evidence. Although they carefully searched the alley behind the store, they didn't come across anything that seemed to have evidentiary value.

Patrol officers, who continued to canvass the neighborhood, finally came up with a possible witness. A woman who lived just across the street from the 7-Eleven said she had gotten up in the night to use the bathroom, and she'd seen all the store's lights go off sometime between 2:00 and 4:00 a.m.

She was shown the suspect from the security camera, but she didn't recognize him as anyone she'd ever seen before. Disappointingly, none of the other neighboring residents recognized him either.

Jerry Trettevik talked to Bubba Baker's mother, who said that her son did have a "mental problem." Bubba himself was eager to talk to the detective. He admitted that he'd been in the store on Sunday night.

"But I left at one fifteen a.m.," he said.

"Were you there any other time that night?"

Bubba nodded. "I was in the store around eleven thirty p.m., just when Julie came to work. I saw a big, black man there. He was very dark-skinned—not like me."

Trettevik showed Bubba the hidden camera's pictures, and Bubba nodded his head vigorously.

"That's the man I seen at eleven thirty."

"Do you know him? Ever see him before?"

"No, sir. I never seen him before."

The canvassing and interviewing spread out, casting a wider net over the neighborhood. Myrle Carner and Al Lima talked to patrons in nearby taverns. They showed the photo of the man in the fatigue jacket and cap to customers at the Jolo Tavern. Some of the regulars said the man was "vaguely familiar," but no one could put a name to the face.

They had better luck at the 19th Hole tavern at South Columbia and Beacon. The female bartender there remembered that a husky black male had been in on September 24 at 11:00 p.m.

"He sat at the counter and ordered wine. I'd never seen

him before. He left but he came back about forty-five minutes later and bought a bottle of beer to take with him."

"What'd he look like? How was he dressed—beyond
the jacket?" Carner asked.

"He was about five feet eleven and weighed more than
two hundred pounds. I'd say he was maybe thirty-five.
Had a full mustache and a goatee."

Shown the photo, the woman nodded. "Yes. I'm positive that was the man who was here on the twenty-
fourth."

The stranger hadn't seemed nervous or angry or in a
hurry. He hadn't been back since that Sunday at midnight.

Now more witnesses were forthcoming. Another tavern
patron recalled a black man wearing a jeans jacket—but he
was with another man. "I had the impression that the two
men were together. The second guy wore a fatigue jacket
and a blue cap with a bill. He had a goatee, mustache,
glasses."

Carner showed him the security camera photos, and he
quickly identified the man shown. "He was the second man
that I saw here at the 19th Hole."

Larry Stewart and Jerry Trettevik received information from two patrol units that had worked First Watch on
Sunday–Monday. They had been dispatched to the 7-Eleven
on Beacon Hill at 4:00 a.m. Monday morning, shortly after
they'd begun their shift.

"It was a 'suspicious circumstances' call," one officer
said. "A passerby phoned it in. When we got there, the
store was dark, and we saw no activity in or around it. We
assumed that everything was all right. We figured they'd
just closed up early on Sunday night."

Detectives located the man who'd called the police. He said he and a friend had gone to the 7-Eleven a little before 4:00 a.m. to buy cigarettes and found nobody behind the counter and the lights mostly off.

"I walked in anyway, and this black guy wearing a green fatigue jacket and a cap came out of the back room to tell me the store was closed.

"I told him all I wanted was a couple of packs of cigarettes, and he grabbed them and gave them to me. He charged me a dollar a pack. When I got home, I got to thinking about it, and it seemed really strange. I called 911 and asked for somebody to go by and check it out."

Shown the photos, both the complainant and his friend agreed that the alleged robber was the man they had seen in the store—but they hadn't seen Laura Baylis at all.

"The guy kept his right hand in his pocket the whole time, and he was really nervous. He kept looking back at the back of the store. The big store sign was out then, but the store lights were still on."

Citizens were trying to help. They searched their memories for anything peculiar or disturbing that might have happened on Sunday night–Monday morning. A Beacon Hill resident called Trettevik and Stewart to say that he, too, had gone into the 7-Eleven between 3:00 and 4:00 a.m. "I picked up a couple of bags of sunflower seeds and put them on the counter. I looked around, but I didn't see anyone. Then this black guy came out from the back room and said the store was closed. I saw that the till was open and empty, so I left the seeds on the counter and walked out."

If Laura Baylis had been in the rear of the store—and

she certainly must have been—she was either too frightened to call for help, or bound and gagged—or unconscious. In the worst case scenario, she might have been dead. And yet detectives hadn't found one drop of blood in the place, not one indication of a struggle.

The robbery detectives wondered again if there was another side to Laura's personality. Was it possible that she'd been in cahoots with the man in the fatigue jacket?

No. They agreed that was impossible. She and Jack had been too happy, and all her acquaintances said she saw no one but him. She always went straight home from work.

Where was she?

Laura Baylis's picture appeared in all local papers, as did the picture of the unknown man in the cap and jacket. If someone out there knew more about the baffling case, no one called the police.

Jerry Trettevik and Larry Stewart went door-to-door in the area, trying to find someone who had seen something else that night, and they came up empty-handed.

Holter and his detectives tracked down the *real* Julie Costello in Missouri. She admitted that she given Laura Baylis some ID but said she hadn't heard from her since she'd left Kansas City.

Julie Costello said that Laura Baylis had a pattern of leaving cities precipitately—telling her friends and employers all kinds of stories about why she had to go. She had told Julie that she could never stay long enough in one spot before she worried that immigration authorities would check on her.

Julie knew very little about Laura's background, only

that she spoke with an English accent and that she had relatives in England.

Back in Seattle, Laura remained missing. The probe into her vanishing continued. Calls poured in from people who thought they recognized the man in the pictures.

Each name mentioned was checked out and eliminated.

Jack Atkins told Larry Stewart that if Laura had any friends in America whom she might contact, it would be a young man in Minneapolis. He had been a good friend of hers. Jack gave them Ben Calkins's* address and phone number, which he'd found in Laura's papers. Ben was living in a fraternity house. Stewart phoned the fraternity and found that Ben was currently in England and had been for several months. Next, he called Ben's family and spoke to his parents in Minnesota.

After Stewart explained the situation, Ben's mother said, "Yes, we know Laura, but Ben's lost track of her. She left some of her papers here. Would that help?"

It certainly was more than the detectives from the Robbery Unit had found so far. The woman mailed Laura's passport (in her real name) and various other documents to Stewart.

Her birth certificate indicated that Laura Anne Baylis had been born November 30, 1955. She had emigrated from Suffolk, England, to Canada in 1976. Her Canadian passport was valid until 1982, but it didn't allow her to cross U.S. borders or work in the United States.

Trettevik and Stewart asked an official of the Immigration and Naturalization Service for assistance in contacting Laura Baylis's parents. Special Agent Anthony Provenzo contacted offices in London and asked that the parents of the missing girl call the Seattle Police Department.

A short time later, the Seattle detectives received a call from Mrs. Bessie Baylis. The distraught mother confirmed what the detectives had feared: She had no idea where her daughter was, had had no word at all from her since Laura's last letter on September 15. At that time, her daughter had been happy and contented with her life in America.

"She didn't mention anything about planning to leave Seattle or Jack."

Laura Baylis's family was extremely concerned. They promised to do whatever they could to help in the mystery that continued to grow. Mrs. Baylis said she would look for any medical or dental records that might help to identify Laura. She knew that the American detectives meant *if her body was found*, but they were as kind as they could be and didn't spell it out. They even said that Laura might be suffering from amnesia, or that she might be headed for England.

Spokane detectives reported that they had found the body of a Jane Doe, but that victim turned out to be a sixteen-year-old local girl.

Weeks passed with no sign of Laura Baylis. And then, on October 14, her whereabouts were finally, tragically, discovered.

Alva Marsh,* who owned several properties in the neighborhood, stopped to check on a vacant house he owned in the 6300 block of Beacon Avenue. The run-down residence was located only a mile from the 7-Eleven where Laura Baylis vanished.

Marsh had been inside the house a few times in recent weeks and he'd noticed a strange, repugnant odor he couldn't identify. On this October day, he had decided to search for the source of the nauseating smell.

And he had come upon a body in a closet beneath the stairs leading to the basement. It appeared to be that of a woman. She was wearing blue jeans.

Shocked, Marsh ran up the stairs and headed for the nearest phone to call police.

It was shortly after noon when homicide detectives Duane Homan and Mike Tando, and their sergeant, Craig Vandeputte, were summoned on a "questionable death" call. When they viewed the victim and noted the clothing she wore, they recognized that it was identical to the garments worn by the missing girl in the case Lieutenant Holter and Detectives Trettevik and Stewart were working in the Robbery Unit. Accordingly, they asked that Trettevik and Stewart respond to the scene.

It was a warm Indian summer day with no hint of rain as the crew of investigators moved through the vacant house. Alva Marsh said that the house had been boarded up for at least two years but that he had had problems with people breaking in and vandalizing. He had been about to begin cleaning up the premises and the yard when he discovered the body.

The house was a three-story frame structure, full of clutter. The entrance to the basement was on the south side of the house, accessible by four steps from the yard. All the basement windows were boarded up and intact, but the hasp on the basement door lock had been pried from the frame. There was no artificial light at all in the cellar and the detectives brought in auxiliary lighting to augment the thin gray rays that leaked through the boarded windows.

Now they could see streaks of blood on the outside of the closet door. The woman's body sat slumped over just inside. The young woman had been dead for some time; she still wore the clothes Jack Atkins had told them she wore as he walked her to her bus on Sunday: blue jeans, a blue shirt, and a blue ski jacket with a red lining. Her jeans were pulled down below her buttocks and her other clothing yanked over her head. She appeared to have been stabbed, but the decomposing body would require an autopsy to try to verify time and cause of death.

They walked up the steps to search the upper floors of the abandoned house, almost feeling the presence of ghostly spirits from its past and, now, from its present.

There was some graffiti sprayed on walls and other clutter that indicated someone had been using the old house as a hangout. They also found spots where someone had tried to torch the house. It had been a failed attempt; the little piles of paper and boards were scorched, but then any flames had dissipated.

The empty house should have gone up in a major conflagration. It was full of the debris of what looked like fifty years or more. Former tenants or owners—or maybe trespassers—had left a lot behind: broken furniture, yellowed newspapers, food wrappers, garbage.

But none of the trash littering the upper floors appeared to have any immediate connection to the dead woman. In some areas, the floors were two or three feet deep with detritus; to sift through it all thoroughly would take weeks—even months.

Deputies from the medical examiner's office removed the body from its lonely, cluttered tomb and transported it downtown to await autopsy. Detectives placed police locks on the doors as they ended the first day's probe into what now could be called a homicide.

Although it seemed that the body found was surely that of Laura Baylis, dental records would be necessary to make absolute identification. And those would have to come all the way from England.

Early the next morning, Detectives Duane Homan, Mike Tando, and Larry Stewart returned to the vacant house to continue processing it. This time, they were accompanied by Jean Battista, a fingerprint expert. They dusted every inch of the basement for latent prints but found none. The basement walls were too rough to hold fingerprints, and nothing useful for evidence turned up.

Criminalist Battista did recover two hairs that didn't match the blond hair of the victim. One was short, black, and curly.

The three detectives were inclined to believe that the victim had been killed somewhere else and brought to the basement closet within a few hours of her death. Lividity is a purplish-red striation pattern formed in newly deceased bodies. When the heart stops pumping, blood no longer circulates and sinks to the lowest level of the body, where it eventually etches a series of permanent bright stripes— *unless* it is moved before lividity is set.

In that case, detectives and medical examiners see *two*

"stainings." There will be the first lighter pink shading and then the final lividity stripes, marking a new position. That part of a body that rests on a hard surface is blanched white. Once lividity is complete, the body can be moved without any change in the pink to purplish markings.

Due to the paucity of blood where her body had lain and the pattern of lividity on her body, the detectives agreed that the victim had been killed somewhere else. They also felt that whoever carried the body in had not gone beyond the basement area. This was probably going to be the only area in the house that would give up any physical clues.

Back in the Homicide Unit, they placed a call to Laura Baylis's parents in England and told them gently that the body of a young woman had been found. "We're not positive yet," Duane Homan said, "but we have reason to believe that we've found Laura."

Bessie Baylis said she hadn't been able to locate any of Laura's medical or dental records. "But I'll keep searching," she said, with tears in her voice.

Robbery detectives Jerry Trettevik and Larry Stewart attended the postmortem examination of the unidentified victim. The dead girl had succumbed to nineteen stab wounds of the neck and torso. It was far too late to estimate measurements of the murder weapon or to determine if she had been sexually assaulted, although the way her clothing had been disarrayed certainly suggested rape or a rape attempt.

Stewart and Trettevik retained the girl's clothing for evidence. They watched as the forensic surgeon removed her fingertip skin, which slipped off as easily as gloves from her desiccated hands. There was a good chance that criminalists from the crime lab could rehydrate the skin, at least enough to obtain usable prints.

The detectives were almost positive that the dead woman was Laura Baylis; everything matched, right down to the two gold necklaces her boyfriend had described. But Laura Baylis's parents were having difficulty finding records that could validate that this was Laura. Her dentist had died and his records disposed of. They had nothing with her fingerprints on it. English law doesn't require that babies' footprints be taken at birth. All of the best ways of identifying a nameless body at the time were unavailable to the investigators.

In the Western Washington Crime Lab, ID technician Marsha Jackson was finally able to obtain fingerprints from the victim by "plumping" the fingertip tissue with liquid. She then matched these prints to a single print on an identification card Laura had once obtained in Kansas City. The name on the card was Julie Costello, but the photograph it bore was of Laura Baylis. She had been an attractive young woman who might well have inspired fantasies in the mind of someone who was emotionally disturbed. In fact, she looked a lot like Genie Francis of the popular soap opera *General Hospital.*

Anyone who had seen Laura would probably remember her. Customers of the all-night market did, and they wanted to help catch her killer, but no one had any more information about Sunday night, September 24.

Now the detective team knew for sure that they had found Laura, but her killer had a three-week head start. All they had was a black, curly hair and the picture of the man in the billed cap and fatigue jacket taken by the surveillance camera.

On October 16, they received a vital lead through an anonymous phone call. A woman, who refused to give her name, called Larry Stewart to say that she had seen the picture of the man they sought.

"I saw it in the newspaper, and I think it's a guy named Clarence who lives in the Sixty-one hundred block of Beacon Avenue. If it isn't him, it's a dead ringer for him. He moved into that house early this year with his wife or his girlfriend."

Before Stewart could question her further, she hung up.

Stewart and Jerry Trettevik checked Seattle City Light records for the block and found that one billing in the area was to a Clarence E. Williams, who was employed at Todd's Shipyard. They ran Williams's name through police computers and got a hit. Clarence Williams was described as a black male, thirty-three, five foot eleven, weighing 215 pounds.

He had been on parole after serving prison time for convictions on burglaries, carrying a concealed weapon, and narcotics charges. But he hadn't been supervised directly by a parole officer for two years. That would mean he'd kept out of trouble during his active parole and didn't have to report to anyone currently.

Obtaining Williams's mug shot, the two detectives met with Lieutenant Holter, and they all agreed that he was a close look-alike to the man they sought. He did not wear glasses, however, and his driver's license didn't stipulate corrective lenses.

But anyone can put on a pair of glasses with clear glass lenses.

They checked with Todd's Shipyard and learned that Clarence Williams was employed there as a sandblaster, working the night shift beginning at 4:00 p.m. Ordinarily, he would finish work about 3:00 or 4:00 a.m.

Stewart and Trettevik drove to Williams's residence. There was no response to their knocks, except for a snarling Doberman pinscher who lunged at the window with teeth bared. They looked up and down the street and failed to see any cars parked nearby that matched Williams's known vehicles.

When the Second Watch detective crew arrived for work at 3:45 that afternoon, they went to Todd's Shipyard and showed the photo taken by the hidden camera to employees in the personnel office. They all agreed that it closely resembled Clarence Williams.

But when they were asked if he was working at the moment, the personnel clerk checked and said that Williams hadn't appeared for his shift.

It was October 18 when robbery Detective Jerry Trettevik and homicide Detective Hank Gruber met with Clarence Williams face-to-face at the shipyard. When he walked into the personnel office, they were both struck by his startling resemblance to the pictures they had memorized. Williams even wore an olive green fatigue jacket, its collar rolled just like the jacket collar in the security photos.

At the moment, Williams wore an orange hard hat and carried clear safety glasses. The glasses were not at all similar to those in the photo, however. Clarence Williams's facial hair was almost identical to that of the man they sought.

Williams seemed nervous, but he readily answered the detectives' questions. He said he lived alone, as he'd separated from his wife on September 1. "I gave her my car and I catch a ride every day with a friend—Mercina Adderly.*"

"You ever been in that house where they found Laura Baylis's body?" Gruber asked Williams.

"Never. I saw those pictures in the papers and I knew right away that I look like him," Clarence said anxiously. "I've been in trouble in my life, I'll admit, but never for nothing violent."

Williams said that his own wife had called him after seeing the picture in the paper and asked him flat out if he'd killed the girl.

"I had a hard time convincing her that it wasn't me."

Williams wasn't enthusiastic about taking a lie detector test, because he didn't trust them. But he finally agreed to face a polygraph.

The whole interview was unsettling. Stewart and Gruber were staring at a man who looked exactly like the man in the photographs, who even wore a jacket identical to that man's—and yet he continued to insist that he knew nothing at all about Laura Baylis.

Was it possible that he *wasn't* lying? Clarence Williams was soft-spoken and polite and said he had no idea why he looked so much like the suspect they sought. He was as puzzled as everyone else.

A number of tipsters wanted to get information to the investigators, but they were either frightened or didn't want to get involved. Homicide Detective Wayne Dorman received the next anonymous phone call.

"I been seeing that picture on the TV and in the papers," a voice that could be either male or female said. "I know it's Clarence Williams, and I know for a fact he's been in that house where they found that girl. He ripped that house off three times. I might call back and tell you my name after I think about it."

And then *click* and the line went dead.

Detectives talked to Williams's neighbors, who said he came and went at all hours, and that his Doberman barked continually.

Todd's Shipyard's security officers said that the shipyard kept a box of all kinds of safety glasses on hand at the yard, some of them similar to those in the photo. "Williams would have had access to those glasses."

Hank Gruber and Jerry Trettevik talked to the suspect's estranged wife. She was adamant that Clarence *was* the man caught by the camera and that he had a hat and jacket like those in the picture.

They already knew that. They'd recognized his clothes, too.

"Look," she said firmly, "he's got so many pairs of safety glasses, and some of them are just like that guy in the 7-Eleven store wore.

"I *know* my ex was in the house where they found the body."

"How is that?" Gruber asked.

"I've gone there with him!" she said, much to their surprise. "He was thinking about buying that house and he wanted to show me. He knew his way around it, and we went through it in the dark. I mean, like he knew every inch of it."

She gave Hank Gruber a key to their family car, but, after a thorough processing, he found nothing of value to the case in it.

Williams's wife wasn't surprised. "He couldn't have driven it from the middle of September to the first week of October, anyway, because it was broken down."

Since Laura vanished on September 24, it was understandable that Williams had probably hidden the car and told people it was in the shop. He would have had plenty of time to steam-clean everything from the upholstery to the engine. Or maybe it *was* in need of repair, and he'd borrowed a car.

Despite Williams's protestations of innocence, there were just too many coincidences. Armed with an arrest warrant, Bob Holter, Larry Stewart, Jerry Trettevik, and Jimmy Nicholson went to the Rainier bowling lanes on the evening of October 20. Clarence Williams was a top-ranked bowler, and he was competing in league play there.

The robbery detectives sat quietly in the spectator section until Williams recognized them and walked over.

"What're you gonna do?" he asked.

"Arrest you," Holter replied succinctly.

"I expected it. Can I finish bowling first?" was Williams's surprising reaction.

"Okay. Go ahead," Holter said. "We'll wait right here."

Williams bowled his remaining three games, but he was distracted and his performance dropped with each frame. When he was finished, he submitted meekly to his arrest on suspicion of murder, kidnapping, and robbery. He was advised of his rights and booked into jail on $100,000 bail.

With a new search warrant, and his Doberman locked safely away, detectives and criminalists searched Clarence Williams's home. It was just three structures away from the vacant house where Laura Baylis's body was found, and one mile from the 7-Eleven where she had last been seen alive.

It was within the realm of possibility that Clarence Williams had forced Laura Baylis to walk from the store into the darkness of the wee hours. Even if he didn't have a car, she might have been so frightened by a knife against her body that she didn't dare scream. Lights would have been out in most houses along the way to the empty shell of a house where she was found. It was chilling to picture her walking to her death, while all the time frantically thinking of some way she could escape the tall, powerful man who held her captive.

The investigators carried out bags and boxes of possible evidence from Williams's rented house: a dark cap with a bill, a box containing numerous knives, jeans with a belt that held a knife sheath, a box of ten pairs of safety glasses, a .38-caliber revolver, a pair of boots bearing dark red stains, and two bank bags similar to the bags used at the convenience store to carry cash to the bank for deposit.

Williams's locker at the shipyard yielded a khaki fatigue jacket and more safety glasses. And finally, they found a billed cap that was identical to the cap the kidnapper/killer had worn when he was caught by the security camera. It had been stashed in an empty locker six spaces away from Williams's own.

On the advice of his attorney, Clarence Williams changed his mind about taking a polygraph examination. He had trimmed his facial hair so that it no longer matched that of the man in the photo.

In a lineup held on October 23, Clarence Williams was identified by the man who had gone there to purchase cigarettes.

"Number three is the person I saw in the 7-Eleven store on the morning of September twenty-fifth," he said.

The bartender at the nearby 19th Hole tavern picked Williams as the man she had poured wine for around midnight on the 24th. A patron who was in the tavern that night picked Williams out of the lineup, too.

They obtained a search warrant for Mercina Adderly's car. The woman who had driven him to work most days had lent Williams her car on several occasions during the vital time period when his own car was inoperable. She couldn't remember exactly which days he had asked to borrow it but said she would try to think back.

As they processed her car, they found some long, blondish-brown Caucasian hairs in the trunk. Mercina was black, and so were Clarence Williams and his wife. Criminalists, using a scanning electron microscope, found that these hairs were alike in class and characteristics to Laura Baylis's hair. This made them a probable match—but not a positive one.

Again, in 1978, DNA was still a brave new world in forensic science.

Mercina Adderly told detectives that Clarence had been suffering great emotional upheaval after his wife left.

"He said things that worried me," Mercina said. "Just

before that girl disappeared, he was very distraught and he told me he wanted to 'hurt someone.' I didn't think he meant it literally, and I finally put it down to his state of mind."

"How long before?" Hank Gruber asked.

"It was summertime—I remember that—but I couldn't say if it was August, or even July."

It was fitting perhaps that it was Halloween when formal charges of first-degree robbery, first-degree kidnapping, and first-degree murder were filed against Clarence Williams in the Laura Anne Baylis homicide.

The man who'd once wanted to buy a seemingly haunted house didn't see the irony in his being charged on the spookiest holiday of the year.

The first problems the prosecution would face at trial were the blurry security camera photos. The State had to convince a jury that they were of Clarence Williams, and they were sure the defense would quibble over that.

Professor Daris Swindler of the University of Washington's Anthropology Department studied pictures taken of Clarence Williams and compared them to the photographs of the man caught by the camera. Swindler often helped police identify victims or suspects, sometimes working with only a skull denuded of all flesh and tissue.

Now he took meticulous measurements to scale of the security photos *and* photos of Clarence Williams. The measured distance from the two subjects' ears to the mandible (jaw), the length of the noses, the placement of cheekbones, the width of the foreheads.

Swindler's conclusion based on comparing the facial characteristics was that all of the photos were of the same person: Clarence Williams.

Williams went on trial in mid-January 1979, in Superior Court Judge Nancy Ann Holman's courtroom. It was to be a trial with one of the most unusual conclusions I've ever heard.

Williams defended himself by telling the jurors that the person in the picture was not him; it couldn't have been.

"I was home asleep at the time they say it happened," he said earnestly. "But once I saw the picture, I was sure they would come and talk to me."

He admitted that he had been in the house where the body was found because he was thinking about buying it.

"But I hadn't been in that house for a long time before that girl disappeared. I've been in the convenience store on Beacon Hill a few times, too, but I never recall seeing any clerk named Laura or Julie or whoever she was. I just didn't know her at all."

The defense was not without ammunition. One of their strongest witnesses was Larry Wilkins, an athletic director for the Seattle Parks Department, and brother of Lenny Wilkins, then coach of the Seattle Sonics, the champion basketball team that was in the midst of its glory days.

It was Larry Wilkins who had seen two suspicious men in the 19th Hole tavern on the night Laura disappeared. He had identified the *second* man as the one in the vital camera pictures. But he testified that that man was not Clarence Williams.

"You saw someone you knew sometime later at the Veterans Hospital, didn't you?"

"Yes."

"Who was that?"

"I don't know his name, but he was the second man in the tavern that Sunday night—the twenty-fourth. He was the man in the security photo.

"He was much heavier and taller than Williams," Wilkins added.

Wilkins testified that he'd known Clarence Williams slightly before the kidnapping incident. He'd played on a local softball team. "If it was Clarence Williams in the tavern that night, I would have recognized him, and he probably would have recognized me."

In the end, it didn't really matter whether or not Clarence had been the man in the tavern. It was much more important that he had been in the 7-Eleven, and he was still connected to the victim in so many ways. The prosecution team wondered if the jurors would see that.

The jurors deliberated for almost four days. The vital question was identification. Were they to believe the report of Dr. Swindler, their own eyes, and the plethora of circumstantial evidence, along with the criminalist's testimony on the hair matches?

Or were they to believe the defense contention that Clarence Williams was merely an unfortunate victim of mistaken identity?

When they returned to the courtroom, their verdict was that Williams *was* guilty and they convicted him on all three counts.

Judge Holman studied the jury's verdict, and what she

did next stunned the gallery and the attorneys present. For the first time in her nine years on the bench, Nancy Holman reversed a verdict!

She hadn't been convinced beyond a reasonable doubt of Clarence Williams's guilt, and she wanted to be sure that an innocent man wasn't convicted.

She ordered a new trial.

Judge Holman's reversal of the jury's verdict was a shock and tremendous disappointment to Lieutenant Bob Holter's crew of detectives who had worked so hard in the investigation. It also was in total disagreement with the King County Prosecutor's Office. Judge Holman asked prosecutor Norm Maleng to continue investigating Laura Baylis's murder, but the prosecution team was absolutely convinced the right man had been convicted. Holman set a new trial date, but it was a moot point; the Court of Appeals affirmed Clarence Williams's conviction.

"I feel like I'm being made an example for somebody else's crime," he said bitterly as he was sentenced to life in prison on all three charges. At the time, that meant three consecutive sentences of just over thirteen years each. His first parole hearing wouldn't come until about 2016.

Most people forgot about Clarence Williams; he'd never been a high-profile felon who garnered tall headlines. And he'd been sentenced to all those life terms. He virtually vanished behind prison walls and was eventually transferred to a Midwestern penitentiary when Washington State's prisons became overcrowded.

Laura Baylis, who had lived her short life as she pleased, who wandered happily throughout the country she chose to embrace as her own, lay buried in her native England. I wrote the story of her life—and her death—for one of the fact-detective magazines for which I was a regular stringer covering Northwest crimes.

There were an inordinately large number of murders in Seattle in 1978, far more than the city would see after the millennium, and I wrote about almost all of them. Overworked homicide detectives worked on their unsolved cases whenever they had a break. There were no cold case squads in the seventies or eighties, possibly because it was rare for new physical evidence to show up, and there would be no DNA to match until well into the nineties.

I, too, put this case on a back shelf in my mind, but I always felt that none of us had heard the whole story of Clarence Williams or of Laura Baylis. Someday, sometime, I believed the whole story would surface.

Maybe then I could update it.

Was Laura a chance victim of a man who "wanted to hurt somebody" because his marriage had shattered?

Or did Clarence have more secrets to unveil?

Was Clarence as innocent as his judge believed?

Was Laura taken away by someone else, someone who never surfaced?

Another case has tormented me, staying with me throughout the decades, popping into my mind unbidden. People sometimes ask me if I get sad and depressed writing in the true-crime genre. With some of the cases, the answer is yes. That's particularly true when homicide victims are young, many of them as young as my own five children at the time I covered the cases. It was almost impossible for me to research and write about them without becoming emotionally involved. I never said to their parents, "I know how you feel," because I didn't; I could hardly imagine. How could I dare to presume to know how they felt?

Many of the national and worldwide headlines in 1978 sounded very much like today's news—only the celebrity names and songs were different. Thirty years flying by like dry leaves in the wind. *Animal House* drew large audiences. The Bee Gees were hugely popular with "Stayin' Alive" and other hit songs from the smash movies *Saturday Night Fever* and *Grease.* It seemed that disco dancing would go on forever. John Travolta's hair was thick and shiny black then and his body was chiseled.

The first test-tube baby was delivered alive and well in England, and Martina Navratilova and Chris Evert were at the top of their games.

That same year was also a year of infamy and horror in many ways. The "Reverend" Jim Jones convinced nine hundred of his devout followers to commit suicide in Guyana by drinking Kool-Aid laced with cyanide, and his guards killed a California congressman and network reporters and photographers who had come, too late, to investigate what was going on; *Hustler* publisher Larry Flynt was shot and left a paraplegic; police found the bodies of twenty-one young men under John Wayne Gacy's house in Chicago; David Berkowitz, "Son of Sam," was sentenced to 365 years in prison; and Ted Bundy was recaptured in Pensacola, Florida, after his escape from a Colorado jail.

ANN RULE

America was saturated with serial killers, it seemed—
but that term had yet to be coined. That would take another
five years. After I'd met with detectives from all over
America to try to catch this "new" kind of killer, I suggested to my then-editor that I write a book about serial
murder. He said, "Don't bother. It's a fad like the hulahoop
or trampolines. By the time you finish a book, nobody will
be interested in serial killers."

He was, of course, wrong.

As always, 1978 had its share of unrest and insurrection
in far-off nations. None of the foreign news had much impact on a young girl who had her whole life ahead of her.
But she worried about those people in *her* world who were
unhappy and she tried to help them.

Her name was Sara Beth Lundquist, and she was the
kind of teenager that any parents would be proud of: innocent, a little naïve, concerned for other people, a lover of
animals, and as freshly beautiful as an apple blossom that
had just unfolded.

Sara Beth was at the center of one of the more baffling
unsolved cases in Seattle's criminal history. I've kept her
photographs at the top of my "unsolved" file, hoping that
one day there would be an end to her story, and that end
would have to be the arrest of someone yet unknown.

Sometime in the summer of 2007, I was signing books
at a huge Costco store, and a man stopped by to say he
hoped for the same thing I did, for a long-dormant case to
be solved.

"Which case is that?" I asked.

He began to say the name of his niece, but he didn't
even have to finish his sentence. It was Sara Beth. She had

been on my mind too, and I always remembered her in the summer. Her family had waited so long with no answers. I told her uncle that I hoped one day to write the end of her story.

Sara Beth's story began shortly after midnight on Sunday, July 2, 1978, and no one could have foreseen how long it would take justice to arrive for her.

In 1978, the Fourth of July came on a Tuesday, and a lot of people were taking a four-day weekend, finding excuses not to come to work on Monday. As often happens in the Northwest on Independence Day, the weather looked as though it would fail to cooperate and the weekend before the big day was marked by gray clouds and drizzle. Those who had planned picnics started to look for alternative locations and kids who had a stash of illegal fireworks worried that they would get too soggy to light.

Sara Beth lived in the Ballard neighborhood in the northwest part of Seattle, a proud and venerable community where there are more Scandinavians per square block than anyplace else in Washington. Many of its residents make their livings commercial fishing, heading up to the dangerous waters of Alaska. Boating is probably the main avocation in Ballard. During rush hour, the Ballard Locks are jammed with motorboats and sailboats traveling between landlocked Lake Washington to the east and Puget Sound to the west. On days when the wind is right, the brightly hued spinnaker sails of private boats dance like butterflies on the waters of Elliott Bay.

Ballard has always been a family community, with

homey-looking bungalows, a local theater that features serials and second-run movies, parades and festivals on both American and Norse holidays—a good place to raise youngsters and a part of the city with a relatively low crime rate.

Sara Beth Lundquist grew up there. At fifteen, she wasn't very different from her peers. She got good grades at Ingraham High School where she was a sophomore—when she studied—but she could be distracted by so many more fun things to do. She worked part-time as an aide in a convalescent home, and her soft heart hurt to see so many elderly people whose families had left them there, alone, and never came to visit. She tried to spend extra time with them.

Sara Beth lived with her mother, Lynne, and her sister, Melissa, in a home divided by divorce. Her ten-year-old brother, Lee, lived much of the time with their father, Robert. The children were close to one another, and Sara Beth saw her father often. She actually *liked* her little brother and often let him tag along when she was with her friends, even though five years was a big age gap.

Sara Beth liked to cook, especially experimental dishes. She made her own Christmas gifts, and was sewing some pretty aprons. She loved her mother and told her so often. Sometimes, Lynne would find notes on her pillow that Sara Beth had left for her, saying, "I love you."

She was as natural an ice-skater as if she'd been born and raised in Sweden or Norway. She played the piano and taught Sunday school.

And she loved to laugh and to make her family laugh. Sara Beth was at that crystalline point between being a child and a woman; she was past the early pubescent years when mothers and daughters sometimes lock horns, and she hadn't yet reached the pseudosophistication of an older teen.

And yet Sara Beth was different from a lot of teenagers. She was extraordinarily beautiful. She had even features, very large blue eyes fringed with incredibly thick, dark lashes, and a perfect rosebud complexion. She was slender and exquisitely proportioned.

She seemed unaware of how pretty she was. When she wore makeup, she looked older than fifteen and could have passed for eighteen or twenty.

Tragically, she would never grow any older than fifteen. Someone stalked Sara Beth Lundquist in the shadows of a rainy July night. Maybe he had been stalking her for a long time and waiting for his chance to take her away from where she was safe. Perhaps he'd just spotted her and become obsessed with the idea of hurting her or taking sexual advantage of her.

Sara Beth's best friend was Minda Craig,* also fifteen. They'd known each other since kindergarten, and they'd been best friends for a year. They had plans for Saturday night, July 1. They were going to see *Damien: Omen II*, about a thirteen-year-old devil child purported to be the Antichrist, and they looked forward to being a little frightened.

Sara Beth was excited about getting out. Three weeks earlier, she'd been diagnosed with mononucleosis, a common teenage illness. At first, she felt quite sick, and later she'd been prevented from working at her job at the convalescent center where she'd been a therapy aide for nine months. Finally her doctor had declared her "no longer contagious." She looked forward to returning to work. Her elderly friends there had missed her as much as she'd missed them.

The movie was one of her first social outings for weeks.

The two teenagers took a bus to downtown Seattle a little before nine in the evening. Minda rode down the hill from her house, and Sara Beth got on at 24th NW and North 85th Street. "I remember the driver was new," Minda recalled, "a really nice black woman who showed us how to get to the Coliseum Theatre."

As she'd promised, Sara Beth called her mother right after the movie to let her know they were okay and would probably be on the midnight bus to Ballard.

Outside the theater, some teenage boys "hassled" the girls, dancing around them, blocking their paths, and asking for their names and phone numbers. They were annoying, but they weren't frightening, and they didn't follow Sara Beth and Minda onto the bus. But they did make them too late, so it was a little bit after 11:30 when the girls caught the next bus back to Ballard.

Depending on how many stops it made, they would be in their home neighborhood around a quarter after midnight.

The Seattle Transit bus got to Sara's stop at 24th NW at 12:20, and she hopped down the steps, waving to her friend. Sometimes they called each other after they got home, but if not, they would be on the phone together the next day—as they always were.

Reassured by Sara Beth's call saying she would be on

the midnight bus, her mother had drifted off to sleep. She was very tired and thought she would hear Sara Beth come in; her daughter was always good about curfews and getting home when she said she would. And she had only to walk through a family neighborhood to get to her house.

On Sunday morning, the phone rang and Lynne Carlson went to Sara Beth's room to tell her she had a call. She was surprised to see that she wasn't there. At first, she wondered why Sara Beth would have gotten up so early and had already made her bed.

Then it dawned on her: *Sara Beth hadn't come home the night before. . . .*

She immediately checked with Minda to see if Sara Beth had stayed overnight at her house, but Minda told her that Sara Beth had gotten off the bus alone at her regular stop and started walking in the direction of her home.

The next call Lynne Carlson made was to the Seattle Police to report her daughter missing. On that Sunday morning, there was still a possibility that Sara Beth had changed her mind and stayed overnight with another girl-friend. Patrol officer LaVerne Husby, who came to take Lynne's report, asked about the possibility that Sara Beth had run away, but she was adamant that Sara Beth would *never* do that.

More frightening was a scenario where Sara Beth had been hit by a car, fallen, or been involved in some other kind of accident and was in the hospital. But a check with Seattle hospitals indicated there were no young "Jane Does" who had come in during the night.

A half hour passed, but it seemed like a day, and Lynne Carlson felt cold fear with every passing moment. Each time the phone rang shrilly, she prayed it would be Sara Beth with an explanation about where she was.

On Leary Avenue Northwest, three miles from where Sara Beth lived, a crew of family members were spending the holiday weekend helping Bill of Bill's Tire Exchange finish transforming a deserted gas station into his new business. The weather had held the day before when they painted the exterior of the station, but now rain had started to fall. They were preparing to finish the paint job on the interior.

It was shortly after noon when Bill's teenage nephew opened the men's room door to get some tools they had stored there. Or rather, he *tried* to open the door. Something was blocking it from inside. Puzzled, he looked down and saw a small hand with perfectly polished nails. The hairs stood up on the back of his neck, and he backed away and called his uncle.

Bill knelt to examine the hand. It felt cold and stiff to his touch. As he told detectives later, "There was just no life in it at all. I knew—I've seen bodies before—and the way that hand lay, I knew someone was dead in there."

He called 911, and Officers Warren Lisenby and LaVerne Husby, and Patrol Sergeant G. S. Perkins responded to the stark report of "a body in a service station."

They had no idea who it might be, although they were inclined to think it was probably a homeless person who'd found a place to get out of the rain. From the description of the body's hand, it was probably a female, maybe a "bag lady" who lived outdoors because she had no money for a room or an apartment.

Still, this area wasn't a neighborhood where many street people hung out.

The three officers peered through the crack in the door. As their eyes adjusted to the dim light inside, they could make out the figure of a young woman. She lay on her back in the six-by-eight room.

The officers immediately put in a call to the Homicide Unit.

All unattended/suspicious deaths are considered homicides first, suicides second, and accidental last. If this young woman had perished through homicidal violence, the patrol officers didn't want to risk losing any physical evidence.

Detective Sergeant Don Cameron's team was working the weekend shift, and he and Detective Mike Tando responded with the homicide van.

"All we know now is that she wasn't here when the painting crew left last night about eight thirty," Sergeant Perkins told the detectives. "The owner doesn't know her, and neither do the others here."

Officer Husby stepped forward. "I think I may know who she is, although I wish I didn't. I took a missing persons report this morning from a woman who lives at Eighty-fourth and Twentieth, about three miles from here. She was worried sick because her daughter Sara Beth didn't come home last night."

"How old is she?" Cameron asked.

"Fifteen. And from what we can see, the girl in the

men's room is wearing clothes that match the clothes Sara Beth was had on last night almost exactly."

Cameron and Tando—the only homicide detectives working on a skeleton crew that holiday—reached tentatively through the opening in the restroom door and touched the dead girl's arm. She was cold and had apparently been dead for many hours.

As they eased the door open, they encountered what looked like a scene from a movie, not the usual ugliness of a homicide scene. Even in death, the girl was beautiful. She wore a silk print blouse, and a jean outfit. A little dried blood marked her face, but her expression was serene and unmarked by fear.

Except for the blood staining her blouse, and the cluttered and inappropriate spot where she lay, she might only have been sleeping, sprawled out with the careless grace of the young. Her chestnut hair fanned out around her head and then was caught in the dried pool of blood beneath her body.

Despite the macho image we see on TV, a good homicide detective never looks at a victim's body without feeling a pang of regret for the loss of a human life. Still, some cases bother them more than others. This girl—was it Sara Beth?—shouldn't be dead, murdered, tossed aside in a pile of flaking plaster. She was so young. She should be going back to school in the fall, maybe riding on a homecoming float or wearing her first corsage to a prom.

But homicide detectives don't make the rules and they can't change the ending of a tragic story; they can only pick up the raveled strands of mystery that are left behind and try to weave some pattern out of them.

The teenager in front of them appeared to have suffered deep stab wounds to the chest, but they couldn't tell how many. One of her hands was cut as if she'd tried to defend herself.

Cameron, who had a daughter of his own the same age, put in a call for Dr. John Eisele of the Medical Examiner's Office and requested that a fingerprint technician be dispatched to the scene. He had to keep concentrating on his job, not on his emotions.

The owner of the building said that the restroom doors hadn't been locked. All the fixtures had been removed.

"Someone broke the lock a while back, and there seemed no need to replace it right away," he said. "Nothin' worth taking."

The small frame building was located in a commercial area where there was little likelihood that anyone would have been around late on a Saturday night to hear screams for help, if, indeed, there had been any. The detectives' chances of finding an eyewitness or an ear witness were slight, so they made every effort to glean what they could from the scene itself.

Detective Lieutenant Bob Holter and Detectives Don Strunk and Paul Eblin, along with senior ID technician Marsha Jackson, joined the solemn-faced group at the tire store.

Even though they knew it might be futile, patrol officers began a door-to-door canvass of businesses in the neighborhood while Marsha Jackson dusted the outside of the restroom door for latent prints, lifting several. They might be vital, or they could have been left by any of a dozen workmen on the site.

Then they completely removed the door itself after lifting out the pins.

The girl's body was now revealed in its entirety. They took photographs and measurements, and bagged what might be useful physical evidence and marked it with their initials and the date.

As much as forensic science has moved forward in the last hundred years, there is one axiom that never changes. It's been handed down to those processing a crime scene from the famed French criminalist Dr. Emile Locard: "The criminal always leaves something of himself at the scene of his crime—something perhaps too infinitesimal to be perceived by the naked eye—and he always takes something of the crime scene away with him."

This rule of thumb surely held true in the grimy washroom of the remodeled gas station. They just had to identify what had been left and what had been taken away. Tando and Cameron slipped more than three dozen bits of evidence into glassine bags and vials and marked them for lab technicians.

The officers doing the door-to-door canvass found that a nearby tavern had been open until just after 2:00 a.m., but it was now closed. If the apartment above it was rented, nobody answered the door. A woman who lived nearby said that her dog always barked at unusual sounds. "But he didn't bark at all last night," she said, "and I'm the only one who lives around here—all the rest of it is shops and businesses."

She lived eighty yards from the gas station–tire shop. She was the only private resident around, and she admitted she sometimes got jittery when all the businesses closed and the workers went home.

"I would have noticed if anyone screamed in the night," she said emphatically.

Medical examiner Dr. John Eisele arrived and knelt beside the dead girl. He commented that rigor mortis was fully established in the body, which indicated the victim had died sometime during the night—at least twelve hours before she was found.

"I can tell you the time of death more closely after we begin the post," he commented. "The cause of death is apparently deep stab wounds—too many for me to count here—but that can also be more precisely defined at autopsy."

If rape had been the motivation for the murderous attack, it might not have been accomplished; the girl's jeans were in place, and her shirt, though opened several buttons in the front, was still tucked into the waistband. Her shoes were gone, and the detectives found no sign of a purse or wallet near the body.

Robbery? Hardly likely. Teenage girls don't carry that much money, and the victim still wore relatively inexpensive jewelry. Revenge? Jealousy? Maybe. They didn't know the victim at all at this point, or what her world had been like.

But they would. Like all exceptional detectives, the six investigators who worked quietly throughout the rainy, gloomy Sunday would come to know Sara Beth Lundquist as well as they knew anyone in life.

After Sara Beth's body was removed. Marsha Jackson

dusted the inside of the room for fingerprints. She succeeded in raising several more latents from the smooth wall surfaces.

There was still doubt that the dead girl was Sara Beth Lundquist, and they needed her fingerprints, too, for comparison.

The puzzle of Sara Beth's missing shoes and purse was solved at 3:00 p.m. when word came that a widow living in the area of 19th NW and 83rd—very close to Sara Beth's home—had found a pair of clog shoes and a purse. Someone had tossed them in her driveway and in the alley behind her house. The purse still held Sara Beth's ID.

Detective Don Strunk left at once to talk with Mrs. Lorraine Olsen.

"Something woke me up last night," Mrs. Olsen told him. "I don't know what time it was, but I heard a woman's scream. Just one. Nothing more, no car, nothing. I listened awhile and it was quiet. I wondered if I'd been dreaming, and I finally went back to sleep.

"In the morning, I went out to move my car, and I found the shoes and purse. "I called one of the numbers inside and I got Mrs. Lundquist. Then I took the purse and shoes over to her."

For Sara Beth's mother, the sight of her daughter's shoes and purse was chilling. They had been found along the route that Sara Beth would have taken after she got off the bus. At that point, she was just a few short blocks from home.

Strunk talked with Minda Craig. He had to tell her that her best friend was dead, murdered. Tears sprang into Minda's eyes and ran down her face. Strunk waited while she tried to deal with the terrible news.

"Try to remember everything you can about last night," he asked gently. "Was there anyone you might have noticed who was watching Sara, bothering her, anything that she might have been afraid of?"

Minda shook her head.

"Did anyone get off the bus at the same stop she did?"

"No, she was the only one. There was a young guy on the bus who talked to us, but he got off about two blocks later. He couldn't have doubled back and caught up with Sara because she would have been almost home by then."

"Did anyone get off at your stop?"

"I can't remember anyone."

Minda said she had gone home and right to bed. She had no idea what might have happened to Sara Beth after she'd walked out of the streetlight's glow near the bus stop.

"Did Sara have any enemies? Anyone who didn't like her?" Minda, still in shock, shook her head. "No. Oh, no— she's very popular at school. She was nice to everyone."

"Did she date?"

"Different boys, but nothing serious. She wasn't going steady or anything. I think lots of guys like her, though."

At a quarter to five, the detectives cleared the scene and returned to homicide headquarters to review what they knew of the case so far. Someone had to have grabbed Sara Beth Lundquist shortly after she got off the bus. Her shoes and purse were found in the driveway and the alley behind Lorraine Olsen's house, and she had heard a cry for help.

"I think that's where he—they, maybe—abducted her," Cameron said. "Mrs. Olsen didn't hear a car, but he probably had one. It was three miles to where he left her in the tire shop. But I think he killed her somewhere else, possibly in a car, because there wasn't enough blood where we found her."

The question was: Had someone known that Sara Beth would be on that bus, someone who waited for her until she was alone and virtually helpless? Or had a stranger seen her that evening, hopped on the bus without either Minda or Sara Beth noticing him, and exited through the back door? Minda could be confused when she said Sara Beth was the only one who got off the bus. Two teenagers busy talking about the movie they'd just seen, and talking with the young man on the bus, could have failed to be aware of someone who didn't want to be noticed.

And there was always the chance that she had encountered evil in the few blocks she had to walk to get home. A chance meeting with a monster? It happened, and it was the hardest kind of case to solve.

Don Cameron sent a request to patrolmen working out of the North Station about the murder and asked them to look for vehicles that had bloodstains on the upholstery or even on the exterior, or drivers with bloodstained clothes.

"Even if it seems far-fetched, look for any evidence or anyone who acts suspicious that might tie in with this girl's murder," he noted. "If the killer's weird, he might still be wearing the same clothes. And look for any vehicle fires. They may be arson. He could have torched his car to hide any residue of this homicide."

He ended his memo by asking that it not be broadcast

over police radio (where citizens with scanners could pick it up) but that it be relayed only at roll calls when shifts changed.

Detectives contacted Metro Transit to ask for the name of the driver of the bus the girls had taken the night before. Homicide partners Wayne Dorman and Dick Reed talked with the bus driver.

The man searched his memory. "There were a lot of people on the bus coming from downtown, that time on a Saturday night," he said. "I can remember two sets of teenage girls. One set of 'em were both wearing blue. I think one girl got off at Eighty-fifth and Twenty-fourth."

"Anybody get off with her?"

"Maybe. I seem to recall a good-looking young fellow— maybe twenty-two or twenty-three, rides the run a lot, very friendly, six feet, slender, longish brown hair. He talked with the girls and he might have got off with the first one. I can't be sure.

"The other girl rode on up the hill and I think she got off the same time as a middle-aged white guy."

Odd. Minda Craig was positive that Sara Beth got off the bus alone. Detectives figured she would be more likely than the busy bus driver to notice a man getting off with her friend.

Minda examined the purse recovered in Lorraine Olsen's driveway and verified that it was Sara Beth's. "It's got six dollars in it, and that's how much she had when we left the movie."

As far as she could tell, the contents hadn't been disturbed since the last time she'd seen Sara Beth open the purse.

Dick Reed and Wayne Dorman asked Minda about Sara Beth's boyfriends. She said the victim had mostly dated a foreign student at the University of Washington, the son of a very wealthy Iranian family.

"He told Sara Beth that they owned a lot of oil fields or something," Minda said. "I think he was pretty rich, but he didn't make a big deal of it."

"Where did she meet him?"

"At the I. Faces Disco on Second Avenue. She really liked him, and he treated her great. But he's gone home on vacation now. He left for Iran five days ago."

Detectives learned that, in the fairly recent past, Sara Beth had dated other youths, including Ricco Sanchez*— whom she'd also met at the disco—and two brothers, sons of a wealthy family that had a business in the north end: Benny and Frankie Aldalotti.*

According to Minda, Sara Beth was drawn to foreign-looking youths with black hair, dark eyes, and tan complexions.

But Nouri Habid,* the Iranian boy, was the only one she was serious about. She dated the American teenagers on a casual basis, and Minda couldn't remember any of them being jealous.

Sara Beth wasn't perfect, and Minda admitted that she smoked a cigarette once in a while and occasionally sipped a drink, although she never finished the whole thing.

"She wouldn't touch drugs, though," Minda said. "Not even marijuana. She said it made her sleepy when she tried it once, but she mostly just didn't believe in it."

Lynne Carlson said that Sara Beth was very careful to

follow curfew rules set up in their home. "She always called me if she would be even a half an hour late."

Don Cameron's team checked juvenile records, but there were no hits on either Sara Beth or Minda. They were good, normal, "straight" kids.

At 8:15 on Monday morning, July 3, Don Cameron, Mike Tando, and ID tech Marsha Jackson attended Sara Beth's autopsy. Jackson took Sara Beth's fingerprints so that she could differentiate them from the many latents she had lifted in the tire garage.

Sara Beth was five foot four and a half and weighed 130 pounds. Dr. Eisele found that she had been stabbed through her clothing twenty-one times. Her killer had plunged his knife into her upper back, the midline of the chest, and the top of her head. She had numerous defense wounds: palm cuts and bruised knuckles, as if she had fought her killer. There was one through-and-through wound in the soft tissue of her right forearm.

The cause of her death was exsanguination: bleeding to death. The knife had perforated her aorta, her lungs, her liver, and the pericardial sac surrounding her heart. Her skull had been fractured by the head wounds with resultant bone chipping, and another thrust had sliced bone off the spinal column.

Whoever had done this to her had been full of rage.

Eisele commented that it would have taken a killer with tremendous strength to inflict wounds of such force and depth. He was unable to tell if the murderer had been right-

or left-handed, as he had reversed the blade in successive thrusts.

"One thing I'm sure of," the ME said. "She wasn't killed in the restroom. We can account for less than a pint of blood on the floor, less than a pint in her clothing, and another pint in the body cavity. She lost two pints more than that; it's probably in the killer's car or at the site of the actual murder."

"Did she die instantly?" Tando asked.

"Almost. She could have lived for a very short time, but five of her wounds were potentially fatal if she didn't have immediate medical attention."

And no one had come to help her as she lay mortally wounded. It was likely that she was already dead when her killer hid her in the dark cubicle.

It was Dr. Eisele's opinion that Sara Beth had not been raped, or, rather, that her killer had not finished an act of rape. There was no evidence of spermatozoa or semen in her vaginal vault. There was no damage whatsoever to her pelvic area and no bruises on the inside of her thighs.

That was some small comfort to her family.

The investigators wondered if Sara Beth's attacker had hated her for some obscure reason and killed her in an act of perverted revenge.

But who could have been that angry at a sweet fifteen-year-old girl? It was far more likely that her path had crossed that of a sadist on the prowl.

Detective Mike Tando was given principal responsibility for the case; it was one of the rash of homicides that hit the Seattle Police Department in early July 1978, and they didn't have enough detectives to put two of them on the case full-time. The young detective with the wild Afro found himself working twenty-hour days for almost a week, running down the deluge of leads that came in once the story hit the evening TV news and the front pages of Seattle papers.

Tando asked the investigators in the Sex Crimes Unit to go through their files and look for any cases of assault that seemed to mimic the MO of the baffling murder. They did, but they didn't find many with similarities to the murder of Sara Beth Lundquist.

While Tando fielded the plethora of tips coming in, patrolmen and Crimes Specific officers fanned out more widely in the neighborhood where Sara Beth lived and near the remodeled gas station where she was found. They would eventually talk to almost three hundred households—and still glean pitifully little that might help find her murderer.

One man near the alley where her clogs and purse were found recalled hearing a "shout" after midnight and a car revving up its motor and driving away immediately after.

A woman a few blocks from there discovered that some old mattresses in her garage had been uncovered and disarranged. But they had no blood stains on them.

Several homeowners said their dogs had barked frantically at something in the middle of the night. But anyone who owns a dog knows they bark at myriad things—from other dogs to raccoons, to the wind, to actual intruders. The list is endless.

One young woman told a patrolman that she had been out with her boyfriend on the night Sara Beth was killed. "We ran out of gas at Eighty-fifth and Twentieth. I waited alone in my boyfriend's car for him come back with the gas, and this weirdo came out of the dark and tried to get in."

The man, who appeared to be in his twenties, had approached the car and tested all the locked doors. Then he proceeded to masturbate at the window next to her, while she cowered inside. After he ejaculated on the window, he disappeared. This had happened at about ten minutes to one.

Another bus driver—on the alternative Ballard run— said he'd passed by a huge beer party going on near 85th and 15th. It had lasted for most of the night, with scores of young people in all stages of sobriety wandering around. "My last run through was about twelve thirty p.m. and they were still out there then."

On July 4, a resident living at 86th and 22nd NW reported that he'd found a large knife caught in the tall laurel hedge that bordered his yard. The knife had dried dark stains on the blade and handle. Mike Tando picked up the knife, only to find that laboratory analysis showed that the stains were food and animal blood. It had been washed, so the possibility that it had once had human blood on it wasn't ruled out. The criminalists were doing further tests.

Sara Beth's funeral was on July 6. Mike Tando and other detectives mingled unobtrusively among the mourners, watching for someone who looked out of place or whose emotions seemed inappropriate. But there was no one there who raised their antennas.

A few days later, Tando talked at length with Lynne Carlson in an effort to find something, anything, that might point to her daughter's killer. But he learned nothing that could help the investigation.

Sara Beth and her mother had had a warm relationship. She had never run away or balked at her family's house rules. She was happy. She would never, ever have gotten in a car, or gone with someone she didn't know. Her mother confirmed Minda's opinion that Sara Beth was frightened of alleys after dark. She wouldn't have taken a shortcut home after midnight, but she would have fought hard for her life if someone grabbed her and dragged her into an alley.

Sara Beth had planned a trip on Sunday, July 2, with the Aldalotti family, and their sons Benny and Frankie, the two brothers she dated casually. Frankie had come by to pick her up on Sunday morning. Told that Sara Beth was missing, he had decided to go on ahead to his parents' lodge on the Olympic Peninsula. The Aldalottis had called later that day to see if Sara Beth had returned safely. Her mother told them that she was dead. They were stunned and saddened.

Mike Tando was a little put off that Frankie Aldalotti hadn't initially been very worried when he heard Sara Beth was missing. Perhaps some of the young men Sara Beth considered to be platonic friends didn't see it that way. Jealousy has always been a motive for murder.

Still, Sara Beth's mother and sister confirmed that her current romantic interest was Nouri Habid, the Iranian student who was currently visiting in his native country. And she hadn't dated Ricco Sanchez for a month or more.

Sara loved to go dancing at I. Faces, but she usually went there with her girlfriends.

Mike Tando answered tips and offers of help that continued to pour in. As time passed, however, they grew stranger. As it happens with most high-profile murder cases, real and self-styled psychics offered to help with the case.

One man insisted that he'd had a remarkably clear dream where *he* had experienced Sara Beth's feelings as she was being killed. He had his dates wrong, and he was under the impression she had been shot. Tando sighed and put this "tip" into the "220 File." (This is Seattle police language for mentally disturbed people; in the early 1900s, officers were paid a $2.20 bonus when they were dispatched to this kind of often dangerous call. In California, the code is "51/50" for someone mentally off balance.)

A group of psychics offered to hold a séance and promised to get back to Tando with whatever "clues" they turned up. Evidently they didn't find any because he never heard from them again.

Because Sara Beth's killer could be *anyone*, there was an invisible veil of panic in Ballard. Women of all ages who were approached by men they didn't know expected the worst and called 911. Patrol units were kept busy. Most of the incidents turned out to be friendly, would-be pickups, but everyone was running scared.

A receptionist at the Asian Services Center reported that she'd received a call from a youth who'd rambled on and finally confessed that he'd "killed a girl in Ballard." But he had the details of Sara Beth's case all wrong.

Hers was the kind of murder case that pulled kooks out of the woodwork.

Two patrol officers were in the area of the tire store a

few nights after the murder. Shortly after 11:00 p.m., they watched a man loitering near the restroom. He was drunk and sobbing, and they were somewhat surprised when he asked them for a flashlight.

"He told us he was Sara Beth's neighbor, and he said he'd found her shoes."

The man was Sven Olsen—the thirty-five-year-old son of Lorraine Olsen, who had found Sara Beth's purse and clogs! They wondered what he was looking for in the place where her body had lain.

It was enough to make detectives look more closely at Olsen. He was showing excessive sorrow over her death. They learned that, twice, he had attempted to see her body at the mortuary. When they talked with him, Olsen agreed that it was he who had found Sara Beth's shoes and purse and brought them into his house. He'd felt very guilty ever since, wondering if she died because of inaction on his part.

"I thought I should call someone, but I didn't know who. I went to bed instead," he said, wiping away a tear. "Maybe I could have saved her somehow."

Sven Olsen had known both of the Lundquist girls since the time he'd clerked in a 7-Eleven in the neighborhood.

It was hours later—on Sunday afternoon—when he showed the clogs and purse to his mother, and she called Lynne Carlson.

Sven Olsen's coming home about the time Sara Beth was murdered and his overwhelming emotional reaction over the death of someone he didn't know *did* make him a likely suspect for a while. Still, further investigation showed only that he was an unhappy man with a drinking problem, employed, somewhat ironically, as a bartender.

Detective Mike Tando talked with patrons at the Blue Gill tavern where Olsen worked. Those who were there on Saturday night were positive that Sven had never left the tavern between the time he came on shift in the early evening of July 1 and 2:00 a.m., when it closed. Whoever had seized Sara Beth had to have attacked her within five or ten minutes of when she got off the bus at twenty minutes after midnight.

Tando was hitting all the catch-22's that go along with murders with no obvious suspects. Anything was possible, and it was always a question of how far he should go on which tips. In retrospect, what is essential to solving a murder seems obvious. From the other end, it isn't that easy.

A photographer who worked at I. Faces called in. "I take slides of the dancers, and then we project them on a giant screen at the disco," he said. "I'm sure that Sara Beth and Minda were at I. Faces both Friday and Saturday nights. I have pictures of Sara to prove it."

But he didn't. Mike Tando looked carefully at all the slides in question and failed to find any photos of Sara Beth, although he saw a few that resembled her.

"We weren't there," Minda insisted when Tando asked her about the previous weekend. "We went out for a Coke on Friday night at a restaurant in the north end, and then we talked to some boys we knew in a park. And on Saturday night, we went to the movie, but you already know that."

Another promising lead ending nowhere.

It wasn't that people weren't trying to help. Seattleites had taken Sara Beth to their hearts, even though they hadn't known her. The slightest change in ordinary behavior alerted them. Neighbors even reported one man who'd been seen washing down his back porch and steps the morning after Sara Beth was murdered. That wasn't really guilty behavior, but Tando talked to him anyway. "I'd washed all the windows in the back and got dirt on the porch," he said. "So I just decided to wash it."

His housemates verified this. "He was home with us all of Saturday night."

With more leads coming in almost hourly, Mike Tando was astounded at the number of weirdos who apparently resided within the tightly populated, circumspect community of Ballard. It was as if someone had lifted the roofs off scores of houses, and the secrets once safely hidden inside were exposed for everyone to see.

But that holds true for *any* area; everyone has hidden, private things—some more peculiar than others.

The mother of a teenager in Ballard called to say that her fifteen-year-old daughter and a girlfriend had been terrified during a recent bus ride. A man in his twenties chose a seat across the aisle from them, and then he'd removed a long knife from his waistband.

"He was enjoying how scared they were," she said worriedly. "He kind of pantomimed how he could hide the knife in his work glove and up his sleeve."

"Did they know him?"

"No. They never saw him before. Now they're afraid to get on a bus, and I'm afraid, too."

She agreed to call Tando if they saw the man again, or if anyone knew who he was.

The homicide file on Sara Beth's case grew thicker every day. Detectives got a call from the manager of a motel on Aurora Avenue North. The area was becoming low rent, but it wasn't yet a regular stroll for teenage prostitutes that it would become one day.

"One of our maids started to clean a unit," the manager said excitedly, "and she said it was 'awash with blood.' That's just how she put it!"

When investigators arrived, however, they found only isolated spots of the dried brownish-red. The manager and the maid had exaggerated. Now that he was calmer, he admitted that he'd just learned that a family had had a drunken free-for-all in the unit over the weekend.

A special agent with the FBI, assigned to Seattle, was much more believable. He reported that he regularly commuted downtown on the same bus run in Ballard that Sara Beth and Minda had taken on Saturday, July 1. His position made him more observant than most people, and he'd become concerned.

"On several occasions, I've noticed a dirty white car following close behind that bus," he said. "I've tried to get a license number, but the tag's always covered with mud. I'll keep watching for it."

A thirteen-year-old junior high student found a knife in the street near 83rd and 24th NW. Unfortunately, he played with it for a day before calling the police, contaminating most of the evidence that might have been on the knife. Even so, like the other found knife, it was retained for lab tests.

Many readers of mysteries and true crime know that an unknown killer is usually someone who moves in the same circles as the victim—a lover or spouse, a relative, friend, coworker, classmate. Good detectives do start with those closest to the victim and work their way through ever-widening possibilities.

Sara Beth had been quite close to the Aldalotti family, and was said to have gone out with both their sons. Benny, the younger brother, said he had seen Sara Beth the night before she was killed. "And I talked to her on the phone several times. We were mostly talking about how she was going to ride to our cabin on Sunday with Frankie."

Frankie Aldalotti, nineteen, was living in another state, but he flew home to visit his family on Saturday evening, July 1. He was the brother who had planned to pick her up the next morning for the vacation trip and who first learned that she was missing.

Benny Aldalotti wouldn't speculate on who might have killed Sara Beth.

"But she seemed nervous about something when I talked to her in front of her house Friday evening," Benny said. "She told me she really wanted to go up to our cabin for the Fourth of July weekend, but she didn't think it would look right for us to date.

"I asked her, 'What are you talking about?' 'Cause it wasn't a date. She seemed confused about where we stood. Maybe she felt like she'd be cheating on Nouri. I know Sara Beth hadn't dated Ricco Sanchez for almost two months."

Frankie Aldalotti had to be interviewed by phone; he'd already flown back home.

Detectives wondered about the location of Sara's Beth's rich boyfriend from Iran. Had he *really* left America? They checked with customs in both countries and verified that he had, indeed, left the country on June 28, arrived in Iran, and hadn't yet returned to the United States.

The only other boyfriend that Sara had seen regularly in the months prior to her death was Ricco Sanchez. Mike Tando found that Sanchez worked at a Black Angus restaurant when he was dating Sara Beth. He didn't own a car, so he had picked her up in a taxi for their dates. A check at the Black Angus revealed that Sanchez had quit his job. His last day was either the Wednesday or Thursday after the July Fourth weekend.

Detectives Duane Homan and Paul Eblin went to Sanchez's address and talked with his mother. She promised she would have him contact detectives as soon as possible.

On July 20, Ricco Sanchez appeared at headquarters, ready to talk with homicide detectives. Ricco, sixteen, said he was eager to help in the investigation of Sara Beth's death.

"I only knew her for about a month. We went out a couple of times—to the movies and the drive-in. I met her at I. Faces. I used to call her a lot—just to talk."

"Where were you on the Saturday night Sara was killed?" Mike Tando asked abruptly.

"A friend and I went camping in the Cascade foothills on June 29—Thursday—and we didn't come back until Sunday when we were rained out," Ricco said. "I didn't know about what happened to Sara until that night when my friend called and told me to look in the paper. I was shocked. I still am," he finished, bowing his head.

"Did you kill Sara?" Tando asked.

"No, sir. I didn't."

"Why would someone kill Sara Beth?" Paul Eblin asked.

"The only reason I can think why anyone would kill her would be over jealousy. If somebody who wanted to go out with her—only she wouldn't—is all I can think of."

Asking a suspect for his opinion on how to solve a crime is an old and effective technique; actual murderers tend to enjoy the cat-and-mouse game that puts them in the role of experts on the subject. As they pontificate on what detectives should look for, they often reveal more about themselves than they mean to.

Was Sanchez telling them that *he* had been jealous when Sara Beth stopped dating him? They didn't think so, and he knew that they would check on his camping story. He impressed the detectives as sincere. He seemed to be playing it straight with them.

And, of course, they checked his alibi about the camping trip and found it to be true.

In most homicide cases, there aren't enough suspects. In the case of Sara Beth Lundquist, there were too many. Old boyfriends, new boyfriends, peculiar neighborhood characters, strangers who might have been attracted to the exquisite teenager, and possibly sexual predators who chanced upon her when she was all alone.

Detective Pat Lamphere of the Sex Crimes Unit talked with Mike Tando about one of her cases. A seventeen-year-old girl had been abducted at knifepoint and raped by a man who drove a van. The victim was walking home after dark on a street not too far away from where Sara Beth was last seen alive.

"The interesting thing is," Lamphere said, "our victim

goes to I. Faces to dance all the time. Look at her picture; she's almost a twin of Sara Lundquist."

The rapist Pat Lamphere sought had gotten away clean because his victim was too upset to think about checking the license plate as he sped off.

July 1978 was coming to an end, and the case file on Sara Beth Lundquist was now as thick as an encyclopedia. Mike Tando started another file. Practically everyone who had ever known Sara Beth had been interviewed, as well as occupants of homes for many blocks around the alley where she was thought to have been attacked. Her girlfriends were frightened, too, and reported every call they received from boys or men they didn't know.

On July 28, Nouri Habid called from Iran and talked to Lynne Carlson. He was worried because Sara Beth hadn't written to him as she'd promised. Lynne had to tell him that Sara Beth had been dead since two days after he'd left. Brokenhearted, Nouri said he would fly at once to the United States.

On August 7, a woman walked into the Public Safety Building and asked to talk to a homicide detective. She seemed distraught and said that something had been bothering her for a long time.

Detective George Marberg ushered her into an interview room.

"I live on Fifteenth and Northwest Fiftieth," she began. "On July first, or very early on the second, I heard my dog barking at something outside, and I couldn't get him to be quiet. Then I noticed a car in front of my house. I saw two young men and they were either carrying a young woman or helping her into the car. I just thought that she'd had too much to drink at the tavern, but then I got to thinking about the girl they found in the garage."

It might have been just the lead that Detective Sergeant Don Cameron's crew had been waiting for, but they were disappointed when the woman said she suffered from glaucoma, which rendered her eyesight only marginal. She'd been able to see that the men had been about the same height and dressed in dark clothing, but her failing vision had blurred their features.

It might make sense. At 130 pounds and in good physical shape, Sara Beth could have put up a good fight against one man; she would have had little chance against two.

But why? Her autopsy hadn't indicated that a sexual attack had been the motive. She wasn't robbed. She wasn't involved in drugs. And she had been perfectly honest in her relationships with the young men she dated. She hadn't told her mother, her sister, or her friends that she was afraid of anyone. Her killer or killers had to have been consumed by an abnormal mental state, perhaps driven by an obsession kept hidden until that midnight as July 1 turned into July 2.

The only motive that really made sense was that Sara Beth had been murdered by someone in a mighty rage; the "overkill" from so many stab wounds pointed to an out-of-control killer.

Enough residents had heard that one "scream" or "shout" close to 12:30 a.m. near the bus stop where Sara Beth got off to convince detectives that she had been seized almost as soon as she left the pseudoprotection of the streetlight. She had then been dragged into the alley, losing her purse and clogs along the way.

But there was no blood in the alley. There were two pints of blood still unaccounted for. She had probably been grabbed, her mouth covered after she managed to scream only once, and forced into a car. The blood that would have coursed from her wounds was undoubtedly in her killer's car or truck. If that vehicle could be located, surely traces of her blood would still be present. No amount of cleaning could remove them. Nor was it likely that her murderer had avoided getting blood on himself and his clothing.

But they had no suspect. They had no vehicle with suspicious stains.

Don Cameron and Mike Tando clocked the mileage from the alley to the tire garage. It was 3.1 miles and the trip took five and a half minutes at normal driving speeds in average traffic. It was almost a certainty that Sara Beth was unconscious or dead when she was placed in the restroom.

Detectives believed that someone other than the killer knew about his crime; it didn't seem something that he could keep to himself. They believed he had probably been violent in the past and would almost certainly be violent again—unless he was stopped.

And that belief disturbed them mightily.

I wrote the article about Sara Beth Lundquist's unsolved murder thirty years ago, and I asked that anyone who might have new information contact Detective Sergeant Don Cameron and Detective Mike Tando in the Public Safety

Building in Seattle. There was a $5,000 reward for information leading to an arrest and conviction.

Along with many other investigators who worked so hard to solve Sara Beth's murder, Don Cameron is dead. Mike Tando's Afro is long since tamed, and he has retired from the Seattle Police Department. None of the men and women who were assigned to some part of the Lundquist case are active police officers now. Even the Public Safety Building is gone, reduced to rubble to make way for a newer building. I have a chunk of marble from the "very modern" structure where I worked as a rookie cop. It has a treasured place in my garden now.

But over all these years, no one who followed this case has ever forgotten Sara Beth Lundquist, even though it seemed there would be no answers. Her mother, Lynne, often wondered if she would die herself before she ever learned who had taken away her precious daughter. Her little brother, Lee, has turned forty, and Sara Beth's friends are well into middle age now as she herself would be—had she been allowed to live.

When the answer did come, I was astounded. Perhaps I shouldn't have been. There were remarkable similarities between Sara Beth Lundquist's murder and another homicide that occurred that summer of 1978. Today, the truth shines through the years like a beacon, but it was obscured back then, a pale light covered by the fog of too many cases, a certain failure to communicate among and between diverse police departments, misleading autopsy results, and the state of forensic science at the time Sara Beth was killed.

As I said earlier, it's so much easier to view a homicide

puzzle in retrospect. Everything can fall into place perfectly when you're looking back. When certain facts or information aren't available, seeing clearly ahead in a baffling case with too many "witnesses" can, indeed, be like trying to negotiate a cleverly designed maze.

In major cities all over America, police departments have established cold case squads, where detectives search through dusty files and blurry carbon copies written by their predecessors years before. Combining long-unsolved homicides with modern forensic science and fresh eyes, these cold case investigators have been far more successful than anyone could hope. Over the past few years, the Seattle Police Department's cold case squads have successfully closed several cases dormant for more than three decades. Greg Mixsell, Richard Gagnon, and Mike Ciesynski have used DNA matches and other forensic science near-miracles to take another look at physical evidence carefully preserved in the huge warehouse that replaced the police department's Property Room of the fifties and sixties.

And that evidence has given up untold secrets.

The evidence warehouse became necessary in 2004, having outgrown its former location in the Public Safety Building. It includes everything from specks of blood to entire walls that have been sawed out of crime scenes. A room-sized freezer preserves biological evidence: blood, bloody clothing, saliva, semen.

Sergeant Cindy Granard, one of the custodians of this massive collection of evidence, is passionately protective of it, and for good reason. "We want to arrest the right person, or be able to exonerate someone. The public needs to know the great care we take to protect these items."

Unless detectives agree to have evidence that is no longer needed destroyed, everything in the warehouse must be kept sacrosanct for *eighty years*!

Was it even within the realm of possibility that Sara Beth Lundquist's killer would ever be caught? Might there be something left to examine that couldn't be tested when she was killed because the expertise wasn't there then?

As Greg Mixsell and Richard Gagnon moved on, Detective Mike Ciesynski has become "Mr. Cold Case" in the Seattle department. He wasn't that much older than Sara Beth Lundquist back in 1978 when he was growing up in Chicago. Mike always wanted to be a cop. He joined the force in Calumet City, Illinois, and then moved west to be a police officer in Casper, Wyoming. Eventually, he and his family moved even farther west. He joined the Seattle Police Department and added more years of law enforcement experience. He now has served twenty-five years as a cop and a detective.

In 2005, Mike worked cold cases for the Seattle Police Department.

On March 9, 2005, Ciesynski received a phone call from Lee Lundquist, Sara's younger brother. Lee was close to forty then, not the kid brother that she had treated so kindly. Ciesynski could tell that Lee Lundquist would never rest until he found out who had killed her.

Lee believed that Frankie Aldalotti, who was supposed to drive her to his family's cabin on the July 4th holiday, was her killer.

"I think there was a limo driver involved, too," Lee said. "His nickname might be 'Junior.'"

Mike Ciesynski pulled Sara Beth's case out of the archives and reviewed it. It became a priority for him. Twenty-seven years had passed since she was killed. As he pored over the files, he looked at the crime scene photos and memorized the picture of a lovely young girl who never grew older than fifteen.

Ciesynski saw that there were many, many homicides in 1978, and most of them had been solved years earlier. He tried to connect unsolved cases with other murders in that time frame—to see if there might be similarities that would stand out.

He then went to the warehouse where 162,000 pieces of evidence waited for a time they might be needed. He was gratified to find that the physical evidence that had been carefully preserved in July 1978 was still there. Sara Beth's clothing remained intact, sealed against age and loss—her jean jacket and slacks, her silky shirt, her clogs, her undergarments. The chain of evidence had been maintained.

Ciesynski reached carefully into one pocket of her denim outfit and pulled out the ticket stub for *Damien: Omen II*.

Suddenly he was back in 1978.

As Ciesynski turned the clothing inside out, he spotted a stain and some dark pubic hairs on her leotard. The stains might be semen or saliva. It would be a miracle if something carrying DNA still existed. But if Sara Beth's killer had prematurely ejaculated before he could carry out rape, that faint stain *could* be semen.

He packaged the clothing with delicate caution. To a homicide detective, it might be as precious as diamonds. To be absolutely sure of what he had, Mike Ciesynski needed to find samples of blood and semen preserved from Sara Beth's body.

There he was stymied. There were no samples from her in the evidence warehouse, nor were there any medical records that might lead to Sara Beth's genetic profile.

But he'd heard that sometimes the King County Medical Examiner's Office preserved swabs and slides after postmortem examinations. To Ciesynski's great relief, the ME had saved just such items for almost thirty years.

On March 25, Ciesynski picked up three anal, oral, and vaginal slides that had been retained from Sara Beth's autopsy. He sent them to the Washington State Patrol crime lab. Even the tiniest speck of DNA can now be replicated infinitely, so small samples are no longer in danger of being destroyed by the tests for a genetic profile.

While he waited for the results from the lab, Ciesynski looked for phone, address, or Internet listings for a woman named Penny Martin,* who was an ex-girlfriend of Frankie Aldalotti. He found a listing in that name, but the woman who answered the phone said she didn't know anyone named Aldalotti.

"I've heard of another Penny Martin, though," she said. "I think she works for the Kent School District."

The second Penny wasn't the right woman, either.

The cold case detective was disappointed but not ready to give up. He was elated, and a little surprised, when he heard from a Washington State parole officer in late May. Frankie Aldalotti hadn't exactly lived a crime-free life in the years since Sara Beth was murdered.

"We know him," the parole officer said. "My partner and I went to arrest him after he abducted and raped his girlfriend back in the seventies. We picked him up at his parents' house and transported him to the King County Jail. When we got there, he pulled out a six-inch .357 revolver and held us hostage for several hours."

The parole officers had emerged unscathed, but it was a very dicey period for them.

Ciesynski located another former girlfriend of Frankie Aldalotti. He spoke with Maggie Cochran* in August 2005. She vaguely remembered being interviewed by detectives about Sara Beth back in 1978, although she had tried to put Frankie out of her mind after a terrifying relationship.

"I remember Frankie," she said. "Since he shot me, I guess it's to be expected I'd remember him very well."

Maggie and Frankie's romance was mercifully short and soon disintegrated into violence, although she found it hard to get away from him. She said that Frankie had abducted her twice and taken her to his father's cabin, where he raped her.

"One time he beat me up," Maggie said. "He threw me against a wall and fired a dart gun at me. The next time he forced me up there, he put a gun in my mouth and raped me. He also threatened me with a long screwdriver."

The only way she had gotten away after the second rape was to convince him that she'd go back to dating him if he would just drive her back from the cabin to her home.

"I didn't report the first two rapes," Maggie said, "but Frankie was getting progressively worse. I broke up with him and was relieved to be done with it. But then he smashed my bedroom window and fired at me with a twenty-two."

"Were you injured?" Ciesynski asked.

"The bullets hit me in my thigh and my buttocks."

That had been the absolute last straw. Frankie had done some prison time—for the crimes against Maggie and also for holding two parole officers hostage.

"I never saw Frankie again," Maggie Cochran said, "and that was just fine with me!"

Maybe Lee Lundquist was right about Frankie Aldalotti. He certainly sounded like a dangerous man with an uncontrollable temper. Ciesynski needed something with Aldalotti's DNA on it to send to the crime lab for comparison. He and Greg Mixsell drove to the latest address listed for the suspect.

Casually, Mike walked past the house, pretending he was looking for an address. There was a white Chevrolet pickup truck parked in front of the residence. He spotted three cigarette butts lying in the street just next to the driver's door. Without skipping a beat, he reached down and scooped them up. To an onlooker, he seemed to be tying his shoelace, but he held what might be vital evidence in his hand. After he was back in the detective's "sneaker" car, he slipped the butts into an envelope and sealed and labeled it.

If the traces of saliva on the cigarette butts matched the DNA that was being tested on Sara Beth's clothes and in the medical examiner's samples, they would have evidence against Aldalotti.

It seemed to be a shoo-in.

Months passed, but the Washington State Patrol forensic lab had a long backup of testing to do on more recent cases. It was September 18, 2006, when Mike Ciesynski finally received a phone call from William Stubbs, a forensic scientist employed there.

"We have a match," he said.

Ciesynski held his breath. He expected it to be Frankie Aldalotti.

But it was no shoo-in. Frankie Aldalotti might have been an undesirable boyfriend, but he was not the man who had ejaculated on Sara Beth's clothing and on her person.

It was a major disappointment for the cold case detective. Everything had seemed to fit perfectly. Stubbs said that he had been able to obtain a DNA typing profile from one of the anal swabs at the medical examiner's office. "We searched it against CODIS [Combined DNA Index System] and it matches the DNA of a Clarence E. Williams. Now we need a reference sample from Williams."

At that point, Mike Ciesynski didn't know who Clarence Williams was, but he located the old case file and read about Laura Baylis's murder. She had been abducted and killed thirteen weeks after Sara Beth died. He ticked off the similarities between Laura and Sara Beth's homicides.

Ciesynski read that a witness in the Baylis case, Mercina Adderly, had told detectives that Clarence Williams had talked about "wanting to hurt someone" sometime "in the summer" of 1978. Ciesynski wondered if that was before Sara Beth's murder or before Laura Baylis's murder.

According to the Washington State Corrections Department, Clarence Williams was currently housed in a prison in Monroe. Mike Ciesynski made plans to pay Williams a visit, but first he compared the two cases, detail by detail. There were, indeed, similarities:

- Both were attractive young females.
- They had both been stabbed multiple times, almost equally divided between their breasts and their upper backs. Laura had suffered nineteen stab wounds. Sara Beth had sustained twenty-one. The patterns and number of stabs were almost ritualistic.
- Each had been attacked on a weekend.
- Both were Caucasian.
- Both appeared to have been seized in one place, killed in another, and left in a closet-sized space, with little blood evident.
- Initially, there appeared to have been no conclusive signs of sexual attack in either murder.

There were, of course, other variables that *didn't* match. Laura was a world traveler, used to taking care of herself, and Sara Beth a naïve girl in her midteens. The MO of the crimes matched—but the neighborhoods where the young women were abducted were more than twenty miles apart. The distance from Ballard to Beacon Hill was significant. Ballard was in northwest Seattle, while Beacon Hill was in the southeast. One of the most convincing ways to link a single killer to a pattern is finding that he picks the same type of victim, uses the same MO, and operates within a specific area.

But not always. Gary Ridgway, the "Green River Killer," usually stayed near Sea-Tac Airport or the Aurora strip to find his victims, and disposed of them in rugged, wild areas inside a haphazard "circle" around Seattle. But Harvey Carignan, the "Want-Ad Killer," killed women from Alaska to Minnesota, marking their body sites with red crayon circles on a map. Serial killers came in two categories: cross-country travelers trolling for victims and those attached to one area.

Maybe there was a good reason that Sara Beth's killer had strayed outside his "comfort zone."

Ciesynski called the Monroe Correctional Complex. He wanted to be sure that Williams was still there. He was. Corrections investigator Bob Hoover e-mailed a photo of him as he looked twenty-eight years after Laura died. He was the same man who appeared in the lineup photos viewed by people who had come into the 7-Eleven on Beacon Hill the night Laura disappeared. But now he was an old man, grizzled with gray beard stubble.

The cold case probe moved ahead rapidly. There was a real sense of urgency; Clarence Williams would be up for parole in fewer than eight years, when he was seventy-one. At that age, and after almost forty years behind bars, there was a good chance the Washington State Parole Board would release him.

Reading over Laura's and Sara Beth's files, Ciesynski was convinced that Clarence Williams would still be dangerous—probably murderously dangerous. Mike Ciesynski agrees with other experts on serial murder; as long as they are physically able and free, serial killers continue to take lives, and it doesn't matter how old they are.

In February 2007, Mike Ciesynski and Detective Weklych drove to the Monroe Complex armed with a search warrant. Weklych read Clarence Williams his Miranda rights, and he signed the form that showed he understood and was willing to talk with them.

Ciesynski advised Clarence that he was under investigation for the murder of Sara Beth Lundquist. There was little reaction from the suspect. He shrugged his shoulders and said, "I didn't do either of those murders."

"We've matched your DNA to Sara Beth," Ciesynski said.

Again, Williams shrugged. "I picked up a seventeen- or eighteen-year-old girl on Pike Street and paid her twenty dollars for sex," he said almost casually. "I dropped her off around the Fremont Bridge. I picked up a lot of prostitutes around Pike Street, and I had regular sex and sometimes oral sex with them. I didn't use no condom."

Mike Ciesynski managed to hide his distaste for the prisoner as he told Williams that explanation wouldn't wash. "Sara Beth Lundquist wasn't a prostitute. She was a young girl in high school, a virgin.

"Are you familiar with the Ballard area?" he asked next.

"No."

The detectives knew that was a lie. Ciesynski had checked Williams's work record, along with job applications. He listed Foss Shipyard as a former employer. Foss Tugs and Foss Shipyard were located on the waterfront in Ballard.

"Sara Beth was found at Bill's Tire Store. You said you worked for Seattle Disposal, too. That's at Thirty-four hundred Phinney North, *exactly* one mile from Bill's."

"Okay," Williams said, annoyed. "You want me to say I killed her. I killed her. I picked her up on Pike Street, drove to the tire store, and dumped her. Is that what you want? I don't need another homicide beef."

It was, in a sense, a confession, but it probably wouldn't hold up. Clarence Williams was being sarcastic. Ciesynski and Weklych left, with a promise to be back. They would bring along the DNA results and let Williams read them for himself.

On March 16, Mike Ciesynski returned to the Monroe complex. He handed a copy of the DNA report to Williams. He scanned it and then said, "You're asking me to remember something that happened thirty years ago." He shrugged once more and said, "What can I say?"

He didn't say anything. When Ciesynski saw that Williams had shut down again, he concluded the interview. Handing him a card, he said, "Give me a call if you ever decide to talk."

Four days later, Frankie Aldalotti finally called the cold case detective. He was no longer a suspect, but Ciesynski was interested in talking with him anyway. He might have some bit of information that would add to the strength of murder charges against Williams.

He didn't. Frankie said that Sara Beth had really been Benny's friend. "I didn't know her very well, and I never dated her or was interested in dating her. We didn't have any type of relationship and I don't know anything about her background."

Mike Ciesynski was confident that they were close to bringing murder charges against Clarence Williams, close enough that he felt safe in letting Lynne Carlson know that. He called and updated her.

To be absolutely, totally armed with DNA evidence, Ciesynski sent Sara Beth's panties to a private lab, Forensic Sciences Associates. Technicians there confirmed the match. There was a tiny area of spermatozoa on the back of the panties. It had emerged from a male with a specific analysis of the amelogenin gene.

"The calculated genotype frequencies," the report read in a language few understand, "indicate that it is unlikely that more than one human has ever possessed this genotype array."

The buccal (cheek) swab that Ciesynski had taken from Clarence Williams was identical in genotype array.

There were possibly other witnesses who would tie up the case. So many of those involved in 1978 had passed away. Dr. Eisele, the original forensic pathologist who had done the autopsy on Sara Beth, had died, along with several homicide detectives. But Mike Ciesynski had found Minda Craig, Sara Beth's best friend, who remembered that Saturday night in 1978 as if it were yesterday. Her sadness over the loss of her friend had never faded, and she said she would be glad to testify.

He didn't expect, however, to find Lorraine Olsen, the neighbor who heard Sara Beth scream that night. She'd been past middle age then.

But Lorraine Olsen was alive and in a wheelchair, being cared for by her son who had found Sara Beth's shoes and purse, and she was over eighty.

"But I think she can testify," her son assured Ciesynski. "I think she will want to do that."

During the summer of 2007, Clarence Williams was one of four hundred convicts who'd been moved to the Prairie Correctional Facility in Appleton, Minnesota, because of overpopulation in correctional facilities in Washington.

Mike Ciesynski flew to Minnesota on October 23. Prison guards at the facility led him to an empty mess hall, a huge room. Other than some men cleaning the serving counter forty feet away, and a guard at the door, he was alone with Clarence Williams.

He found Clarence Williams disgruntled because he believed that the cold case detective had orchestrated the Minnesota transfer. He had not. It would have been more convenient for the investigation to have had Williams remain in Monroe, only thirty miles from Seattle Police headquarters.

Read his rights once more, Williams signed it and asked wearily, "What now?"

"You're going to be transferred back to the King County Jail in Seattle."

"I never asked to come here in the first place." Williams didn't ask why he was being sent back. He undoubtedly knew why.

Ciesynski outlined the similar stabbing pattern—and number of wounds—found on both Laura Baylis and Sara Beth Lundquist.

Williams sighed and shrugged, his usual reaction. "I've got nothing to say about that. I didn't stab that other girl."

All unconsciously, he had admitted for the very first time to stabbing Laura Baylis.

It was obvious, though, that he wouldn't admit to anything else. Ciesynski stood up and said, "See you in Seattle."

Senior Deputy Prosecuting Attorney Kristin Richardson, who heads the Cold Case Division of the King County Prosecutor's Office, oversaw filing charges against Clarence Williams, now sixty-two. He was charged with rape, kidnapping, and first-degree murder in Sara Beth's death. He was extradited from Minnesota to face the charges in Seattle, and he was arraigned on November 20, 2007.

His court-appointed attorney was taken off guard when Williams attempted to take an Alford plea without consulting him. The Alford meant that Williams would tell the judge that he would not admit guilt, but that he believed he would be found guilty if he went to trial.

His attorney hastily intervened and the judge agreed to accept "no plea" until there was agreement between Williams and his lawyer.

He formally entered an Alford plea on December 3.

Sara Beth's family watched from the gallery as the tall, muscled man who had killed her stood within feet of them. They felt some relief to know that he had been locked behind bars during all the years they wondered who he was. At least he hadn't killed anyone else after Laura Baylis's murder. Nor would he ever be free to kill again.

Six days before Christmas 2007, those who loved Sara

Beth told Clarence Edward Williams what he had done when he ended the life of a girl he "couldn't remember."

She would never go to college, never fall in love and get married, never have children or grandchildren—never have a chance to live out the seventy-plus years that she might have expected. All the Christmases, Easters, birthdays that should have been ahead, washed away like letters carved into a sandy beach.

Kristin Richardson read the letter that Lynne Carlson had written, while Williams sat without expression or acknowledgment: " 'There will be no language to describe the depths of my grief . . . no words to describe my pain in seeing my other children suffer. You took the life of a sweet and innocent child, but you can never take her spirit or her laughter, or her precious love, from me.' "

Clarence Williams declined to make a statement before he was sentenced. To paraphrase him, *"What could he say?"*

On December 17, 2007, Clarence Williams was sentenced to 361 months to life in prison, to run consecutively to the eight years he still had to serve for Laura Baylis's murder. It was, for a sixty-two-year-old man, a life sentence.

Clarence Williams came to Seattle from Milwaukee and lived there four years. Mike Ciesynski is still looking at other long-dormant homicides that occurred in the Seattle area during that time frame. And he has alerted Milwaukee authorities that if they consider Williams a possible suspect, they may find answers to *their* unsolved cases in the sixties and seventies.

For Sara Beth Lundquist and for Laura Baylis, there is, at long last, a bleak justice. The man who abducted and murdered them will never walk free again. And yet he lives and breathes, eats, sleeps, watches television, exercises, may have friends and family.

And they do not. Although Laura and Sara Beth never met, they share a sisterhood. I suspect that each of them would have fought to save the other if there had been two of them facing a violent sexual predator.

But neither of them had a chance.

NOT SAFE AT
HOME

This is an alarming story because most of us feel safe when we arrive home and bolt the doors to the outside world, and, even if we live alone, home is supposed to be a safe harbor. As we saw in the Mauck case, that isn't always true.

My own "security system" begins with three very large Bernese mountain dogs who are devoted to me and are very suspicious of strangers. I have an alarm system, too, but their low growl and angry barking is the earliest warning. Not to mention my "attack cat," Bunnie, who thinks he is a dog and is tougher than any canine.

I'll admit that I want to frighten readers just a little as I tell my most memorable true crimes—but only to make you all wary and prepared with an almost automatic plan of what to do if someone stalks you or attacks you. Those who survive sudden attacks are invariably those who react within seconds. Rapists and killers don't want to attract attention; their favorite targets are would-be victims who are stunned into passivity and silence until it is too late to save themselves.

The woman who was watched surreptitiously and

stalked in the following case would never have suspected *who* the phantom in her world was, and that was when she lost her advantage. Without really noticing the date when this investigation occurred, I was a little shocked to realize that I had inadvertently chosen a crime that had taken place on the very same July 4th four-day holiday in 1978 when Sara Beth Lundquist vanished. The victims had no connection at all, save the date that each encountered a different sadistic sociopath.

Strange. I have no idea why I happened to go back to that weekend thirty years ago. I picked these cases because they fit a pattern—and didn't look at the date. This case— and Sara Beth's murder—happened years ago, but similar crimes still occur somewhere in America every day.

I hope "Not Safe at Home" will make my readers more cautious and enable them to file an instinctual response deep in their thought processes until it's so solidly implanted that it becomes like a tattoo on the brain.

Traia Carr found herself at a crossroads in her life when she was in her fifties. She'd never expected her marriage to end in divorce. After all, they'd been together for thirty years, and it seemed they would celebrate their golden wedding anniversary together. But life can change suddenly and take sharp turns when we least expect it. Even though the divorce was amicable and she and her ex kept in touch often, it wasn't the same. Traia had never lived all alone in her life.

Traia had managed to cope with those changes. She adjusted to life as a single woman, and the pain that had been as sharp as glass shards a few years earlier slowly softened. She was an attractive woman who appeared to be in her early forties, not her late fifties. After a while she started to date, and she had many invitations.

Her home was a neat bungalow on Third Street in Marysville, Washington. Marysville is a small town just five miles north of Everett, the Snohomish County seat. Traia's hometown was adjacent to I-5, the interstate freeway that runs from California to Vancouver. Most travelers know it as a good place to stop for lunch or supper, but they know little else about Marysville: a workingman's town where ostentation is rare. Most homes are like Traia's, with wood siding or shingles. You don't find mansions in Marysville.

From the freeway, those who bother to look out their windows at the landscape from Everett to Marysville can see rivers and ponds—wider and deeper in the rainy months—lumber mills, and sprawling commercial farms growing trees, pumpkins, and all manner of produce. There are mountains and forests and Indian reservations near Marysville. Sometimes the area seems engaged in a tug-of-war between burgeoning civilization and what Snohomish County once was when its only residents were Native Americans.

Traia Carr tended to a large yard full of mature fruit trees, a vegetable garden, and bright flowers. She found a job as a clerk in a small bakery, a job she truly enjoyed. She wasn't worried about finances, though. She had a regular income from payments on the sale of a tavern she and her ex-husband had owned and operated for decades, and she also received Social Security checks, her share of her former husband's benefits.

She had numerous friends and as active a social life as she chose to participate in. Yet Traia had had her share of heartache. She found one man she truly cared for, and they dated almost daily for a year after he separated from his wife. And then one day, he simply stopped calling her. She eventually learned that he had gone back to his wife to try to make their marriage work. He hadn't had the nerve to tell Traia, so she waited for the phone to ring, agonizing, wondering what had happened to him.

Traia was inconsolable for a long time. She wondered how he could move out of his apartment and disappear without telling her what was wrong, or explaining his plans to her. She shed the tears that all women suffering from unrequited love do, but gradually she regained her sense of proportion and began to date other men—but only casually.

In the spring of 1978, it looked as though Traia was going to have her happy ending after all. Her lover told her that his reconciliation with his wife hadn't succeeded. He wanted to come back to Traia, and she welcomed him with open arms.

Disappointments in love may cut cruelly for young women who have never had their hearts broken before, but a woman approaching sixty has the added sense that romance might never come again for her. Traia felt that way, and she'd loved Tom Scott* more than any other man she'd ever known. And now he was back in her life.

Her ex-husband, grown children, friends, and coworkers at the bakery noticed a profound change in Traia. She smiled a lot, and she hummed softly as she worked. She knew that she and Tom might have only ten or twenty years left to be together, but that didn't matter; Traia would cherish every day of that time.

And yet Traia had a niggling premonition. It had nothing to do with Tom. It was more a sense of doom that she couldn't put into words. Finally, she told a close friend, "I don't know why—and it probably sounds silly—but I just have this terrible feeling that something is going to happen to me—"

"What do you mean?" her friend asked. "What could happen?"

"I really don't know. It seems to me as if my children are spending so much more time with me, and they're being so good to me—almost as if I won't be around much longer."

"Traia, shame on you," her friend said. "I don't think you can accept being happy. You're looking for something to be worried about, and you don't need to. You're healthy, Tom loves you, and you have all the time in the world."

Traia Carr nodded nervously. The only other worry she had was a direct contradiction to her fear of dying young. She sometimes wondered what would happen to her if the payments on the tavern ran out before she was eligible for her own Social Security checks. That was five years away. She lived comfortably on her bakery salary and the tavern payments, but she couldn't make it if she lost either monthly stipend.

She loved Tom Scott, but he had walked away from her once, and she had yet to be convinced that he wouldn't do it again. She knew she would regain her complete trust in him, but she was still apprehensive. So many older women without men were one or two paychecks away from losing their homes. She'd seen it happen to friends.

Basically, however, Traia was happy. Tom was kind and supportive emotionally, and she realized her fears for the future were only ephemeral—nothing she couldn't deal with in the light of day. She knew she would deal with what she had to, if indeed, her anxieties ever came true.

What Traia didn't mention to anyone was something she couldn't explain: When night fell, she often felt as if someone was watching her. That sounded paranoid, but

she had the definite sense that someone might be just outside her windows, somewhere out there in the blackness.
When she tried to peer out, she saw only her own reflec-
tion. She kept her shades and curtains drawn at night.

July 4, 1978, was a good day, one she'd looked forward to.
To celebrate the holiday, Traia and a woman friend went to
a picnic at Traia's daughter's home, and they had a wonderful time. It was shortly before seven that evening when
Traia drove her friend home. Invited in, Traia and her
friend had two drinks apiece as they discussed the day's
festivities and the great potluck lunch they'd enjoyed.

It was a little after 8:30 when Traia left for her own
house, which was only about ten minutes away. Both
women were tired, a little sunburned, but relaxed.

Traia was due at the bakery to work the day shift on the
morning of July 5.

The workweek started that Wednesday, and a steady
stream of customers stopped by the bakery. The owner was
kept busy boxing and bagging orders, and putting bargain
prices on some "day-old" items that were left over from
the holiday closure. She kept glancing at the door, wondering where Traia was; she really needed her. Traia was never
late, and she always called in if she was ill or wasn't able
to come to work.

But there was no word at all from her.

When the owner got a break, she called Traia at her
home, but the phone rang and rang and no one answered.
Her boss stood with her hand on the phone and a puzzled

look on her face. That just wasn't like Traia Carr. When she called someone to come in to take Traia's place, both women were concerned.

"Traia would have called us," the other bakery clerk said. "I wonder if she's fallen or something?"

"I don't know, but I think we'd better check on her. I'll call her daughter, and if she hasn't heard from Traia, I'll call her ex-husband. If they don't know where she is, we're going to lock the store and go over there. Maybe she's been taken ill and she needs help—but she can't get to her phone."

Ominously, neither Traia's former husband nor her daughter had heard from her since the July 4th picnic the day before. They suggested that the Marysville Police be called. Officer Herm Mounts agreed to meet Traia's boss and fellow employee at her home on Third Street.

From the outside, Traia Carr's house looked normal enough—except for the fact that her car, a 1970 Pontiac, was not in its usual spot. It wasn't anyplace on her property. Her front door was locked, but her daughter produced a key.

Inside the house, nothing was normal. Traia was a meticulous housekeeper. She never left dishes to soak, she hung up her clothes immediately after taking them off, and her floors sparkled with fresh wax.

Now her frightened daughter and her coworkers looked around her house with dismay. The clothes she'd worn to the picnic the day before had been tossed inside out on the living room couch. They appeared to have been removed hurriedly.

"My mother wouldn't have left her clothes that way," Traia's daughter exclaimed.

"Maybe she was in a hurry to go somewhere," officer Mounts suggested.

"No, you don't know my mother," her daughter insisted. "She just wouldn't have. She *always* hangs everything up. And I've never known her to undress in the living room."

"Traia?" they called as they walked through the silent house.

There was no answer, only a faint echo of their own voices. They opened all the interior doors, peered into closets, and searched the yard and sheds outside, too. If Traia Carr had been taken ill, it hadn't been in her home.

She wasn't anywhere on the property.

On the other hand, there was no sign of a struggle, no blood droplets or streaks, nothing overt that shouted that there had been violence inside this quiet home.

There was still a good possibility that Traia was safe and well but had been called away suddenly. Her car was gone, and that might be a good sign. Maybe she'd even eloped with Tom Scott, or left hurriedly to help a friend in trouble—someone her daughter didn't know. Parents don't tell their grown children *everything*.

As Herm Mounts and the group left Traia's home, they noticed a Snohomish County Sheriff's patrol car parked at the house next door. Two of the county's major crimes detectives—Bruce Whitman and Dick Taylor—had been dispatched to the residence, a large two-story, older home that was currently occupied by a widow with many children. Whitman and Taylor were investigating an incident that had taken place at a teenager's party. One of those attending had suffered a superficial knife wound.

Gabrielle Berrios* had been widowed fourteen months before when her husband, Luis Sr.,* died at the age of fifty. Luis Berrios Jr.* was seventeen, one of the oldest of Gabrielle's children. Now, the two Snohormish County detectives spoke to him about what had taken place the day before. They determined that he hadn't been involved and he said that he'd never carried a knife.

"But there's a kid—my mom lets him live here," Luis said, "and he has a really big collection of knives."

As Whitman and Taylor left to return to their headquarters in Everett, they commented on what a coincidence it was that *two* local law enforcement agencies had reason to show up at the same time at houses next door to one another. Marysville was hardly a hotbed of crime, with its population of 5,000. The 1600 block of 3rd Street was a residential neighborhood where it was rare for either the Marysville police or the sheriff's office to be summoned.

At this point Whitman and Taylor knew nothing of Traia Carr's disappearance—but they soon would.

Longtime Marysville officers knew Traia's house: They had sad memories of a violent event that had occurred there a decade earlier. In 1968, a Marysville patrolman was killed in the house when he went there to settle a family fight—one of the more dangerous calls police officers deal with. This was long before Traia moved in. Possibly she wasn't even aware of the sudden death in what later became her home.

As Marysville detectives conferred, they agreed that the situation in that same house didn't sound good. A dependable woman was suddenly gone, her family was distraught because this wasn't her pattern, and her clothing was left behind, inside out as if someone had ripped the garments from her body. From what her daughter could determine, no other clothing was missing from Traia Carr's closet.

It all added up to something far more menacing than a woman deciding to take a vacation on a whim. Because the Marysville Police Department had only a dozen sworn officers, who were rarely called upon to investigate circumstances as bizarre as Traia's vanishing, they asked for assistance from the Snohomish County Sheriff's Department. As it happened, Bruce Whitman and Dick Taylor handled all violent crimes in the county—and they certainly knew the neighborhood where Traia lived.

Marysville officer Jarl Gunderson was heading the probe, and he thought the two county detectives with their vast experience and training would be of great help in finding Traia.

At 4:30 on Wednesday afternoon, the trio of investigators returned to Traia Carr's home. Nothing had changed, and there was still no word from Traia. They moved from room to room, looking at the most minute signs that something chilling had happened here.

A glass of milk, drained of its contents, sat on the kitchen stove. The mattress was slightly off-kilter on the box springs in Traia's bedroom, and her spread was askew. Several of her wigs were scattered on the floor.

They picked up the phone in her bedroom and found there was no dial tone. Following the cord, they discovered that the line had been cut.

Someone had wanted to keep Traia from calling for help.

Traia's daughter followed the detectives' directions as she walked through the house. She looked more carefully than she had earlier. She had been so frightened then that something had happened to her mother. She still was, but she grew calmer.

"I can see now," she said, "that there are several things missing. Her clock radio is gone, and she has an old antique radio from the thirties. That's not here."

She pointed to her mother's dresser top, where necklaces and brooches were tangled together. "She keeps her dresser as neat as everything else—not like this."

"Is anything missing?"

She shook her head. "I'm not sure. I'll have to go through her jewelry box and the drawers to be sure."

Traia Carr had a small safe, which had been pried open. Oddly, the detectives found three hundred dollars in cash still inside. But the money was hidden from view.

"Someone who wasn't familiar with this safe could have missed this," Bruce Whitman said.

"My mother has a special ring," Traia's daughter said. "She keeps it in this safe. It was made especially for her—with the birthstones of all her grandchildren. There isn't another one just like it. But it's gone. . . ."

"What about clothing?" Dick Taylor asked. "Can you look more closely and tell us if anything—anything at all—is missing?"

She carefully searched her mother's neat closet, shaking her head. "Nothing's gone—but wait! Her purple robe isn't here. That's her favorite."

It didn't look good. No woman disappears voluntarily wearing only her bathrobe.

Traia's daughter had noticed recently that her mother was inordinately cautious about whom she let into her house.

"She keeps her doors locked—all the time. And she has this chain on it. Even if she's expecting someone, she always checks through the peephole before she'll open the door. She would never let a stranger in."

"Is she afraid of anyone?" Jarl Gunderson asked. "Has she mentioned anyone to you—by name?"

The young woman shook her head. "No, no one. But that's like her; she never wants to worry me. She might tell one of her friends if she's scared of someone. But she was in such a happy mood yesterday at our picnic. She didn't seem worried about anything."

But perhaps she had been. Searching the outside of her house, they found crushed flowers beneath several of her windows and footprints in the dirt outside her bedroom window. Someone—perhaps a voyeur, perhaps somebody looking for a way to get in—had obviously stood close to her windows, watching her when she didn't know it.

The detectives realized that if someone *had* abducted Traia Carr, it almost had to be someone she knew—and trusted—or she never would have let him in in the first place. Her daughter didn't think she was afraid of anyone, but she admitted her mother wouldn't want to scare her.

Still, Traia was gone. And so was her car and many of her belongings.

* * *

445

A door-to-door canvass of all the houses in the 3rd Street neighborhood produced negative results. One neighbor said he'd heard loud voices on the night of July 4, but he paid them little attention. With so many teenagers living at the Berrios residence, loud music, shouts, and laughter— even screams—were more usual than unusual.

Like most small-town cops, Jarl Gunderson knew almost everyone in Marysville. He knew that Traia's divorce had been friendly and that she and her ex-husband were on good terms. And he knew that Traia had a good reputation; the men she chose to date were primarily those she had known for a long time. Some of them were a good deal younger than she was, but there was no crime in that. She was attractive enough to appeal to men in their forties.

Gunderson talked with one of her bakery coworkers who seemed to be close to her.

"Was there anyone who frightened Traia?"

"No, I wouldn't say exactly *afraid*," she mused. "But she told me about this one guy she'd had trouble with. He was at her house, and he was kind of 'liquored up' and I guess . . . well, he made a pass at her that she didn't appreciate. She said she pushed him out the door and locked it. She said she wasn't going to let him come over anymore."

The witness didn't know the man's name.

"Was he angry?" Gunderson asked. "Did he ever try to see her again?"

"Not that she ever mentioned. Traia was pretty firm with him."

Traia Carr's Pontiac sedan was found first. A Marysville police sergeant discovered it at 1:30 a.m. on Thursday,

July 6. It was barely half a mile from her house, parked on 3rd Avenue.

When they found her car, the investigators knew that their fears for her safety were accurate. The upholstery on the back of the driver's seat was literally drenched in blood, which had now dried completely.

DNA matches were unheard of at the time, but the Western Washington Crime Lab would be able to compare blood type, enzymes, and RH factors if they could find any samples or records of Traia's blood values.

After daylight dawned, Dick Taylor and Bruce Whitman processed the Pontiac for evidence. They found more blood in varying quantities on the hood, throughout the interior, and on the doors. There was so *much* blood that, if it had all come from one person, they sincerely doubted that that person could still be alive.

Once again, they surmised that the killer—or attempted killer—probably lived close by. He could have easily dumped Traia's car and walked to one of the many houses that spread out from both sides of 3rd Street.

There was no purse in Traia's car, nor her missing purple robe. The two detectives couldn't find anything that might have belonged to the person whose gun or knife had caused all the bloodshed.

And they still didn't know where Traia Carr was.

They lifted a number of latent fingerprints that might prove to be invaluable *if* they found a suspect whose prints could be compared to these unknown prints. In 1978, AFIS didn't exist. The FBI didn't keep single fingerprints three decades ago—except those that belonged to felons on the Ten Most Wanted list.

Forensic science has advanced a great deal since the seventies, when computers weren't yet standard household equipment. Looking back, 1978 CSI techniques seem archaic now.

There was just one man whom Traia Carr was extremely close to, and he lived in her neighborhood. That was Tom Scott, the ex-lover who had recently come back to her. His apartment was several blocks up the street from her house.

Jarl Gunderson, Dick Taylor, and Bruce Whitman studied Scott as they questioned him. He appeared to be very distraught and grief-stricken over Traia's disappearance. They believed his emotions were real and not manufactured tears meant to take suspicion off of him. But they also knew that sociopaths were quite capable of feigning grief when it served their purposes.

"I'll do anything in my power," Scott said, sobbing, "to find out what happened to Traia. I just keep praying she's still alive, waiting for us to find her."

The three investigators didn't believe that she was still alive, but they didn't comment on it; Scott was upset enough as it was.

"Try to think," Bruce Whitman urged. "Think of anything unusual that may have happened in the past few months—anything, even if it didn't seem important at the time, that might have caused Ms. Carr to be afraid or nervous."

But Tom Scott said the only thing he could think of was actually a crime where *he* was the victim.

"I was over at Traia's house for the evening, and somebody ripped off stuff from my truck—they took some tools, fishing gear, and some blank checks. I was mad. I figured it was probably somebody from the house next door. There's a bunch of teenage kids over there, and it seemed like it was the kind of thing kids would pull. I wanted to go over there and confront them, but Traia begged me not to. She said she had a good relationship with the family, and the kids had never bothered her. She thought I might stir up trouble if I accused them. So I didn't."

Gunderson nodded. "We've been working on that," he said. Later, he told Whitman and Taylor that he felt Scott's suspicions were probably true.

"Those missing checks are popping up around town, and the makers have been traced to the Berrios house next door. Luis Jr.'s name is on some of them, but there are also some from other kids his mother lets live there."

The Marysville Police Department was very close, Gunderson said, to filling charges against the forgers when Traia Carr disappeared. Still, he doubted that there was a connection.

They tended to agree. Why would anyone from the Berrios house hurt Traia? She hadn't approached them about the theft from Tom Scott's truck, and she'd convinced him not to accuse them, either. She had bent over backwards to keep a peaceful relationship with her next-door neighbors. And the forgers had no idea yet that they were about to be arrested.

No. Abducting the pretty divorcée made no sense at all. Surely, even as attractive as Traia was, she was much too old to tantalize teenage boys—and much too circumspect even to consider doing so.

Five days passed, and there were no calls or letters from Traia. Her relatives and her lover were desperate for news of her as the hottest weather of the year burned grass brown, and Traia's trees dropped pears, peaches, and early apples on the ground, where they rotted. Ordinarily, she would have been canning and freezing the produce for the winter ahead.

The Marysville and Snohomish County detectives were convinced now that they were probably working on a murder case. They had eliminated almost everyone in Traia's world as suspects. Tom Scott had a solid alibi for the vital time period when his sweetheart vanished, and he was doing everything he could to help them.

He had loved Traia—that was clear—and he was deeply saddened as day after day passed and there was no word from her or *about* her.

The amorous suitor who made unwanted sexual advances to Traia when he was drunk had been far away from Marysville on July 4. The detectives verified that.

If Traia had received obscene phone calls, she hadn't mentioned it to her friends or to Tom Scott. She had been afraid at night—but of whom?

They had worked their way through Traia's world. Except for someone unknown who had frightened her, there was no one else who would conceivably have wanted to hurt her.

If a stranger had come to her door, she would never have let him in.

"Traia's feisty," one of her relatives told the investigative team. "She could handle troublemakers in the tavern; she'd eighty-six them if they didn't shape up. But she valued her life, and she wouldn't have taken any chances with it. Once she saw a stranger in the peephole of her door, she wouldn't let him in. I know that."

At 4:30 in the afternoon on Wednesday, July 12, Traia Carr had been missing for a full week. A logger was finishing work for the day off an isolated dirt road on the Tulalip Indian Reservation, which is very close to Marysville. Working alone, he was cutting and yarding—pulling fallen fir trees out of the woods.

He'd been in the area for a few days, and he'd caught occasional whiffs of a nauseating odor. He recognized it as decaying flesh. That wasn't unusual in the deep woods, and he figured some animal had died close by and was decomposing rapidly.

He hooked a turn (two logs together) and dragged them down along the road. Glancing back, the logger caught a glimpse of "something light." He hopped off his rig and walked back to see what it was.

Traia Carr had been found.

Bruce Whitman and Dick Taylor processed the body site. Without the logger choosing just this area to work in, the missing woman might never have been discovered. The undergrowth was as thick as if they were in a jungle.

The female body before them was completely nude and lying facedown. Despite the decomposition caused by a week's intense heat, and the fact that the huge fir trees had actually passed over her body—crushing it—the detectives could still see many puncture wounds in her back. And, when they gently turned her over, more knife wounds marred her breasts. Someone had stabbed her again and again in an almost classic example of a rage killing.

Traia's purple robe and slippers were gone, although tracking dogs would later turn up a torn piece of purple cloth in the brush not far away.

Dr. E. Bitar, a forensic pathologist, performed the postmortem exam on Traia Carr. The knife thrusts had entered her heart and lungs, causing several fatal wounds. Some were shallow, but the deepest wounds measured five inches. She had been stabbed at least fourteen times—five in her back and nine in her upper front torso.

"See this bruising impression here," Dr. Bitar pointed out to the detectives. "The weapon used had a guard at the end of the handle. The guard made the bruises. The murder weapon was a knife with a wide curving blade, tapered at the point."

Because Traia was nude when her body was found, her robe ripped to pieces, Jarl Gunderson, Bruce Whitman, and Dick Taylor agreed that the motive behind her murder could very well be sexual. And Dr. Bitar confirmed that theory. Acid phosphotase turns bright reddish-purple when it comes in contact with semen, and this test on Traia was positive for semen and for sperm (now dead).

The most bizarre and shocking discovery at autopsy, however, was that her killer had packed her vagina with leaves. There was no other way for leaves to have entered her vaginal vault so deeply unless someone had deliberately shoved them there.

But why? Was it a kind of symbolic rape? That wasn't likely because the killer hadn't been impotent—he had left semen behind. It could only have been a gesture of contempt.

The three investigators looked harder at the occupants of the house Gabrielle Berrios rented next door to Traia. They were closing in on an arrest for the theft of Tom Scott's belongings and checks, and Jarl Gunderson needed to obtain a search warrant to find possible evidence in that case.

They didn't believe that a teenager would have kidnapped Traia Carr and killed her in this grotesque fashion. They would find the answers to check theft first—if they could—and bide their time on the homicide probe. The very proximity of the two houses was a factor that couldn't be discounted. Nor could the juvenile records of many of the residents in the sprawling Berrios home.

They got their search warrant, and the items it listed were Tom Scott's tools, fishing gear, and blank checks. They entered the Berrios residence and found it cluttered and messy, not unusual for a place where numerous teenagers lived.

Bruce Whitman searched upstairs. He observed a number of knives in the small bedroom of one of the boarders, but none of them matched the description of the murder weapon.

Jarl Gunderson's search area was a washhouse located on the back of the property. He was looking for the blank checks that hadn't yet turned up. When he reached into a cardboard box, he came up with a small jewelry chest. He showed it to Taylor, who pulled a list out of his pocket; it was an itemized tally of Traia's missing jewelry that her daughter had given him that morning.

"Gold ladder used to hold earrings," he read.

"It's here."

"Ring made of birthstones—"

"That's here, too," Gunderson said. "And there's a payroll stub from the bakery, from a check made out to Traia Carr."

Both investigators were stunned.

"Until that moment," Rick Taylor recalled, "we weren't sure at all that anyone in that house was connected to Traia Carr's murder. We were leaning the other way—we really felt it was probably someone else entirely, probably an older man who was fixated on her."

They wanted very much to continue their search, but search warrants are strictly defined to protect the rights of citizens. Their current warrant didn't list any of Traia's belongings. If they continued to search now, any evidence discovered that was linked to her murder might well be deemed "fruit of the poisoned tree"—evidence found without a search warrant—and be thrown out of court.

Frustrated, but knowing it was the only legal way, they immediately stopped their search of the Berrios property and set about getting a search warrant seeking evidence in Traia Carr's homicide. They certainly had probable cause now to believe that someone living in Gabrielle Berrios's house might be the killer.

While they awaited word that a new search warrant had been granted, the three investigators talked to possible witnesses in the house about the theft of Tom Scott's property.

As the detectives were pulling scorched and partially burned checks out of a burn barrel, Luis Berrios Jr. came strolling up the alley behind his home. He had a wary expression on his face as Dick Taylor looked up and said, "Hi."

Luis didn't say anything.

"You're under arrest for possession of stolen property," Taylor said and advised him of his Miranda rights.

He didn't mention Traia Carr's murder, and Luis visibly relaxed, taking a deep breath. The detectives had seen that same relieved look on the afternoon of July 5—after they'd told Luis they were investigating the juvenile fight at the party in Everett. When they came out to question him the day after Traia vanished, Bruce Whitman and Dick Taylor had been completely unaware of Traia's disappearance.

Several young men in their late teens had been living next door to Traia Carr, and Luis Jr. was known to Jarl Gunderson as, at most, a penny-ante crook. He wasn't very big at five foot eight, but he weighed 165 pounds, and that made him considerably taller and heavier than Traia. Still, she'd been forty years older than he was, old enough to be his grandmother. He was hardly a likely candidate as her rapist-murderer, but he might know something that he was afraid to tell.

Luis didn't seem concerned about the theft charges. He answered questions about Tom Scott's missing property, but his responses were vague. They took him into the house and sat down at the dining room table.

"We don't want any conversation," Taylor said, and Luis looked confused. But as the minutes passed, he grew anxious again. If they'd come to talk to him about a burglary, why weren't they asking him more questions?

Once they were informed that a second search warrant had been signed by a judge, Taylor, Whitman, and Gunderson led Gabrielle Berrios out to the washhouse in the backyard. She was stunned when they showed the search warrant that now allowed them to look around her property for items of Traia Carr's that were still missing.

"We have reason to believe that someone living in your house is aware of what happened to Mrs. Carr—"

"We *all* know what happened to the poor lady," Gabrielle interrupted, crossing herself. "She was murdered."

"No," Jarl Gunderson said. "We think someone who lives in your house may have *guilty* knowledge about her abduction and her death. We need to talk with Luis Jr."

She stared back at him, uncomprehending. And then a shadow crossed her face as she understood. "That's all right," Gabrielle said. "I can see why you might want to. He knows just about everything that goes on here—but he doesn't always tell me."

A uniformed officer led Luis Jr. out to the washhouse, and he was interviewed in the presence of his mother, after he was once more advised of his rights—this time in the case of Traia's murder.

Luis Jr. finally admitted that he had some of his neighbor's things. "But I only had them because some Arab gave them to me at a party the night of July Fourth."

It seemed to be a contrived story, but there were a large

number of Middle Eastern students attending Everett Community College at the time.

Gunderson left the interview to speak with people Luis said were at that party. He learned that Luis had been there, all right, but witnesses said he arrived after midnight—not earlier in the evening, as he said.

Jarl Gunderson outlined all the evidence—both physical and circumstantial—that indicated Traia Carr's killer probably lived in his house. He stared hard at Luis. "Luis, I've known you for a long time," he said. "And I know when you're lying."

Luis looked at the floor.

"You're lying now, aren't you?"

Faced with the information that Gunderson had uncovered, all the bravado went out of Luis Berrios Jr. He heaved a great sigh. "All right," he said softly. "I did it."

"What did you do?" Gunderson pressed.

"What you think I did. I killed her."

The investigators were surprised. They had expected him to tell them about someone else who was Traia's killer.

Luis Jr. was now ready to fill in the blank spots in their reconstruction of the victim's last hours. The three detectives listened avidly as he told them he had felt sexually turned on by his fifty-seven-year-old neighbor. He'd kept track of her comings and goings and come to know her habits. Often, he'd peered into her bedroom window as she undressed for bed.

"She never knew I was there," he said.

"Maybe she did," Whitman said flatly. "But I doubt she knew it was you."

Luis continued with his story of what happened the night of July Fourth. His mother and younger brothers and sisters had gone to see the fireworks display, and his friends had all gone out, too.

"I was talking to my girlfriend on the phone about twenty minutes after eight," he recalled. "We had a fight and I hung up on her."

Luis said he'd been angry and bored. "I was the only one in our house," he said. "I saw Traia come home from her picnic and go into her house. I watched while the lights went on. I knew she was probably alone."

"You kept that close track of her?"

"Yeah. I could tell if she was alone or if her boyfriend or her daughter was over there."

Luis said that he'd looked around his house for some money "to do something with." He'd searched through a number of rooms in the big old house.

"That's when I stumbled across the knife. And I began to think about the neighbor next door—Traia—and about raping her. I went over and circled the house and I peeked into her windows. I could see that she was alone."

Then Luis had gone around to the front door and knocked. Traia had looked out the peephole and recognized him, and she'd opened her door with a smile.

"I asked her if she'd like to watch the fireworks from my house, and she was happy. She asked me, 'Yes, that would be nice. Where are they—out in back?'"

For some reason, Traia had begun to shut her door—maybe to remove the chain from its slot, maybe because she wanted to change clothes.

"But I pushed it open," Luis said. "And I pulled out the

knife and slipped inside. She was shocked and asked me what I was doing and if I wanted money."

Traia *would* have been shocked: This was the kid next door, from the family she'd done so much for—from bringing day-old doughnuts home from the bakery for the kids to giving them odd jobs when they needed money. She had tried so hard to welcome them to the neighborhood and avoided arguments at all costs. She'd felt kind of sorry for the recent widow with so many kids and so little money.

"So she asked me did I want money," Luis said. "And I told her I wanted sex."

She saw that he meant it, but it was, of course, unthinkable. Traia had tried to talk Luis out of having sex with her, and she'd offered him money if he would just leave.

"I told her I meant it when I said we were going to have sex. I held the knife close to her and told her to take her clothes off."

Trembling, Traia had taken her clothes off and placed them on the couch in the living room.

"I told her to go into the bedroom. She was really scared and she started to cry, but that didn't change my mind. Then she said her boyfriend was coming over at eleven thirty."

At that point, Traia Carr may have sealed her doom. She had feared something like this, as she'd sensed someone watching her—always—but she had never been able to explain, even to herself, what it was that terrified her. And she had no idea *who* it was who watched her. She just knew that *someone* was.

"That changes things," Luis recalled saying to her. "If

your friend is coming over, we'll have to get out of this house and go somewhere else."

"No . . . no," she said, weeping. "He's not coming over. I was just saying that, hoping you would go home and forget this."

"But now I can't believe you," Luis had told her, playing sadistic mind games. "I can't believe anything you're saying, so you'll have to come with me."

Traia had pleaded with him to be allowed to dress first, and Luis had finally agreed to let Traia wear her robe. "She threw that on, and some pink slippers, and she grabbed her purse."

Her phone line was cut, there was no one next door, and it seemed as though the whole town was someplace else, watching the fireworks that lit up the sky and boomed in the dark night. As Luis led Traia out to her car, she must have looked around frantically for someplace to run, for someone to call out to.

But there'd been no help around.

"I drove out behind the Thunderbird Drive-In to the Indian reservation," Luis said. "Then I parked and told her to get in the backseat."

And there, in the pitch black of the night on the lonely reservation road, Luis Berrios Jr. had raped Traia Carr, still holding the sharp Buck knife to her flesh so that she dared not struggle or fight him.

When he had finally finished with her, Traia asked, "Can we go now?"

"I told her, 'Yes. Yes, we can.' "

She believed that the ordeal was over and that she was

going to live, after all. Luis was going to let her drive home. She bent over to turn the key in the ignition.

Luis had been standing by the open driver's side door. He seemed to be back at the scene of Traia's death as he continued to describe what happened in the woods on the Indian reservation.

"I knew I had to kill her so she wouldn't say anything to anyone," he said. "I stabbed her in the back, all the way in. She was quite surprised. I pulled my knife out and stabbed her again. She fell out of the car onto the ground and started making a funny noise. I panicked, I guess, and I just kept stabbing her. Then she stopped making noise. The knife got caught in her robe, and it made me angry, so I just cut it off her and threw it in the brush."

His tone was so matter-of-fact that the listening detectives felt a little sick.

Luis Berrios said that he had stuffed leaves into Traia Carr's vagina.

"Why?" Jarl Gunderson asked him.

"I figured that would erase any trace of rape. Kind of cover it up—"

And then Luis had gotten into Traia's car, sitting in her wet blood in the driver's seat, and driven away.

"What did you do next?" Bruce Whitman asked him.

"I went to Smith Island and I threw her purse out. Then I drove around for a while and went back to her house. I went in and took some things I wanted."

The seventeen-year-old boy appeared to have no conscience at all. He betrayed no regret or guilt over what he had done to a woman who had been only kind to him. His choice of what to take from the dead woman's house was strange: the radios, Traia's jewelry, and food.

"I took some canned goods and some fresh vegetables. I was kind of thinking of running away, and I thought the food might come in handy.

"I put the box full of her things in the backyard on the ground, and then I took her car up about three blocks, parked it, kept the keys, and walked back home. I put the box of stuff in the washroom, and then I took the knife and put it in the flower bed. I stepped on it until it was buried."

But Luis was still restless. He regretted that he hadn't taken the liquor that Traia had. "I went back to her house and took some bottles. I went to the party, drank her liquor, and got so drunk that I passed out. I woke up about four a.m. Then I came home."

Once Luis Berrios Jr. began to talk, his confession was a geyser of words. Maybe he did have a conscience and needed to get the ugly story out. He led the three detectives to the flower garden where he'd buried the death weapon beneath the petunias. He pointed out a few items in his family's washhouse that the investigators had failed to find.

Luis led them unerringly to where he'd left Traia's body, even though it had changed somewhat because of the logging that had occurred since her murder. Then he took them to a sewer lagoon on Smith Island where the blackberry vines had grown ten feet high in the summer heat.

"That's where I threw her purse—and her slippers."

*   *   *

There was no question that Luis had killed Traia Carr. The investigators recovered physical evidence in each area he led them to. K-9 Unit's dog Tracer wriggled through the thick and thorny Himalayan blackberry vines and emerged with her slippers and her purse.

"I took her money, but I left her credit cards in there," Luis said, almost as if he wanted a pat on the back for being honest.

"Why did you kill her?" Gunderson asked him. "She didn't fight you—you got what you wanted from her. Why didn't you let her go home?"

"You know I couldn't," Luis said. "She would have reported me to you guys for raping her. I couldn't risk that."

He commented that it was kind of funny that she was really afraid he was going to kill her all during her ordeal. "But she was turning the car key at the end, and I could tell she thought she was going to live. She really thought I was going to let her go.

"She was sure she was going to die when we left her house, but when I told her to get in the front seat and turn the key, she believed everything was going to be okay. I think she was even going to give me a ride home."

Luis told the detectives that he thought he'd been caught for sure when they showed up at his house the day after the Fourth of July. "I thought you guys had found her body already. I was relieved when you were only asking about the guy that got stabbed at the party. I didn't touch him, you know, I just helped clean up his wound—it wasn't anything much, anyway.

"I told you about how I killed Traia. There'd be no point in my lying to you now about that thing at the party."

They were inclined to believe him. He'd been in a number of juvenile scrapes with local police, but nothing in Luis's background indicated a propensity for violence. What had happened to Traia Carr seemed completely out of character for this taciturn, emotionally flat kid.

And yet Luis had admitted to watching Traia for a long time. He had become obsessed with her. It wasn't money he wanted; it was a chance to act out the sexual fantasies that consumed him.

Traia had been touched that the neighbor boy would invite her to his family's fireworks, and then appalled when he broke into her home and told her he intended to have sex with her.

She could never have imagined such a thing. And that, perhaps, was the death of her.

Because Luis Berrios was so close to his eighteenth birthday, the Snohomish County Juvenile Court declined jurisdiction over him, and he was tried instead as an adult on charges of first-degree murder, first-degree rape, first-degree kidnapping, first-degree theft, and taking and riding in a motor vehicle without the owner's permission. The Snohomish County Prosecutor's Office wanted to be sure that even if he were found innocent on one charge, he would face a legal obstacle course with no easy exits.

That turned out to be unnecessary: He was found guilty of all five charges. If he ever gets out of prison, he will undoubtedly be older than Traia was when he killed her.

Tragically, Traia Carr—who would be close to ninety years old now—no longer had to worry about how she would earn a living if her income from the tavern sale ended, or about the arthritis that caused her pain. But she could have dealt with that. When she died so horribly, the saddest thing of all was that she wouldn't have the happy years ahead that she visualized. She'd been given a second chance when her lover came back to her, and they should have had several decades to enjoy a "September Song" kind of romance. Very few people are lucky enough to find that. Traia Carr was one of those lucky people.

But it was all taken away from her when she unlocked her door for someone she trusted.

We all forget to be cautious now and then. But it's wise to remember that strangers aren't the only people who might do us harm. I think most of us are smart enough to refuse to open our doors and our lives to them. If a stranger comes knocking on your door asking to come in to use the phone because there's been an accident, it's easy enough to tell him you will call—and let the police sort it out when they arrive.

But if it's someone you don't know all that well, and if the visit comes unexpectedly, late at night, or if your sixth sense gives you a silent alarm signal, don't open the door. Sometimes those you think you know turn out to be more treacherous than you ever imagined.

Women living alone should be doubly cautious.